Toeing the Lines

Women and Party Politics in English Canada

Second Edition

Sylvia B. Bashevkin

Toronto

OXFORD UNIVERSITY PRESS

1993

Oxford University Press, 70 Wynford Drive, Don Mills, Ontario M3C 1J9

Toronto   Oxford   New York
Delhi   Bombay   Calcutta   Madras   Karachi   Kuala Lumpur
Singapore   Hong Kong   Tokyo   Nairobi   Dar es Salaam
Cape Town   Melbourne   Auckland   Madrid

and associated companies in
Berlin   Ibadan

This book is printed on permanent (acid-free) paper

Canadian Cataloguing in Publication Data

Bashevkin, Sylvia B.
    Toeing the lines : women and party politics in
English Canada

2nd ed.
Includes bibliographical references and index.

1. Women in politics - Canada.   2. Political
parties - Canada.   I. Title.

HQ1236.5.C2B3 1993   305.43′32′0971   C93-093026-6

Contents

Illustrations

Acknowledgements

This second edition grew out of a suggestion by Richard Teleky, then managing editor at Oxford University Press, that I update my original manuscript. Although the text had been declared out of print, we both believed that the subject remained very current. With the cooperation of Phyllis Wilson at OUP and the copy-editing of Sally Livingston, revisions were completed by July of 1992.

This process could not have occurred without the research assistance of Karen Jones. Working to short deadlines, she provided knowledge, perspective and a crucial link to many of the party informants identified in the Appendix. My warmest thanks to Karen and each of these individuals.

A diverse network of people have kept me in touch with women and politics, on many different levels. During the late 1970s, I held office on the executive of the Ontario NDP Women's Committee and worked in a number of routine capacities in NDP campaigns. Since 1987, I have been active in a Toronto group seeking to elect more women, the Committee for '94. Friends in the Committee, particularly Libby Burnham and Wanda O'Hagan, made sure to send copies of every scholarly paper that crossed their desks.

The coordinators of the Women and Politics Worldwide project, Barbara Nelson in Minnesota and Najma Chowdhury in Bangladesh, invited me to participate in a challenging cross-national study. The research director of the Royal Commission on Electoral Reform and Party Financing, Peter Aucoin, encouraged me to write yet another paper on women's party involvement, as did Alain Gagnon and Brian Tanguay, Donald C. MacDonald and Graham White. Marianne Holder and Karen Jones were co-authors in two of those ventures, and I learned a great deal from our collaboration.

Much of what follows has also been enriched by a long round of conferences, workshops, seminars, lectures and media interviews on the subject. Political activists from all parties shared their experiences and insights, while students, colleagues and journalists asked all the hard questions. No author could ask for better preparation.

Finally, this project was aided by the support of the Humanities and Social Sciences Committee at the University of Toronto, and by the assistance of Arlene Bacon, Hyla Levy and Marian Reed in the Department of Political Science. My husband and daughters offered the encouragement every writer needs, along with a necessary dose of impatience.

All errors of fact and judgement remain my own.

Preface

The first edition of *Toeing the Lines* appeared about seven years ago; the research and writing were completed even earlier, in the fall of 1983. In the nearly ten years since, a great deal of new Canadian literature has appeared in the women and politics field. Many of these studies built on older and still valid critiques of the treatment of women in both political thought and empirical analysis.[1]

In terms of new research, Canadian scholars have examined the development of women's movements,[2] the impact of elected women,[3] and constitutional and Charter politics,[4] as well as the obstacles affecting women in their pursuit of public office.[5] Other studies have focused on gender differences in mass-level public opinion[6] and among party convention delegates.[7] Efforts have also been made to present findings from this literature to general readers of Canadian politics, notably in Sandra Burt's pieces for the Macdonald Commission and a leading introductory textbook.[8]

This expansion of the Canadian literature has been paralleled by an outpouring of comparative women and politics research. In the US, Western Europe, Australia and elsewhere, the growing volume of publications prompted one author to claim that 'since 1982 the relevant literature seems to have grown almost exponentially'.[9] Yet this flood of new studies did not prompt any major reorganization of the first edition of *Toeing the Lines*, nor did it lead to a shift in the focus of argumentation. Instead, virtually every sentence and note was altered to reflect evidence that updated the more tentative state of knowledge existing in 1983. New Canadian data were gathered for Chapters 1 through 5, and additional comparative materials were included in Chapters 6 and 7.

The central thesis of the first edition remains intact as of this writing: although Canadian women are becoming increasingly numerous in party organizations, their political mobility and policy gains continue to be tenuous. For the most part, women as a group are still 'toeing the lines' in Canada and other party systems, rather than participating in strategic, legislative and policy work that would transcend their conventional maintenance (including clerical) roles.

The discussion opens with an overview of political history in English Canada. Using the tension between political independence and partisanship as an organizing theme, Chapter 1 addresses the growth of the early suffrage movement as well as developments after enfranchisement that affected social welfare legislation and the right of women to hold public office. It then traces the emergence of second-wave feminism and maintains that a dilemma between independence and partisanship continues to shape women's political engagement.

What are the implications of this historical background? Chapter 2 explores how the circumstances surrounding female enfranchisement and the second-wave women's movement may have influenced attitudes in the general public. It uses theoretical work on the 'dual cultures' of women and men in a single political system to explain the public opinion patterns that are commonly seen as reflecting a 'gender gap'.

Chapter 3 examines the participation of women in major party organizations, including local constituency associations, party conventions and election campaigns. Drawing on data from federal- and provincial-level politics, it suggests that although women's involvement has generally increased over time, there remain relatively few females at elite levels of party activity. Under-representation is particularly apparent in competitive political environments, where parties hold or are in a position to challenge the reins of government. Moreover, Chapter 3 demonstrates that many women continue to perform stereotypical types of party work, including clerical or 'pink collar' roles in local constituency associations.

Chapter 4 considers the efforts that have been made to challenge female under-representation, including the introduction of formal rules and regulations as well as informal strategies. Formal responses such as mandatory affirmative action policies are found to be most common in the New Democratic party, while less formal approaches have been pursued in Liberal and Conservative organizations. Chapter 4 argues that without some formal changes within parties and in the larger electoral system, numerical under-representation at elite levels is likely to continue.

Chapter 5 addresses the development of women's groups in the major Canadian parties. Comparison of the goals and accomplishments of these units suggests that many older associations have been replaced by more explicitly feminist women's groups. Newer party women's organizations thus operate according to a mandate that differs from that of their predecessors, involving demands for both increased numerical representation in party activities and increased attention to women's issues in party policy.

Similar types of changes have also occurred in other party systems. Chapter 6 compares the history, attitudes and participation of women in similar Western party environments, and outlines a number of questions—pursued in Chapter 7—that deserve more research attention. It concludes that increased numbers of women are involved in North American and West European politics and are concerned about their position in party organizations. Most, however, remain distant from power and policy influence.

Readers should note that Quebec has been largely excluded from this study for a number of reasons, many of which become apparent in Chapters 1 and 6. First, female enfranchisement in Quebec was strongly opposed by clerical and political interests that were preoccupied with maintaining French Canadian identity in the face of a perceived threat from neighbouring Anglo-American culture. Throughout the first four decades of this century, approximately, women in Quebec were denied many rights that had already been obtained by their sisters elsewhere in Canada, including the right to vote in provincial elections.[10] Therefore, the background to suffrage in Quebec suggests a distinctive political history as well as a disparate set of expectations about attitudes and participatory behaviours.[11] These are best served by a separate study. In fact, if incorporated within a comparative framework, the political history of women in Quebec might most appropriately be included in a study of France, Italy and other nominally Catholic cultures.

Second, in more contemporary terms, the political experiences of women in Quebec are shaped by a social and partisan environment that clearly differs from conditions prevailing elsewhere in Canada. The development of the contemporary women's movement during the late 1960s and following coincided with the emergence of a strong independentist movement, and with growing tensions between Francophones and Anglophones, separatists and federalists, in the province.[12] Although one could argue that a nationalist/feminist dynamic also emerged in English Canada,[13] this dimension was of far greater significance in Francophone Quebec.[14]

Many of the same political organizations that are significant elsewhere in Canada, particularly the Conservatives, New Democrats and newer protest formations, have remained marginal or irrelevant for long periods in Quebec, just as the provincial Parti Québécois and federal Bloc Québécois have not contested office outside Quebec. Similarly, efforts in Quebec during the 1970s to increase women's legislative representation were distinctive because of the virtual political monopoly of the federal Liberals, who held relatively centralized and hierarchical control over nominations to the House of Commons.

These factors help to explain the sustained constitutional and strategic divisions between Quebec and English Canadian feminists.[15] Moreover, they indicate that analyses of women and politics in Quebec deserve more careful and thorough examination than is possible in a single-volume study of this type.

NOTES

[1] Early studies in this area included Thelma McCormack, 'Toward a Nonsexist Perspective on Social and Political Change', in Marcia Millman and Rosabeth Moss Kanter, eds., *Another Voice* (New York: Anchor, 1975), 1-33; Susan C. Bourque and Jean Grossholtz, 'Politics an Unnatural Practice: Political Science Looks at Female Participation', *Politics and Society* 4:2 (1974), 225-66; and Murray Goot and Elizabeth Reid, *Women and Voting Studies: Mindless Matrons or Sexist Scientism?* (Beverly Hills: Sage, 1975). Subsequent Canadian work in this stream includes Caroline Andrew, 'Women and the Welfare State', *Canadian Journal of Political Science* 17:4 (December 1984), 667-83; Jill McCalla Vickers, 'Feminist Approaches to Women in Politics', in Linda Kealey and Joan Sangster, eds., *Beyond the Vote* (Toronto: University of Toronto Press, 1989), 16-36; Chantal Maillé, 'L'approche féministe en science politique', *CPSA Bulletin* 21:2 (May 1992), 68-71; and Thelma McCormack, *Politics and the Hidden Injuries of Gender* (Ottawa: Canadian Research Institute for the Advancement of Women, 1991).

[2]See Nancy Adamson, Linda Briskin and Margaret McPhail, *Feminist Organizing for Change: The Contemporary Women's Movement in Canada* (Toronto: Oxford University Press, 1988); Sandra Burt, 'Canadian Women's Groups in the 1980s: Organizational Development and Policy Influence', *Canadian Public Policy* 16:1 (March 1990), 17-28; Sandra Burt, 'Organized Women's Groups and the State', in William D. Coleman and Grace Skogstad, eds., *Policy Communities and Public Policy in Canada* (Toronto: Copp Clark Pitman, 1990), 191-211; Susan D. Phillips, 'Meaning and Structure in Social Movements: Mapping the Network of National Canadian Women's Organizations', *Canadian Journal of Political Science* 24:4 (December 1991), 755-82; Sue Findlay, 'Facing the State: The Politics of the Women's Movement Reconsidered', in Heather Jon Maroney and Meg Luxton, eds., *Feminism and Political Economy* (Toronto: Methuen, 1987), 31-50; and Jill Vickers, 'Bending the Iron Law of Oligarchy: Debates on the Feminization of Organization and Political Process in the English Canadian Women's Movement, 1970-1988', in Jeri Dawn Wine and Janice L. Ristock, eds., *Women and Social Change* (Toronto: Lorimer, 1991), 75-94.

[3]See Manon Tremblay, 'Quand les femmes se distinguent: féminisme et répresentation politique au Québec', *Canadian Journal of Political Science* 25:1 (March 1992), 55-68; Bernadette Paré, Réjean Pelletier and Manon Tremblay, 'La différence de sexe en politique: les députées et députés du Québec à Ottawa', paper presented at Canadian Political Science Association meetings, Kingston, 1991; and Manon Tremblay, 'Les élues du 31e Parlement du Québec et les mouvements féministes', *Politique* 16 (Fall 1989), 87-109.

[4]See, for example, Beverley Baines, 'Gender and the Meech Lake Committee', *Queen's Quarterly* 94:4 (Winter 1987), 807-16; Anne Bayefsky and Mary Eberts, eds., *Equality Rights and the Canadian Charter of Rights and Freedoms* (Toronto: Carswell, 1985); Kathy L. Brock, 'Being Heard: Interest Representation in the Manitoba Constitutional Process', paper presented at Canadian Political Science Association meetings, Kingston, 1991; Gwen Brodsky and Shelagh Day, *Canadian Charter Equality Rights for Women* (Ottawa: Canadian Advisory Council on the Status of Women, 1989); Sandra Burt, 'The Charter of Rights and the Ad Hoc Lobby,' *Atlantis* 14:1 (Fall 1988), 74-81; Judy Fudge, 'The Public/Private Distinction: The Possibilities of and Limits to the Use of the Charter to Further Feminist Struggle', *Osgoode Hall Law Journal* 25:3 (Fall 1987); Sherene Razack, *Canadian Feminism and the Law: The Women's Legal Education and Action Fund and the Pursuit of Equality* (Toronto: Second Story Press, 1991); and Barbara Roberts, *Smooth Sailing or Storm Warning? Canadian and Quebec Women's Groups and the Meech Lake Accord* (Ottawa: Canadian Research Institute for the Advancement of Women, 1988).

[5]See Kathy Megyery, ed., *Women in Canadian Politics: Toward Equity in Representation*, Research studies of the Royal Commission on Electoral Reform and Party Financing, vol. 6 (Toronto: Dundurn Press for Supply and Services Canada, 1991); and Lucie Desrochers, *L'accès des femmes au pouvoir politique* (Quebec City: Conseil du statut de la femme, 1988).

[6]Published studies include Barry J. Kay, Ronald D. Lambert, Steven D. Brown and James E. Curtis, 'Feminist Consciousness and the Canadian Electorate: A Review of National Election Studies, 1965-1984', *Women and Politics* 8:2 (1988), 1-21; Kathryn Kopinak, 'Gender Differences in Political Ideology in Canada', *Canadian Review of Sociology and Anthropology* 24:1 (1987), 23-38; Peter Wearing and Joseph Wearing, 'Does Gender Make a Difference in Voting Behaviour?' in Joseph Wearing, ed., *The Ballot and its Message* (Toronto: Copp Clark Pitman, 1991), 341-50; and Sandra Burt, 'Different Democracies? A Preliminary Examination of the Political Worlds of Canadian Men and Women', *Women and Politics* 6:4 (Winter 1986), 57-79.

[7]See Janine Brodie, 'The Gender Factor and National Leadership Conventions in Canada', in George Perlin, ed., *Party Democracy in Canada* (Scarborough: Prentice-Hall, 1988), 172-87; and Alan Whitehorn, 'The Gender Gap amongst Party Activists: A Case Study of the New Democratic Party', paper presented at Canadian Political Science Association meetings, Charlottetown, 1992.

[8]See Sandra Burt, 'Women's Issues and the Women's Movement in Canada since 1970', in Alan Cairns and Cynthia Williams, eds., *The Politics of Gender, Ethnicity and Language in Canada*, Royal Commission Research Studies, vol. 34 (Toronto: University of Toronto Press for Supply and Services Canada, 1986), 111-69; and Sandra Burt, 'Rethinking Canadian Politics: The Impact of Gender',

in Michael S. Whittington and Glen Williams, eds., *Canadian Politics in the 1990s* (3rd ed.; Toronto: Nelson, 1990), 208-20.

[9] Vicky Randall, *Women and Politics: An International Perspective* (2nd ed.; London: Macmillan, 1987), xi.

[10] See Chantal Maillé, *Les Québécoises et la conquête du pouvoir politique* (Montreal: Editions Saint-Martin, 1990), part 1; Micheline Dumont, Michèle Jean, Marie Lavigne and Jennifer Stoddart, *Quebec Women: A History* (trans. Roger Gannon and Rosalind Gill; Toronto: Women's Press, 1987); and Sylvie d'Augerot-Arend, 'Why So Late? Cultural and Institutional Factors in the Granting of Quebec and French Women's Political Rights', *Journal of Canadian Studies* 26:1 (Spring 1991), 138-65.

[11] Research in this area includes Anne-Marie Gingras, Chantal Maillé and Evelyne Tardy, *Sexes et militantisme* (Montreal: Editions CIDIHCA, 1989); and André Blais and Jean Crête, 'Les ménages et le vote [au Québec]', *Recherches sociographiques* 28:2/3 (1987), 393-405.

[12] See Michèle Jean, ed., *Québécoises du 20e siècle* (Montreal: Presses Libres, 1974); Yolande Cohen, ed., *Femmes et politique* (Montreal: Le Jour, 1981); and Lise Payette, *Le pouvoir? Connais pas* (Montreal: Québec-Amérique, 1982).

[13] See Sylvia B. Bashevkin, *True Patriot Love: The Politics of Canadian Nationalism* (Toronto: Oxford University Press, 1991), chap. 6.

[14] See Diane Lamoureux, 'Nationalism and Feminism in Quebec: An Impossible Attraction', in Maroney and Luxton, eds., *Feminism and Political Economy*, 51-68; and Michèle Jean, Jacqueline Lamothe, Marie Lavigne and Jennifer Stoddart, 'Nationalism and Feminism in Quebec: The "Yvettes" Phenomenon', in Roberta Hamilton and Michèle Barrett, eds., *The Politics of Diversity* (London: Verso, 1986), 322-38.

[15] See Sylvia Bashevkin, 'Building a Political Voice: Women's Participation and Policy Influence in Canada', in Barbara J. Nelson and Najma Chowdhury, eds., *Women and Politics Worldwide* (New Haven: Yale University Press, 1993).

CHAPTER ONE

Independence versus Partisanship: Dilemmas in the Political History of Women in English Canada

The Women's Good Government League . . . stands on the principle of cooperation and is assured that women can best serve their country by keeping out of parties and away from the party machines.

—*Woman's Century*, 1918[1]

I couldn't open my mouth to say the simplest thing without it appearing in the papers. I was a curiosity, a freak. And you know the way the world treats freaks.

—Agnes Macphail, 1949[2]

The political experiences of women in Canada have been shaped by varied influences, some of which are related directly to women, and others of which emanate from broader political processes and structures. Many studies of female political involvement interpret these experiences with reference to two main sets of factors: one psychological, including conventional patterns of gender role socialization, and the second structural, involving discriminatory practices within party organizations.[3]

Although this focus upon role constraints and structural limitations reveals some of the obstacles to female political activity, it has obscured an important historical dimension within the political development of English Canadian women. Boldly stated, the ideological and organizational dilemmas surrounding female enfranchisement in English Canada provide a critical and widely neglected perspective on subsequent political experiences in this culture. The following discussion argues that early feminism and suffragism in English Canada were part of a broader progressive challenge to the traditional two-party system and, furthermore, that these movements became locked on the horns of a political dilemma: on the one hand, early women's groups were attracted towards a position of political independence, which could guarantee both organizational autonomy and purity; on the other hand, they were drawn towards conventional partisanship, which might better ensure their political influence and legislative success. This tension between independence and partisanship within the context of a changing party system helped to define the parameters of women's political history in English Canada for many decades. A similar dilemma continues to shape not only the development of contemporary English Canadian feminism but also the broader relationship between women and the party system.

In practical terms, this tension between independence and partisanship has limited the exercise of effective political power by women in English Canada.[4] Even though females in some regions had the right to vote—primarily in local school board elections—as early as the eighteenth century, and although many were organized into such party affiliates as the Toronto Women's Liberal Association prior to the formal extension of the franchise, few entered the electorate as politically skilled or equal participants.[5]

This situation resulted in part from the ideological position adopted by mainstream suffragists, which began with the assumption that females would spread a mantle of purity from their private domestic sphere to the public, political domain. In the words of the *Woman's Century*, quoted above, new women voters were advised to avoid the corrupting, immoral party organizations and to adopt an independent, non-partisan route to national influence. The limitations of this strategy as applied within an essentially partisan, parliamentary system, combined with women's co-optation into separate auxiliaries within the two major parties, are reflected in Agnes Macphail's experience in the House of Commons. More than fifteen years after the formal extension of the federal franchise, Macphail remained the sole female member of parliament, a 'freak' who reluctantly symbolized the continuing distance between women and political power in Canada.

What was the organizational and ideological background to this dilemma between independence and partisanship? To what extent has the subsequent political history of women in English Canada been shaped by early feminist experiences? And how have women recently begun to question and challenge their lack of political and, especially, partisan influence? These are the main questions that inform our discussion of the political history of women in English Canada.

First, however, one important caveat must be added. The following discussion of difficulties that resulted from the continuing strain between independence and partisanship is *not* intended to direct blame towards individual women or women's groups. Rather, the purpose of this organizing theme is to identify crucial problems of access and influence that face many extra-parliamentary interests in their efforts to shape parliamentary systems. Neither the first nor the second wave of the Canadian women's movement, for example, could adopt the simple integrationist strategy that was more feasible in the congressional environment of the United States; party institutions north of the forty-ninth parallel have remained more structured, disciplined and politically relevant than American ones through the late twentieth century.

Conversely, independent feminism in a parliamentary setting cannot 'win' without moving its policy demands through party-controlled pipelines. Feminism, like other social movements in Canada, has therefore had to exert pressure in *both* partisan and independent directions, and has had to co-ordinate these two streams of activism. If any lessons of history can be drawn from the following discussion, they concern the enormous challenges presented by such an agenda— both to external impact and to internal survival.

ORIGINS OF THE MOVEMENT

The formal beginnings of the suffrage movement in English Canada are generally dated from the founding of the Toronto Women's Literary Society in 1877.[6] Composed primarily of well-educated and professional women of the Protestant middle classes, the Literary Society disguised its suffragist leanings until the 1880s, when Dr Emily Stowe, her daughter (Dr Augusta Stowe-Gullen) and a number of other activists established the Canadian Woman Suffrage Association and a series of similarly directed organizations.[7]

Much of the ideological and organizational strength of English Canadian suffragism developed as a result of ties between this movement and other reform groups operating around the turn of the century. According to Carol Bacchi's research on major suffragist leaders, the movement attracted many men and women who were also affiliated with temperance, urban improvement and civic education activities. Organized pressure for the vote was thus allied with a broader reformist response to the rapid pace of industrialization, urbanization and the perceived decline of traditional values in many Western societies.[8]

In addition, women in Toronto and the western provinces were particularly influenced by feminist and suffragist initiatives in other Anglo-American democracies; they frequently merged elements of the American and British movements with an essentially moderate, non-militant approach that reflected English Canadian culture more generally.[9] Moreover, Canadian feminists also benefited from the increasing opportunities available to middle-class women in education, professional employment and volunteer work; in this respect, they shared a growing international commitment to broadening their own political rights.[10]

What rationale did English Canadian suffragists offer in pursuit of the vote? The historical literature on this subject demonstrates a number of important divisions within the movement, particularly along generational and ideological lines. As in the United States, activists in English Canada included an older 'hard-core' minority who sought to challenge the discriminatory treatment of women in virtually all facets of social life, including education, employment, political rights and, most importantly, the family.[11] Believing that females were entitled to the same degree of individual independence as males, 'hard-core' feminists, such as Flora MacDonald Denison, campaigned outside the more moderate, reformist mainstream of 'social feminism' in English Canada.[12]

The ideological and organizational pivot of Canadian suffragism thus resembled its 'social feminist' counterpart in the United States; the latter linked 'suffrage and temperance and other crusades, such as civil service reform, conservation, child labor laws, mothers' pensions, municipal improvements, educational reform, pure food and drug laws, industrial commissions, social justice and peace'.[13] The argument for 'maternal' or 'social' feminism in English Canada was, as these names suggest, predicated upon a fundamental belief in the necessity for social reform and for women's participation in this process. Unlike more radical 'hard-core' arguments, it elevated Protestant social reform above demands for legal emancipation and claimed that the granting of the vote to women was essential for general social improvement.[14]

The manner in which organized feminism developed held important implications for women's relations with the Canadian political system. For much of its history, the core of the movement remained in Toronto, which served as the headquarters for such groups as the Dominion Women's Enfranchisement Association and the Canadian Suffrage Association. While claiming to be nationwide, these organizations actually 'had few affiliates and even less control outside Toronto'. Ironically, though, it was outside Toronto that the initial legislative successes of the movement were achieved (see Table 1.1).[15]

The regional divisions and conflicts that characterized other Canadian social movements thus affected suffragist organizations in an especially damaging manner, since the latter needed to operate on a region-by-region basis in order to secure the provincial franchise, while they also required an image of national influence in order to achieve the vote federally. These organizational demands were not easily reconcilable; as Catherine L. Cleverdon points out: 'The small but valiant bands of women found it necessary to concentrate their political efforts upon their provincial governments, and this undoubtedly militated against the successful formation of any truly nation-wide suffrage association.'[16] Indeed, in the absence of such a national organization, suffragists relied heavily upon alliances with older, more established and generally conservative women's groups, including the Women's Christian Temperance Union (WCTU), the Federated Women's Institutes and the National Council of Women of Canada (NCWC).[17] In forming such alliances—particularly with the NCWC, which formally endorsed enfranchisement in 1910—suffragists gained an important element of national visibility and credibility; at the same time, however, they became increasingly dependent upon moderate, social feminist strategies that would be acceptable to the NCWC leadership and similar coalition partners.

The organizational features of Canadian suffragism thus held important consequences for the momentum of the movement. Cleverdon's historical study offers abundant evidence that it developed episodically, in 'fits and starts'; enfranchisement organizations were activated, receded into dormancy, and later were reactivated, with great frequency. As rapid legislative progress was made in one region, particularly in the western provinces during the years 1914-17

TABLE 1.1 LEGISLATIVE CHANGES AFFECTING THE POLITICAL STATUS OF WOMEN IN CANADA

JURISDICTION	DATE OF FEMALE ENFRANCHISEMENT[a]	LEGISLATIVE SPONSOR	DATE OF ELIGIBILITY TO HOLD OFFICE	FIRST WOMAN ELECTED
Manitoba	28 January 1916	Liberal gov't	28 January 1916	29 June 1920
Saskatchewan	14 March 1916	Liberal gov't	14 March 1916	29 June 1919
Alberta	19 April 1916	Liberal gov't	19 April 1916	7 June 1917
British Columbia	5 April 1917	Liberal gov't	5 April 1917	24 January 1918[b]
Ontario	23 April 1917	Conserv. gov't	4 April 1919	4 August 1943
Nova Scotia	26 April 1918	Liberal gov't	26 April 1918	7 June 1960
New Brunswick	17 April 1919	Liberal gov't	9 March 1934	10 October 1967
Prince Edward Island	3 May 1922	Liberal gov't	3 May 1922	11 May 1970
Newfoundland	13 April 1925[c]	Conserv. gov't	13 April 1925	17 May 1930[b]
Quebec	25 April 1940	Liberal gov't	25 April 1940	14 December 1961
Canada	24 May 1918, full female franchise[d]	Union gov't	7 July 1919	6 December 1921

[a]Denotes date of royal assent.

[b]Denotes victory in by-election.

[c]According to this 1925 legislation, female voters had to be age 25 or over to vote, while men could vote at age 21. This disparity was rectified by the Terms of Union of Newfoundland with Canada, 1948.

[d]The Military Voters Act and the Wartime Elections Act, which both received royal assent in September 1917, enfranchised women who were British subjects and who had served in any branch of the military, or who had a close relative serving in the armed forces of Canada or Great Britain.

SOURCES: Catherine L. Cleverdon, *The Woman Suffrage Movement in Canada* (Toronto: University of Toronto Press, 1974) and Terence H. Qualter, *The Election Process in Canada* (Toronto: McGraw-Hill, 1970), 9, 52.

(see Table 1.1), it was expected that a growing momentum would carry the cause from coast to coast. This sense of momentum, however, overshadowed the fact that the women's movement remained small and weak in national terms. Moreover, as its affiliates in Francophone Quebec and Atlantic Canada were particularly slow to develop, the organizational strength of the movement was centred outside those regions where women's traditional roles were most constraining and, in the view of many activists, most in need of legislative reform.[18]

SOCIAL FEMINISM AND THE PARTIES

The major political effects of early feminism in English Canada concern women's relationship with the established party system. Like other reformist movements of the early twentieth century, including those that embraced labour and agrarian interests in the Western provinces, the major streams within Canadian suffragism rejected the evils of 'partyism' in favour of an independent, virtually suprapolitical stance.[19]

This rejection of conventional partisanship grew out of a broader distrust of established political structures, as reflected quite generally in Western Canadian progressivism. According to the classic study by W.L. Morton, leading progressive farmers and trade unionists supported direct or populist democracy, based upon citizen-initiated legislation, referenda and recall propositions.[20] Many progressives believed that political corruption and the absence of regional and group representation under existing arrangements resulted from party control over political nomination and election procedures. In Morton's words, progressives endorsed a populist system to replace conventional representative democracy, in order to 'break the hold "bosses" and "machines" serving the "invisible government" of the "interests" were alleged to have on the government of the country'.[21] Many suffragists, especially in Western Canada, shared this belief in the intrinsically corrupting, immoral and impure character of established party institutions.

One of the most vocal critics of this system was Nellie McClung, a nationally prominent suffragist and social feminist who was especially active in Manitoba and Alberta. McClung's diary records her initial impressions of party politics, gathered during a Liberal campaign meeting that she attended in rural Manitoba during the 1880s. Women in the audience were exhorted by provincial Premier Thomas Greenway 'to see that their menfolk voted and voted right and this he said (so even we could understand) meant voting Liberal'.[22] After two questions regarding women's rights were ignored by the chairman, McClung left the meeting with the firm belief that politics was "a sordid, grubby business . . . I do not want to be a reformer."[23]

McClung's subsequent exposure to WCTU activities and Women's Press Club and Local Council work in Winnipeg led her to reverse her earlier view on reform. Nevertheless, as a suffrage activist in the Political Equality League during later years, McClung reflected many elements of her older anti-party attitude.

In fact, like many social feminists in the US, she merged a progressive critique of party politics with social reform arguments in favour of female enfranchisement:

> If politics are corrupt, it is all the more reason that a new element should be introduced. Women will I believe supply that new element, that purifying influence. Men and women were intended to work together, and will work more ideally together, than apart, and just as the mother's influence as well as the father's is needed in the bringing up of children and in the affairs of the home, so are they needed in the larger home,—the state.[24]

Politics was thus perceived by McClung and many of her allies as housekeeping on a grand scale. If women could introduce order, morality and purpose to the domestic household, then they could surely extend this positive influence to 'the larger home,—the state'. The evils of partyism would finally be superseded, following female suffrage, by a reform-oriented system of good government.

Aside from the utopian expectations that were generated by this approach, particularly in the decades after 1918, McClung's argument was important because it cemented the alliance between mainstream social feminism and those parties that were anxious to co-opt progressive interests—including women. In the Prairie region, which is useful for illustrative purposes, McClung established what might be termed an 'arm's-length alliance' with the pro-reform Manitoba Liberals in 1914, on the basis of an agreement that the latter would introduce suffrage legislation once they defeated the governing provincial Conservatives. The Liberals lost the subsequent election despite the efforts of McClung (who noted that she 'never even took car fare from the Liberal party . . . I am a freelance in this fight') and others, but later won power in 1915.[25] The party indeed sponsored suffrage legislation following its election, as did the Alberta Liberals for whom McClung campaigned successfully as a provincial candidate in the 1917 elections.

Perhaps the most troubling aspect of such alliances was their effect upon newly elected suffragists: McClung, for example, grew increasingly uncomfortable in her role as an 'independent' MLA within a distinctively partisan caucus and legislature. Believing in the need for non-partisanship, however, McClung voted her conscience in the Alberta house, which after 1921—when the United Farmers of Alberta formed the government—generally meant crossing party lines to support UFA-sponsored legislation. The frustration that greeted this direct exposure to political and especially parliamentary decision-making, combined with McClung's defeat in the subsequent provincial election, was echoed across Canada as other suffragists and similarly-minded reformers entered the party-dominated system, only to find that both their broader structural objectives and their specific goals (especially prohibition) were marginalized by the very parliamentary system that they had set out to transform. Despite their formal commitments to political independence, therefore, suffragists soon discovered they were wedged within the same partisan political system that they had earlier promised to eliminate, or at least transcend.

THE FEDERAL FRANCHISE

The difficulties associated with operating inside an established party system and, at the same time, maintaining a critical distance and independence from that system are evident in the events surrounding the granting of the federal franchise. Although legislation to enfranchise widows and unmarried women was presented as early as 1883 by Sir John A. Macdonald, it was not until after provincial suffrage was enacted in Ontario and the Western provinces that this issue received serious consideration on the federal level.[26] Suffrage thus reached the national agenda just as women's contribution to Canada's effort in the First World War was becoming increasingly evident, and at a time when the Union government of Prime Minister Robert Borden faced a major electoral and political challenge concerning the issue of conscription.

Although the basic facts of the conscription crisis are relatively well known, only limited attention has been given to the organizational differences within Canadian suffragism during this period and their connections with wartime legislation. One source of internal conflict among English Canadian feminists existed long before 1917, dating back to older generational and ideological differences between the radical 'hard core' Canadian Suffrage Association (CSA) and the more moderate 'social' elements in the movement, including the NCWC, WCTU and National Equal Franchise Union (NEFU).

Racism, conscription and the war itself further divided feminist ranks during the First World War. As historical research by Carol Bacchi and Gloria Geller has demonstrated, the political or hard-core stream represented by the CSA generally resisted the appeals to Anglo-Saxon superiority and purity that were inherent in government-sponsored legislation to permit a limited female franchise in 1917.[27] CSA activists also tended to be urban pacifists who remained suspicious of the government's motives in introducing the Wartime Elections Act. In the words of the CSA president, Dr Margaret Gordon, this proposal constituted 'a win-the-election measure . . . it would be direct and at the same time more honest if the bill simply stated that all who did not pledge themselves to vote Conservative would be disfranchised. This might be satisfactory to some but it is not a Canadian-born woman's ideal of free government, nor can anyone who approves of this disfranchise bill claim to represent Canadian suffragettes.'[28]

By contrast, the more conservative mainstream of English Canadian feminism—particularly the members of its elite—were more willing to adopt racial and patriotic (that is, pro-war) arguments in their pursuit of the franchise. Bacchi points out that the four activists who surveyed women's opinions regarding full versus partial federal suffrage (on behalf of the prime minister) were all married to Conservatives.[29] In addition, it is notable that such pro-reform Liberal women as Nellie McClung agreed with limited enfranchisement and expressed racial and patriotic views in support of this legislation.[30] Mainstream social feminists—

most notably the presidents of the NCWC, NEFU, Imperial Order Daughters of the Empire (IODE) and the Ontario WCTU—thus endorsed what Cleverdon terms 'one of the most bitterly debated and controversial measures in Canadian history'.[31]

The Wartime Elections Act received royal assent on 29 September 1917. It enfranchised only those women who were British subjects of age 21 and over, and who had a close family member serving in the Canadian or British armed forces. In political terms, the effects of this bill were as predicted, since newly enfranchised women helped to re-elect the pro-conscription government of Prime Minister Borden. Once established in its new term, the Union government convened a Women's War Conference in Ottawa and enacted full suffrage legislation in 1918.[32]

While these developments suggest that Canadian women made successful use of the federal party system, it is important to recognize that their 1918 victory entailed major political costs. First, and probably most important for the future relationship between women and political power in Canada, the key arguments of both hard-core (equal rights on the basis of political justice) and social feminists (social reform incorporating the vote) were marginalized in the federal debate, which centred on conscription and the electoral viability of Borden's Union government. Federal suffrage for women was largely achieved through a series of political choices made by, and in the interests of, the government of the day. Suffragists thus found themselves formally empowered within, but substantively distant from, the very system of national party government that they had long distrusted.

Second, the federal victory and subsequent enfranchisement bills in Atlantic Canada left organized feminism with no clear strategy for future action. It is to these post-enfranchisement dilemmas that we now turn our attention.

THE AFTERMATH OF SUFFRAGE

As in the United States, many women voters in English Canada entered the electorate expecting a social and political millennium. The ideology of social feminism emphasized the pure reformist motives of women, and promised a restoration of traditional moral values in both the home and the state. This commitment to uplifting was not easily translated into practical action on a mass scale, however. As Nellie McClung reflected during the 1930s:

> "We were obsessed with the belief that we could cleanse and purify the world by law. We said women were naturally lovers of peace and purity, temperance and justice. There never has been a campaign like the suffrage campaign . . . But when all was over, and the smoke of battle cleared away, something happened to us. Our forces, so well organized for the campaign, began to dwindle. We had

no constructive program for making a new world . . . So the enfranchised women drifted. Many are still drifting.[33]

As McClung observed, the divisions within suffragist ranks that had existed throughout the early decades of the twentieth century deepened during subsequent years. In many regions, feminists and other newly enfranchised women split politically along the same demographic lines that had conventionally divided men. Class, ethnic, occupational, regional and rural/urban differences shaped female political perceptions and often obscured earlier visions of a single emancipated womanhood, united in its goals and experiences.

On an organizational level, these internal cleavages became increasingly visible. Research by Bacchi, for example, reveals the fragmentation surrounding Canadian efforts to establish a separate woman's party in the years immediately after federal suffrage.[34] In 1918, a number of social feminists in the NEFU founded the Woman's party, with the stated goal of extending their political gains as enfranchised women. While the objective of consolidating earlier achievements was probably shared by many feminists, a separate party strategy under the leadership of pro-war, anti-labour and generally Conservative-affiliated women from Toronto received less than solid support. Not surprisingly, the Woman's party was frequently condemned as being urban, elitist and a Conservative front group. Its failure to develop as a viable and autonomous political organization paralleled the fate met by the National Women's party in the United States, where females were similarly constrained by established lines of party organization, political ideology and social class.[35]

What distinguished English Canadian from American feminism, however, was the absence of a strong national organization following enfranchisement. Mainstream social feminists in the United States recognized the importance of political education and a cohesive social reform lobby at the state and federal levels; in 1920, they launched the non-partisan National League of Women Voters (NLWV) to fulfil this mandate.[36]

With one important exception, English Canadian suffragists established few ongoing organizations following enfranchisement, and women generally floundered politically as a result. It was widely believed, even by such prominent social feminists as Nellie McClung and Louise McKinney, that Canadian women voters should return to their homes after the First World War and, using their domestic environment as a base, work to mobilize public opinion around such issues as the minimum wage and industrial working conditions.[37] Unfortunately, the organizational structures necessary to achieve systematic results were generally lacking.

The notable exception to this pattern developed in British Columbia, where social feminists continued to remain active in politics following provincial enfranchisement. As a group, BC suffragists employed their alliance with the provincial Liberals to retain significant legislative influence through the late 1920s. Among the specific actions taken by BC feminists was the transformation of the suffragist Political Equality League (established in 1910) into the post-suffragist New Era League. This move coincided with similar national efforts in the United States, where the pro-vote National American Woman Suffrage Association became the League of Women Voters following 1920.

Many of the major policy concerns of the New Era League paralleled those that had motivated earlier suffragist activities. As summarized by Elsie Gregory MacGill in the story of the social feminist involvement of her mother, Helen Gregory MacGill, the main priorities for reform legislation in BC included prison and family law reform; infant protection; industrial health and safety; minimum wage legislation for women; mothers' pensions; a Juvenile Courts Act; and improved public health, library and education systems.[38]

The ability of BC feminists to ensure government sponsorship and passage of this legislation was related to two factors. First, a number of active suffragists, including the 'high Tory' Helen Gregory MacGill, became party members after the provincial Liberals adopted woman suffrage in their platforms of 1912 and following.[39] In addition, the fact that Liberals in the Prairie provinces also favoured and ultimately enacted female enfranchisement legislation (see Table 1.1) led active suffragists to join the party and to establish the BC Women's Liberal Association during this same period.[40]

Second, along with their partisan ties, social feminists in BC retained an independent women's network through such groups as the New Era League. After a prominent suffragist and founder of the Women's Liberal Association, Mary Ellen Smith, was elected to the provincial legislature in 1918 and later appointed minister without portfolio in 1921 (thus becoming the first female cabinet minister in the British Empire), feminists outside the legislature began to channel their reformist concerns through Smith to the provincial government.[41] Smith's position in the Liberal cabinet, combined with the success of BC social feminists in retaining some organizational continuity following enfranchisement, ensured the passage of significant reform measures, including mothers' pensions and a Minimum Wage Act.[42]

With their active ally inside the chambers of government, social feminists in BC found that many reform bills were favourably received during the critical first decade after suffrage. However, this successful combination of partisan alliances, including the election and cabinet appointment of an active feminist woman, with politically independent and effective women's organizations was the exception rather than the rule for many years following 1918. Indeed, as events on the federal level during the 1920s were to prove, women's rights to vote and to hold public office generally had minimal effects on the broader political system.

THE PROBLEM OF PUBLIC OFFICE

Despite the early success of the Dominion Women's Enfranchisement Association in electing two women to the Toronto School Board in 1892, the election of females to public office was not a high priority for mainstream social feminism in English Canada. According to Bacchi, efforts to elect women faltered as older hard-core feminists became increasingly outnumbered by moderate social reformers, who attached relatively little importance to candidacy and office-holding. In fact, many social feminists questioned whether the majority of married, child-rearing women could devote themselves to any career outside the home, including politics. In the opinion of one activist, there were 'plenty of "unmarried women and widows, and married women with grown-up children"' to work in elections and run for office.[43]

In light of this prevailing view, it is not surprising that relatively few women contested public office, and even fewer held elective office, in the years following formal enfranchisement. On the federal level, for example, only four women were nominated as candidates in the 1921 general elections, representing 0.6 percent of the total federal candidates for that year.[44] The sole woman elected to the House of Commons in 1921 was Agnes Macphail, a 31-year-old unmarried schoolteacher who represented the rural Ontario riding of South-East Grey.

Macphail's political career, including her experiences as an MP and subsequently as an Ontario MPP, is important not only because it confronted many of the psychological and structural obstacles generally faced by women in politics, but also because it reflected a more specific tension between partisanship and independence in the political history of women in Canada. In terms of general barriers to elite-level participation, the nomination, election and legislative tenure of Agnes Macphail had much in common with the experiences of other women in Canada and elsewhere. For example, like many female candidates in competitive ridings, she had to defeat ten males to win nomination initially, and then withstood strong protests from both the constituency organization and the electorate at large because of her gender.[45] In Macphail's own words: 'It took strenuous campaigning for two months just to stop people from saying, "We can't have a woman." I won that election in spite of being a woman.'[46]

Once she had defeated the incumbent Conservative MP in South-East Grey, Macphail's entrance to the House of Commons was treated on the social or women's pages of the Canadian press, where her wardrobe and personal style were closely scrutinized.[47] This treatment as a new MP encouraged Macphail to adopt an increasingly critical perspective toward her own political experiences, even though she had not been active previously as a feminist or suffragist.[48] First, and very importantly, Macphail's legislative work suggested to her that progressive men were not immune to the general biases of males against females in politics; even J.S. Woodsworth (at the time a Labour MP from Manitoba) once confessed: 'I still don't think a woman has any place in politics.'[49] Second, Macphail learned that few policy concerns raised by Canadian feminists received serious attention within legislative bodies. She therefore worked diligently on family allowance, equal pay and women's prison issues, even though her initial priorities had concerned the rights of Ontario farmers.

Third, Macphail's experiences as a provincial and federal legislator led her to speak publicly about the continuing obstacles to female political involvement. During the 1930s, she rejected at least one proposal that would have guaranteed female representation on all new CCF committees, arguing that women could not demand special considerations on the basis of gender.[50] Nevertheless, she believed strongly that males would not easily concede or even share control over political decision-making. In a 1949 article entitled 'Men Want to Hog Everything', Macphail foreshadowed the more recent observations of Liberal MP Judy LaMarsh: 'The old ideas of chivalry justify men in thinking of women as a rather poor choice in human beings. Put her on a pedestal, then put pedestal and all in a cage.'[51]

What was specifically Canadian about Macphail's experiences, however, was the extent to which her own career reflected ongoing political tensions between partisanship and independence. Most notably, Macphail was elected on the platform of the United Farmers of Ontario, a primarily agrarian-based rural organization that rejected conventional 'partyism' in favour of direct group representation in the House of Commons.[52] Her role as a parliamentarian was therefore independent of the two established national parties, neither of which elected female MPs other than the spouses of former male MPs until the 1950s. At the same time, Macphail's work was part of ongoing efforts to challenge Liberal and Conservative dominance through a progressive labour/agrarian coalition at the federal level. Ultimately, the parliamentary alliance with which Macphail was associated formed one basis for the Co-operative Commonwealth Federation, established in 1932.

Macphail's political impact as a legislator was thus constrained by many of the same factors that had affected early feminist activism in English Canada. Like the suffrage movement itself, Macphail rejected conventional partisanship and established her legislative career outside the parameters of mainstream party politics. Although this 'anti-partyism' was consistent with Macphail's progressive beliefs as well as the reformist tenor of Canadian suffragism, such a position tended to limit her influence within an essentially partisan, parliamentary system.

On the other side of the coin, Macphail's commitment to political independence was complicated by a need to form coalitions in order to challenge conventional two-party dominance in English Canada. In Macphail's case, a parliamentary alliance with pacifists and Western Canadian socialists eventually cost her the seat in South-East Grey, since the constituents of this rural riding were unsympathetic towards many of the political partnerships and causes with which their MP was associated.[53]

Moreover, Macphail's ability to fashion an independent position around the rights of women was hampered by both consciousness and organization during this period: not only was there limited understanding of gender inequality and its implications, but most of the established organizations of Canadian women were ideologically opposed to her broader political views. Macphail was generally viewed as an agrarian progressive and, ultimately, as a leading Canadian socialist and pacifist. Her statements in support of the Glace Bay miners and against Canadian military academies, for example, were vehemently denounced by the IODE, the Women's Canadian Club and other established groups that had staked out their positions as the legitimate and representative voices of Canadian women.[54]

It was not until the relatively legalistic matter of female appointment to the Senate was broached that Canadian women began to overcome these internal differences and to pursue a more unified, coherent political strategy. In fact, the judicial victory associated with the 'Persons Case' in 1929 resembled closely the efforts to establish a royal commission on the status of women nearly forty years later, as well as the subsequent constitutional changes won by Canadian women in 1981. It is to the issue of Senate appointments that we now turn.

THE 'PERSONS CASE'

The issue of women's eligibility for Canadian Senate appointments, centred around legal interpretations of the word 'persons', came to public attention during the year following full federal enfranchisement. In 1919, the first president of the Federated Women's Institutes of Canada, Edmonton police magistrate Emily Murphy, received unanimous support from her organization for a resolution encouraging the government of Canada to appoint a woman to the Senate. The NCWC and the Montreal Women's Club passed similar resolutions that were subsequently rejected by the federal Conservative government on the basis of a narrow constitutional reading of the word 'persons'.[55] A specific nominee to the Senate was suggested by members of the Montreal Women's Club, who endorsed Judge Murphy because of her suffragist and social feminist efforts in co-ordination with Nellie McClung, Henrietta Muir Edwards (an activist in the Alberta branch of the NCWC), and provincial UFA legislators Irene Parlby and Louise McKinney.

One difficult problem confronting Murphy and her supporters grew out of partisan divisions among Canadian women. According to Rudy Marchildon, attempts to have the 'persons' issue raised at major party conventions during the 1920s were unsuccessful, largely because many women's groups (including the Montreal Women's Club) were composed primarily of Liberals who objected to petitioning the Conservative government of the day. Once the Tories were defeated federally, fears that a newly elected Liberal government might appoint British Columbia MLA Mary Ellen Smith to the Senate prevented many Conservatives from actively pursuing the 'persons' issue.[56]

Fortunately for the cause of female senators, in 1927 Emily Murphy learned of an obscure provision in the Supreme Court Act that permitted interested parties to request constitutional interpretation of points under the BNA Act. She then enlisted the support of her four suffragist colleagues from Alberta and, on 19 October 1927, all five women petitioned the Supreme Court of Canada. Since their legal expenses were to be assumed by the federal government, Murphy's group selected a prominent Toronto lawyer, Newton Wesley Rowell, to present the case both in Ottawa and, later, before the Privy Council in London. Rowell had strongly supported woman suffrage during his term as Liberal opposition leader in Ontario, and his wife had served during that same period as the first president of the Toronto Women's Liberal Association.[57]

Despite the well-sustained arguments presented by Rowell in Ottawa, all five Supreme Court justices who heard the case concurred in the following judgement, delivered on 24 April 1928: 'Women are not "qualified persons" within the meaning of Section 24 of the BNA Act, 1867, and therefore are not eligible for appointment by the Governor General to the Senate of Canada.'[58] The solicitor-general in the federal Liberal government, Lucien Cannon, supported by Quebec special counsel Charles Lanctot, had successfully argued that the original intent of the BNA Act was strictly for men, as 'qualified persons', to be appointed to the Senate. The federal government position also maintained that if a more liberal and contemporary interpretation were to be attached to 'persons', then such changes would require legislative rather than judicial action.

Undeterred by this defeat in the Supreme Court of Canada, and by the failure of the federal justice minister to introduce amending legislation as promised during the 1928 parliamentary session, Judge Murphy made plans to present her case in London. On 18 October 1929, approximately two years after the initial petition to the Supreme Court of Canada, the Judicial Committee of the Privy Council announced its decision that women were indeed persons and thus eligible for appointment to the Senate. This decision was greeted with 'much gratification' by Judge Murphy and her allies, who believed that the 'persons' judgement at last conferred 'full political rights' upon the women of Canada.[59]

In the years following 1929, neither Emily Murphy nor any of her four colleagues was appointed to the Senate. Apparently their feminist activities and, in Murphy's case, Conservative family connections eliminated them from consideration by a Liberal government unwilling to risk the political costs that might be attached to such nominations, especially in the province of Quebec. The Senate thus became for women what it had long remained for men: a regionally and religiously balanced Upper House that rewarded loyal party activists rather than non- or minimally partisan social reformers.

Not surprisingly, then, the first woman to be appointed to the Senate was a well-known Ontario Liberal, Cairine Wilson, who was nominated in 1930 by the King government. Unlike Murphy, McClung or other feminist women who had entered into strategic alliances with the Liberals, Senator Wilson was a seasoned and reliable partisan who had led the Eastern Ontario Liberal Women's Association, the Ottawa Liberal Women's Club and the National Federation of

Liberal Women. Her father was a wealthy Laurier Liberal from Montreal, who had also held a Senate seat.

Aside from these obvious political credentials, Senator Wilson was an uncontroversial social choice as the first woman in the Upper House. She had raised a large family, was active in church and charity work, and believed firmly in traditional moral and family values. For example, when asked in one interview about her interest in serving on the Senate divorce committee, Wilson replied 'that she had no such ambition, and that she had been so busy with her home and her babies she hadn't time to think about divorce'.[60]

The press response to Wilson's appointment echoed conventional views regarding the civilizing influence that women would bring to public life. The new senator was predicted to become 'a charming and hospitable hostess' in Ottawa, a welcome 'adornment' to the city and the nation's Upper House.[61] In the words of a *Maclean's* journalist, Senator Wilson was 'for all of her wealth and social prestige and political distinction . . . first, last, and always a woman—a wife and mother of eight children'.[62]

The second woman appointed to the Senate was also a party stalwart, but this time a Conservative; Iva Fallis of Ontario, who had served on the national executive of the Conservative Women's Association, was nominated in 1935 by the Tory government of R.B. Bennett. It was not until 1953 that additional women were appointed to the Senate, and not until the 1970s that two publicly prominent women, Thérèse Casgrain and Florence Bird, were named on the basis of their independent, non-partisan contributions to improving the status of women. The latter appointments were more closely related to the second wave of women's rights activism in Canada, discussed below, than to the premature expectations of political equality that accompanied the victory in the Persons Case.

BETWEEN THE MOVEMENTS

In the years following federal enfranchisement, the social reform legislation of the 1920s and the Persons Case, most Canadian women reassumed the traditional domestic responsibilities that they had performed prior to the First World War. The world-wide Depression played a major role in limiting the number of jobs available to either men or women, and prevailing beliefs that whatever work existed should go to male breadwinners had an especially devastating effect upon female employment throughout the 1930s. As Veronica Strong-Boag observes in her study of this period, 'To a large extent there was no great discontinuity with the past.'[63]

As women re-entered the home, frequently with the blessing of such prominent feminists as Nellie McClung, they helped to shape a society that was considerably different from that of earlier years. Perhaps the most significant change affecting women after 1920 was the increased level and acceptability of both female education and employment. As Mary Vipond demonstrates, growing numbers of single girls—especially those of the middle classes—were encouraged to develop career goals for the years prior to their marriage. A sound formal education was viewed as one critical element in such development since, over the longer term, 'a well-educated woman would be a more capable, more self-confident, and therefore a *better* wife and mother'.[64]

The household itself was also transformed during this period as manufacturers introduced a wide array of 'labour-saving' inventions to the marketplace. These new devices, from electric irons and toasters to dishwashers and sewing machines, were advertised as the cure for domestic drudgery. Married women could thus devote the bulk of their energies to the family, and particularly to the declining numbers of children who were born following 1920. The mass circulation magazines of the day reflected the expectation that women should develop a more expert and intense approach to their child-rearing responsibilities.[65]

This modernization of the domestic household, combined with increasing opportunities for female employment and education, held differing political implications for middle- and working-class women. For the former, the inter-war years were generally characterized by organizational continuity within such groups as the NCWC (established in 1893), the YWCA (established in 1894), and the Canadian Federation of University Women (CFUW, established in 1919). These voluntary associations, along with the newer Canadian Federation of Business and Professional Women's Clubs (established in 1930), remained actively committed to the social reformist goals that had earlier motivated mainstream English Canadian feminism. Similarly, the various women's associations within the two older political parties continued to operate through the 1930s, and in general to promote an auxiliary or supportive role for women in politics (see Chapter 5).

By contrast, these same years were a time of considerable ferment within the Canadian left, and particularly among women on the left. Research on the CCF by Joan Sangster and John Manley, for example, suggests that some working-class women rejected both the conventional feminist model of moderate social reform and the traditional partisan model of women as ancillary political workers and primary social and fund-raising organizers.[66] The Women's Joint Committee, which operated in Toronto for approximately six months during 1936, was a forerunner of more recent efforts to establish politically assertive women's groups within the major parties. Although the committee was weakened organizationally by a willingness to co-operate in 'united front' activities, it strongly endorsed leadership training programs for party women, publicly accessible birth control clinics, equal pay statutes and other progressive positions on policies of specific relevance to Canadian women.[67]

This ferment among women on the left, as well as the expansion of voluntary organizations among middle-class women, was temporarily interrupted by the events of the Second World War. Wartime mobilization drew hundreds of thousands of Canadian women into the armed forces, defence industries, service sector and agriculture.[68] Child care facilities and special tax provisions were established to encourage married women in particular to enter the wartime labour force.

Following the end of hostilities, when women's employment was no longer deemed to be 'of national importance', most child care centres were closed and federal tax statues reverted to their traditional format.[69] As in the years after the First World War, women were expected to surrender their jobs to returning veterans—an arrangement to which most willingly consented—and to resume their domestic duties. Therefore, despite assumptions that wartime employment would permanently alter the status of women in Canada, it generally represented only a temporary break from conventional gender role norms and expectations.[70]

An important new influence upon the experiences of post-war women, however, was the economic prosperity and sense of confidence that pervaded North American society during these years. As in the decade after 1918, middle-class women in particular were pressured to become major consumers on behalf of their households, and to provide emotional and personal comforts to their upwardly mobile husbands and 'baby boom' offspring.

The conflict between these domestic pressures and conventional role responsibilities, on the one hand, and the social experiences and expectations of women outside the home, on the other, held important political consequences for later years. That is, as middle-class women were exposed to broader educational and occupational opportunities, many resulting from the enlarged service sector necessary to operate the modern welfare state, they confronted an official as well as an informal ideology that was grounded in older, increasingly outdated social values. This contradiction between the post-war 'feminine mystique' of contented and conventional domesticity and a growing sense of personal restiveness and questioning provided one basis for the second wave of women's rights activism in English Canada.[71]

A renewed feminist movement also grew out of post-war activities on the Canadian left, where the gap between egalitarian socialist ideology and internal party practices—noted earlier by Agnes Macphail and others—continued to widen. As Joan Sangster and Dean Beeby have pointed out in their research on the Ontario CCF, relatively few members of the party's political elite were females, even though the organization claimed to represent the interests of all women (notably, the provincial caucus became the first in Canada to introduce equal pay legislation, in 1949).[72] Moreover, the CCF in Ontario employed the bulk of its female membership in social, fund-raising, canvassing and publicity work, a pattern that was reinforced following the appointment in 1942 of a separate women's committee. Although the professed goal of this committee and a subsequent Status of Women Committee (established in 1947) was to increase female party involvement at all levels, such groups had limited funds and faced considerable suspicion from the mainstream party organization. As a result, they tended to evolve into auxiliary-type associations that specialized in consumer price monitoring, bazaars, cookbook projects and other activities of a stereo-typically feminine nature.[73]

This continuation of conventional role norms and power arrangements within the organized left provided an important impetus for subsequent radical and socialist feminist movements in English Canada.

THE RENEWAL OF CANADIAN FEMINISM

The renewal of organized feminism in English Canada (see Table 1.2) is often linked with the establishment in 1960 of Voice of Women (VOW), a non-partisan, grass-roots association formed to oppose nuclear arms testing and weapons pro-liferation. From the outset, VOW remained a loosely organized group whose main goal was 'to unite women in concern for the future of the world'.[74] The mem-bership of VOW reached approximately 5,000 in 1961, and its leadership included a number of women who were later instrumental in efforts to establish a royal commission on the status of women (Helen Tucker, Thérèse Casgrain) and to pressure for implementation of the commission's recommendations in a national action committee on the status of women (Kay Macpherson).

TABLE 1.2 THE ESTABLISHMENT OF MAJOR CANADIAN WOMEN'S ORGANIZATIONS, 1960-1990

DATE	ORGANIZATION	MAIN PURPOSE
July 1960	Voice of Women (VOW)	'To crusade against the possibility of nuclear war'[a]
April 1966	Fédération des Femmes du Québec (FFQ)	To pressure for legislative reform and a Council of Women
June 1966	Committee for the Equality of Women in Canada (CEW)	To pressure for establishment of a royal commission on the status of women
February 1967	Royal Commission on the Status of Women (RCSW)	'To inquire into and report upon the status of women in Canada'[b]
March 1969	New Feminists, Toronto	'To awaken the consciousness of women as to the nature and extent of their oppression as women'[c]
September 1970	Report of the Royal Commission on the Status of Women	'To recommend what steps might be taken . . . to ensure for women equal opportunities'[d]
January 1971	National Ad Hoc Committee on the Status of Women in Canada	To pressure for implementation of Royal Commission recommendations
April 1972	National Action Committee on the Status of Women in Canada	(Replaced Ad Hoc Committee)
February 1972	Women for Political Action (WPA)	To increase female political participation and political education at all levels of government

DATE	ORGANIZATION	MAIN PURPOSE
May 1973	Canadian Advisory Council on the Status of Women (CACSW)	To report on women's concerns to the Minister Responsible for the Status of Women
February 1979	Feminist Party of Canada	To establish a political party with a feminist perspective
January 1981	Ad Hoc Committee of Canadian Women	To achieve equality for women in the Canadian Charter of Rights and Freedoms
January 1983	Canadian Coalition against Media Pornography	To protest the portrayal of women on pay-television
April 1985	Women's Legal Education and Action Fund (LEAF)	To pursue litigation under the equality rights provisions of the Charter
June 1985	Disabled Women's Network (DAWN)	To act as an advocate for women with disabilities
November 1986	National Organization of Immigrant and Visible Minority Women (NOIVM)	To voice the concerns of immigrant and visible minority women across Canada
March 1988	Women Against Free Trade (WAFT)	To co-ordinate opposition by women's groups to Canada-US free trade

[a]Kay Macpherson and Meg Sears, 'The Voice of Women: A History', in Gwen Matheson, ed., *Women in the Canadian Mosaic* (Toronto: Peter Martin, 1976), 72.

[b]Terms of Reference, reprinted in *Report* of the Royal Commission on the Status of Women in Canada (Ottawa: Information Canada, 1970), vii.

[c]Lynne Teather, 'The Feminist Mosaic', in *Women in the Canadian Mosaic*, 331.

[d]Terms of Reference, vii.

While VOW thus provided 'a significant training ground' for future activists, it also offered valuable lessons in the political tensions that continued to confront independent women's organizations.[75] In 1963, when Prime Minister Lester Pearson reversed his position on the stationing of Bomarc missiles in Canada, VOW split internally over a response to his decision. Activists asked:

> Could one swallow the Liberal decision and still campaign against nuclear weapons without its constituting an attack on the party? The majority decided that such a swallow would gulp away VOW credibility. The organization attacked the policy . . . Many members disagreed; some because they wished to support and vote for Liberals, some because they were convinced that the loss, apparent or real, of an apolitical posture would destroy VOW's effectiveness. Others argued that it was one thing to oppose policies in general, but quite a different and disturbing thing to oppose particular leaders on specific matters. To these latter, open disagreement with father-figures was a new and terrifying sensation.[76]

Voice of Women's external credibility and internal unity suffered a great deal because of this split, as the portion of the organization that survived was increasingly labelled as politically marginal, a captive of the radical left. Despite its claims to political independence, therefore, VOW became wedged by broader partisan conflicts that shaped the debate over war, peace and, specifically, the Bomarc missiles. The transcendence of party politics, promised during the first decades of this century by mainstream suffragists, thus remained problematical within VOW during the 1960s.

The apparent lesson to be drawn from VOW's internal fragmentation was that Canadian women could best coalesce around one carefully circumscribed, relatively non-partisan concern: namely, an official inquiry into the status of women. Demands for such an inquiry were made public on 5 January 1967, when CFUW president Laura Sabia was quoted on the front page of the Toronto *Globe and Mail* as threatening to lead some two million women in a march on Ottawa unless the federal government agreed to establish a royal commission on the status of women.[77] Although this demand seemed sudden and—particularly in the context of Canada and Canadian women—unusually provocative, the discussion of women's status had in fact been ongoing for a number of years within older, middle-class women's associations, including the CFUW, YWCA and Business and Professional Women's Clubs.[78]

As in the earlier example of the Persons Case, the events surrounding the Royal Commission on the Status of Women (RCSW) suggest that disparate groups and individuals could indeed organize around one narrow, well-defined objective. According to Cerise Morris's summary, Laura Sabia employed her position as CFUW president to call together the representatives of some thirty-two other groups, who agreed in June 1966 to form 'a new national women's organization concerned solely with the status of women—Committee for the Equality of Women in Canada (CEW) and, through this vehicle, to press for the establishment of a royal commission'.[79] Supported by a strong editorial that appeared in the July issue of *Chatelaine*, a leading women's magazine, and by the broad-based coalition represented in CEW (which included the VOW, NCWC, IODE, YWCA, Business and Professional Women and the newly formed Fédération des Femmes du Québec), Sabia and sixty-four of her colleagues presented the Liberal minority government with a brief requesting the formation of such a commission in September 1966.[80]

During this same period, the two women who then held seats in the House of Commons pressured the Liberal cabinet to establish a royal commission. One was New Democrat Grace MacInnis, the daughter of former party leader J.S. Woodsworth, who in her youth had modelled herself after Agnes Macphail.[81] When MacInnis probed the government's plans on the floor of the House, she generally received facetious and non-committal replies to her questions.[82]

A considerably more influential MP in these matters was Judy LaMarsh, who held the secretary of state portfolio in the Pearson cabinet. Like Agnes Macphail during the 1920s and 1930s, LaMarsh reluctantly became a consistent supporter and initiator of women's rights legislation: 'No matter how little a suffragette by temperament, circumstances gradually forced me into the role of acting as spokesman and watchdog for women. If there had been a dozen women in the Cabinet, that wouldn't have been necessary, but I had to carry out this dual, unasked for, entirely unofficial and unpaid role.'[83] LaMarsh's pressures within Cabinet, combined with Sabia's organizational abilities and statements to the press, began to take effect by the winter of 1967. On 3 February 1967, Prime Minister Pearson announced the formation of the RCSW, to be headed by well-known journalist Anne Francis (Florence Bird).[84]

Despite numerous doubts about its usefulness and, especially on the part of LaMarsh, its legislative impact, the royal commission was critical in helping to define publicly the issue of women's status in Canada.[85] Many academic researchers, older women's associations, newer status of women groups and private individuals contributed to the hearings and final report; approximately 470 briefs in total were presented during the four years following its establishment. Press coverage of the commission process also ensured its visibility, as did the publication of a well-written, well-organized report that provided one of the first systematic overviews of the contemporary female condition in Canada.[86] In all, 167 recommendations were listed in the final version, presented to Prime Minister Trudeau in December 1970.

In historical terms, it is difficult to distinguish the impact of the RCSW from the influence of concurrent developments on the Canadian left. Not only did the women attracted to the Canadian left during the 1960s tend to be younger than the women associated with the commission—many of whom were middle-aged veterans of older voluntary associations—but they were also far more radical both in their identification of the problems facing women and in the solutions they proposed. According to the prevailing liberal view, the basic problem was an inequality of opportunity that could be corrected by legislative reform. By contrast, those on the left saw women's problems as rooted in a pervasive oppression that could not be corrected without a fundamental transformation of social and economic structures. Since, in their view, legislative reform would accomplish little or nothing, few radical women submitted briefs to the royal commission.[87]

The emergence of a more radical 'women's liberation' movement in Canada can be linked to the experiences of females on the left and, more specifically, to their treatment within such new left groups as the Student Union for Peace Action (SUPA).[88] In common with some CCF women of the 1930s and following, female SUPA activists took issue with their assignment to clerical and fund-raising tasks while the leading political strategists, speakers and decision-makers were men. This rejection of conventional role norms by younger women produced a variety of practical and philosophical responses, ranging from radical feminism, which identified the origins of female oppression in biologically determined gender roles, to socialist and Marxist feminism, which generally focused upon the relationship between class structures and the institutions of the left, on the one hand, and women's social and economic position, on the other.[89]

Throughout most of the late 1960s and early 1970s, older women's rights and newer women's liberation groups competed for media attention, social legitimacy and the loyalties of Canadian women. Signs of a possible *rapprochement* between the two sides appeared in 1972, however, at the Strategy for Change conference that formally established the National Action Committee on the Status of Women (NAC).[90] As an umbrella organization embracing widely disparate groups, NAC set out to see that the major recommendations of the royal commission were implemented, and that the various concerns of its constituent members were presented to parliamentary committees, task forces and the public at large. From the outset, NAC's mandate was explicitly non-partisan; it was to argue forcefully and independently on behalf of Canadian women.[91]

The National Action Committee was initially directed by a Toronto-based steering committee, but this arrangement was criticized by activists in Atlantic Canada, Quebec and the Western provinces who questioned how a group with a decidedly Toronto voice could speak for all Canadian women. In 1980, NAC adopted a regionally-based national board system with specified provincial and territorial representatives. NAC attracted older organizations such as the National Council of Canadian Women along with newer and more radical women's liberation and women's rights groups. As an organization of organizations, it grew from 15 member groups in 1972 to approximately 586 in 1988; by the late 1980s approximately 5 million Canadian women held membership in NAC's constituent groups.[92] At the same time, NAC grew increasingly dependent on funds from the federal government, particularly the Secretary of State Women's Program; by the mid-1980s, it obtained approximately $680,000 annually from federal sources, or about 65 percent of its yearly budget.[93]

In 1973, the Canadian Advisory Council on the Status of Women (CACSW) was established. As recommended in the *Report* of the royal commission, this council was charged with the tasks of undertaking research, developing programs and legislative proposals, and consulting with existing organizations in the area of women's rights. However, contrary to the commission's recommendation, CACSW was made responsible to a single cabinet minister—the minister responsible for the status of women—rather than to parliament as a whole. This jurisdictional matter became the basis for a major conflict between the Liberal government and women's groups during constitutional discussions in 1981, when, as we shall see, the ability of the advisory council to represent independently the concerns of Canadian women was called into serious question.

PROBLEMS OF POLITICAL STRATEGY

The Report of the Royal Commission, published in 1970, highlighted a wide variety of inequalities affecting women in Canada. One of the most troubling of these was the relative absence of females in positions of political influence and, more specifically, the weak representation of women in Canadian provincial and federal legislatures.[94] As British Columbia MLA Rosemary Brown reflected in the wake of both this report and her own political experiences, 'to talk of power and to talk of women is to talk of the absence of power as we understand it today'.[95]

The organized response of Canadian women to this situation has been complex and at times conflictual, encompassing both politically independent and partisan strategies. One early effort to increase female representation at elite levels was the Toronto-based Women for Political Action (WPA), a non-partisan organization established in 1972. Following a series of articles in *Chatelaine* magazine that identified obstacles facing women in politics and presented profiles of '105 potential women MPs', a number of activists in Voice of Women (including Kay Macpherson) and the Ontario Committee on the Status of Women (including future MP Aideen Nicholson) established WPA as a focal point for the growing national network of politically active feminists.[96]

Although a key priority of WPA was the election of more females to public office, there were frequent disputes within the group regarding the best means towards this end.[97] In 1972, prior to the announcement of a federal election, many WPA members favoured the nomination of independent women candidates who, following their election, 'could independently set up a caucus in the House of Commons'.[98] This position in support of independent candidacies was in fact pursued by WPA in 1972, when the organization fielded two of its members in the Toronto federal ridings of St Paul's (Macpherson) and Rosedale (Aline Gregory). While both campaigns mobilized large numbers of newly active women and, particularly in the case of Rosedale, introduced feminist collective organization and consciousness-raising to federal electioneering, neither was successful in winning a parliamentary seat.

These electoral defeats, combined with the inroads that other women appeared to be making in established party organizations, led many WPA members away from political independence and in the direction of traditional partisanship. In the words of one activist in Aline Gregory's campaign: 'There were a lot of people who took the message from these experiences that we should all join the established parties, and become conventional political participants . . . In the years following 1972, many women indeed joined parties.'[99] As more WPA members became active and committed partisans, however, the group's mandate to remain politically independent became increasingly irrelevant to its core constituency. Therefore, until about 1979, WPA existed as little more than a Toronto post-office box address, sponsoring occasional conferences (including a 1973 'Women in Politics' session with Rosemary Brown as keynote speaker) and campaign schools.[100]

The partisan identifications adopted by WPA veterans and other feminists who chose to participate in mainstream party politics were generally New Democratic and, particularly on the federal level, Liberal.[101] Within both parties, feminist activists made impressive gains by the mid-1970s, as task forces and new women's rights organizations were established (the NDP Participation of Women Committee and the Women's Liberal Commission were created in 1969 and 1973, respectively) and as more women became visibly influential, particularly as holders of major party and public office (see Chapter 3).[102] In 1972 three Liberal women were elected to the House of Commons from Quebec; among them was Monique Bégin, who had served as executive secretary to the royal commission and as an activist in the Fédération des Femmes du Québec. In 1974, five more Liberal women took office as federal MPs, including Aideen Nicholson, who had largely built her campaign organization within the Ontario Committee on the Status of Women.[103]

The mid-1970s was also a very hopeful period for women in the NDP. On the federal level, a 1974 women's convention in Winnipeg served as the starting point for a feminist-oriented leadership campaign by Rosemary Brown.[104] As a backbencher in the British Columbia NDP caucus, Brown made a strong and credible showing against interim federal leader Ed Broadbent (see Chapter 4). In addition to marking the first campaign for major party leadership by a woman in Canada, this 1975 convention elected Joyce Nash as the first female president of a major federal party organization. In short, the gains made by Liberal and New Democratic women during the early and mid-1970s suggested that political influence was indeed accessible to all hard-working and committed partisans, regardless of gender.

This promise began to fade, however, as growing numbers of feminists questioned the policy changes that had been effected during the decade since the establishment of the RCSW. Such issues as equal pay, pension reform, abortion, day care and sex role stereotyping in education and the media remained largely ignored by both provincial and federal governments through the early 1980s, even though detailed reports and legislative proposals had been prepared by status of women groups (including NAC), internal party task forces and growing numbers of new policy-oriented women's organizations.[105] Among the specific mandates of the latter were reproductive choice (Canadian Abortion Rights Action League, Ontario Coalition for Abortion Clinics), improved child care provisions (Canadian Day Care Advocacy Association), employment rights (Equal Pay Coalition) and media stereotyping (Canadian Coalition Against Media Pornography).[106]

By 1980 many had come to believe that women's advisory councils, notably on the federal level (CACSW), as well as women's associations within the parties, were too traditional in their composition and strategy to provide effective political leadership in these important issue areas. In addition, the partisan and personality conflicts that developed in such groups as NAC suggested that a systematic, coherent response to government inaction was unlikely to develop within 'independent' women's organizations.[107]

Nor was policy influence the only area of frustration. Canadian feminists also questioned the progress that had been made in electing women to public and party office. The weak showing of Conservative leadership candidate Flora

MacDonald was particularly disappointing, since she had received considerable moral and financial support from many women who were not Conservatives (see Chapter 4). Although her campaign captured the imagination of many politically minded feminists, MacDonald's sixth-place finish at the 1976 leadership convention suggested that major obstacles continued to impede women's participation in elite-level politics.

The establishment in February 1979 of the Feminist Party of Canada, coinciding with the revival of Women for Political Action and early discussions regarding a women's bureau in the federal Conservative organization, reflected the extent to which politically active women had begun to reconsider their accomplishments. One early statement by the Feminist party expressed this malaise in terms of developments over the sixty years following federal enfranchisement:

> Since that time, women have indeed increased their attempts to become elected representatives—the number of women seeking federal office rose from 4 in 1921, to 137 in 1974. But the number of women who won seats in those 53 years rose only from one to nine. The dismal prognosis is that, at this rate, we will need another 842 years to achieve equal representation at the federal level.[108]

The response of Feminist party founders was to create their own 'political party with a feminist perspective'.[109] This goal was complicated early on by fragile internal alliances (that is, Conservative status of women activists combined with radical feminists in a single organization), and by the announcement of two federal elections within approximately one year of the new party's establishment.

Ultimately, the Feminist party was a short-lived coalition that made little direct impact upon female participation in Canadian politics. Like Women for Political Action in 1972, however, it symbolized the continuing attractiveness of independent women's organizations to many feminists, including those who only later recognized their limitations within a partisan, parliamentary system. Moreover, the existence of WPA and the Feminist party pointed towards a fundamental questioning of women's numerical representation and policy impact within the Canadian political process, one that would assume ever greater urgency in the 1980s and 1990s.

WOMEN AND THE CONSTITUTION

The long-standing political discontent of many Canadian women crystallized around a single issue during the years 1980-82: constitutional change. Some English Canadian feminists claimed a particular stake in the renewal of constitutional federalism, since they had sent letters and telegrams of support to the 'Non' forces, and especially to activists in the 'Yvette' movement, during the 1980 Quebec referendum campaign.[110] The success of the 'Non' forces in this referendum, combined with the imminent defeat of the US Equal Rights Amendment, suggested that Canadian women would need to play a major role in discussions over future constitutional arrangements.[111]

Systematic input by women's groups into this process, however, came only after prolonged disputes not only with the federal government but within these same women's organizations. Constitutional conflict in 1981-82 spilled over most directly into NAC, especially after the federal government proposed that provinces be granted jurisdictional control over family law. Women's organizations in Quebec supported this proposal, believing that family law and a host of other matters were best handled by a provincial government in Quebec City that was sensitive to the needs of people in Quebec. By contrast, most women's groups in English Canada opposed this proposal, arguing instead for national standards, uniform legislation and the primacy of the federal government.[112] One the many casualties of this round of constitutional bargaining was French/English cohesion within the National Action Committee; the FFQ withdrew from NAC, although it re-affiliated after constitutional matters had quieted down in the mid-1980s.

Much of the public debate over women and the constitution followed a request by the minister responsible for the status of women, Lloyd Axworthy, that the federal advisory council (CACSW) cancel its planned conference on this subject. Axworthy advised that such a conference could prove politically damaging to the Liberal government, and a majority of council members—who were generally 'safe' Liberal appointees—supported his view. In the words of one approving member: 'I saw that it's about time we started playing games the same way government plays games. We should start being nice to them. So if this conference is going to be an embarrassment, let's play it their way and cancel it.'[113]

Doris Anderson, a former editor of *Chatelaine* who had run unsuccessfully as a federal Liberal candidate in 1978, opposed Axworthy's intervention and resigned from the presidency of CACSW on 20 January 1981. Her unwillingness to cancel the conference came as a surprise to Axworthy and his supporters, as well as to many women who had long doubted the value of the federal advisory council. On an organizational level, Anderson's resignation prompted the formation on 21 January of the Ad Hoc Committee of Canadian Women, which held its own successful constitutional conference in Ottawa on 14 February.[114] The Ad Hoc Committee relied upon a diverse base of volunteer support, similar to those employed earlier in the Persons Case and in the efforts to create a royal commission. This visible core of support, again developing around a single, well-defined political issue, later helped to ensure the inclusion of equality rights provisions in the new, constitutionally-entrenched Charter of Rights and Freedoms (sections 15 and 28).

In political terms, however, the 1981 constitutional crisis tended to exacerbate older tensions between partisanship and independence among Canadian women. Just as a number of Liberal activists felt betrayed by the resignation of Doris Anderson,[115] so many others who were less identified with the party believed that they (along with Anderson) were the victims of government—and especially cabinet—manipulation.[116] These perceptions of betrayal and manipulation were deep-seated and spilled over into other organizations that were also associated with the constitutional process. In the National Action Committee, for example, one assistant to Lloyd Axworthy sponsored a contentious resolution on the Charter of Rights; it was approved after dubious political manoeuvrings.[117] As retiring NAC president Lynn McDonald observed in the wake of these events, 'Women's organizations, with their fragile inter-party compositions, have been sorely tried by the Constitution debate.'[118]

Feminist interventions in the federal constitutional debates of the early 1980s thus demonstrated the ability of English Canadian women to form narrow issue coalitions across party lines, while at the same time evidencing the fragility and temporary nature of these alliances. The decline of the Ad Hoc Committee following parliamentary approval of section 28 suggested that ideological unity and organizational continuity remained elusive goals. Canadian women's political history in the 1980s continued to be enmeshed in a complex and uneasy tension between non-partisanship and independent feminism, on the one hand, and the demands of a party-structured parliamentary system, on the other.

NEW CHALLENGES, NEW FEMINISMS

Among liberal feminists, much of the decade after 1982 was marked by concerted efforts to protect and enhance equality rights provisions in the Charter. The leadership of the National Action Committee was solidly committed to legal rights issues through the early 1980s; NAC co-ordinated its efforts with a growing core of legal policy specialists in the National Association of Women and the Law (NAWL) and the Women's Legal Education and Action Fund (LEAF), many of whom had earlier been active in the Ad Hoc Committee.[119] Increased numbers of female students were admitted to law schools, and in 1982 Madam Justice Bertha Wilson became the first woman appointed to the Supreme Court of Canada.[120]

Feminist lawyers and academics helped to spawn a new field of Charter-oriented research, focusing on the implications of equality rights sections.[121] Yet at least one major study of Charter litigation offered pessimistic conclusions. According to Gwen Brodsky and Shelagh Day: 'The news is not good. Women are initiating few cases, and men are using the Charter to strike back at women's hard-won protections and benefits.'[122]

The limits of legislative and judicial progress were only too clear to feminists familiar with the party system. Within ten years of the founding of Women for Political Action, a new generation of women and politics groups had begun to emerge across the country. Like the Toronto-based Committee for '94, established with the goal of electing women to half the seats in the House of Commons by 1994, these organizations were composed primarily of partisans, journalists and non-partisan activists who were frustrated with the limited numbers and influence of female legislators.[123]

Their multi-party composition and media connections helped these groups to attract public attention, and permitted them to sponsor seminars, books, press conferences, television programs, legislative internships and skills training work-shops.[124] Some proposals for structural reform of parties and elections originated in these groups; the Committee for '94, for example, developed a policy brief calling for complete public funding of nomination contests, elections and party leadership campaigns.[125]

These efforts were increasingly challenged, however, by vocal anti-feminist interests such as R.E.A.L. Women.[126] As a conservative group opposed to abortion and in favour of traditional family hierarchies, R.E.A.L. Women also attracted considerable media attention, and eventually obtained financial support from the same federal government source that funded NAC. Much of this legitimacy can be attributed to the election in 1984 and 1988 of successive Progressive Conservative majority governments, each of which included members sympathetic to R.E.A.L. Women.[127]

Yet the difficulties associated with this struggle against anti-feminism must be juxtaposed with at least three other major developments during the 1980s. First, the organized women's movement (under the auspices of NAC) sponsored a nationally televised leaders' debate during the 1984 federal election campaign. This debate helped to establish a convention whereby 'women's issues' were taken more seriously in campaigns; the 1988 debates did not include a separate women's debate, but sponsoring networks did devote part of the question period to these matters.

Second, NAC intervened in a very public and controversial manner in the free trade debate of 1985-88. Through its involvement in many of the leading national and provincial organizations that opposed this cornerstone of Conservative economic policy, and through its participation in the Toronto-based Women Against Free Trade, the organized women's movement in English Canada became a key player in anti-free trade coalitions. NAC based its opposition on arguments that free trade would not only cause job losses for women employed in manufacturing and service occupations, but also that it would also harmonize Canadian labour and social legislation with less progressive US standards.[128]

The challenge to Conservative policy implicit in NAC's position on free trade became even more explicit with a third development. The Meech Lake Accord, arrived at by eleven male 'first ministers' in the spring of 1987, offered substantial additional powers to all provincial governments—not just the government of Quebec.[129] As in the early 1980s, English Canadian women's groups (including a revived Ad Hoc Committee) tended to oppose this devolution of power, believing that further decentralization was damaging to the cause of women's rights, that the closed-door procedures involved in reaching the Accord were badly flawed, and that the terms of the Accord jeopardized the progress that had been made on equality rights in 1982.[130] By contrast, the FFQ strongly supported the five provisions of the Meech Lake Accord, which had essentially been proposed by the Quebec government. The FFQ once again withdrew from NAC in 1989, and did not renew its membership as a constituent group through the early 1990s.[131]

In short, just as the government of Quebec announced in 1990 that it would conduct direct bilateral negotiations with the federal government and would not participate as 'just another province' at any other federal/provincial meetings, so too did organized feminists in Quebec announce that they were unwilling to speak about constitutional politics under the umbrella of the National Action Committee.

Among leading English Canadian feminists, the collapse of Meech Lake in June 1990 was followed by an intense period of reassessment.[132] What had the 1982 constitutional round accomplished, and what additional gains or protections were necessary in any future round? The nation-wide 'Equality Eve' meetings in which approximately 4,000 women took part on 14 February 1991 were among the efforts undertaken to establish a 'Women's Agenda' for the future of Canada.[133]

This process was in some respects unlike previous attempts to distil a feminist constitutional position. In contrast to the situation that prevailed ten years earlier, feminists in English Canada faced a Conservative federal government whose major priorities they had directly challenged on at least two occasions.[134] Politically, the organized women's movement was in a pariah-like position, faced with significant federal funding cuts as well as continued policy and fiscal threats from R.E.A.L. Women.[135] Internally, the women's movement was also substantially altered: NAC was influenced more strongly by socialist and radical feminism, and the conflicts between them, than by the consensual liberal variants that had dominated it in earlier periods.[136] More voices, and more disparate ones, established their claims under the feminist umbrella, including disabled, aboriginal, visible minority, lesbian and immigrant women.[137]

Ironically, this explosion of diverse voices and NAC's growing political isolation coincided with the election of record numbers of Canadian women to public office. The selection of Audrey McLaughlin as federal NDP leader in 1989, Rita Johnston's brief tenure as BC premier in 1991 and Bob Rae's appointment of eleven women to the Ontario cabinet in 1990 were all significant milestones. Taken together, however, these achievements at the elite political level did not mean automatic success for feminist claims in the public policy realm—that is, with reference to employment, child care, abortion or other issues.[138]

Feminist interests in the early 1990s thus seemed constrained by both new and old challenges. The governing federal party, and many women within it, were tired of sustained conflicts with NAC, an 'independent' English Canadian feminist organization that from their perspective seemed more and more tied to an anti-Conservative, oppositional discourse. By contrast, opponents of neo-conservatism shuddered to imagine the long-term effects of the Mulroney regime. Parties throughout Canada came under increased pressure to recruit more women, but not simply affluent, white professionals who would essentially mirror the traditional male elite. Feminists inside and outside the parties worked to articulate what they wanted in a future Canada, beyond basic participation in the process and protection of hard-won Charter provisions. Not surprisingly, many wondered what repercussions would follow from the arrival of new parties on the political scene, including the Reform, Confederation of Regions and Bloc Québécois organizations.

Was partisanship or, conversely, political independence a better strategic choice in this environment? From the perspective of the early 1990s, both routes appeared equally necessary, since on their own neither seemed likely to render women a politically effective entity. But even together, the discordance among women's voices clearly threatened both internal cohesion and external influence.

CONCLUSIONS

This chapter has examined the political history of women in English Canada, focusing upon the long-standing tension between non-partisan independence and more conventional political partisanship. Our discussion has emphasized the importance of this tension in shaping the political experiences of women in English Canada, from the suffragist era through enfranchisement to the present.

In order to evaluate the implications of this historical development for political attitudes and involvement, a variety of empirical materials will be considered in Chapters 2 and 3.

NOTES

[1] *Woman's Century*, 1918, as quoted in Jean Cochrane, *Women in Canadian Politics* (Toronto: Fitzhenry and Whiteside, 1977), 37.

[2] Agnes Macphail, 'Men Want to Hog Everything', *Maclean's Magazine*, 15 September 1949, 72.

[3] For a concise treatment of constraints on female political participation, see Jeane J. Kirkpatrick, *Political Woman* (New York: Basic Books, 1974), chap. 1.

[4] A useful definition of political power is presented by Robert D. Putnam, who writes that power constitutes 'the probability of influencing the policies and activities of the state'. See Putnam, *The Comparative Study of Political Elites* (Englewood Cliffs, NJ: Prentice-Hall, 1976), 6.

[5] See Catherine L. Cleverdon, *The Woman Suffrage Movement in Canada* (Toronto: University of Toronto Press, 1974).

[6] See Carol Lee Bacchi, *Liberation Deferred? The Ideas of the English-Canadian Suffragists, 1877-1918* (Toronto: University of Toronto Press, 1983), 26. In *The Woman Suffrage Movement in Canada*, Cleverdon reports that the Toronto Women's Literary Club was established in 1876 (20).

[7] These subsequent organizations included the Canadian Woman Suffrage Association (CWSA), established in 1883; the Dominion Women's Enfranchisement Association (DWEA), founded in 1889; and the Canadian Suffrage Association (CSA), established in 1906.

[8] See Bacchi, *Liberation Deferred*; as well as Mariana Valverde, *The Age of Light, Soap and Water: Moral Reform in English Canada, 1885-1925* (Toronto: McClelland and Stewart, 1991).

[9] On the international ties of the Canadian suffragists, see Deborah Gorham, 'English Militancy and the Canadian Suffrage Movement', *Atlantis* 1 (1975); and Deborah Gorham, 'Singing Up the Hill', *Canadian Dimension* 10 (1975).

[10] Richard Evans, *The Feminists* (London: Croom Helm, 1977).

[11] The terms 'social' and 'hard-core' feminism were introduced in William L. O'Neill, *Everyone was Brave: A History of Feminism in America* (New York: Quadrangle, 1971). A similar distinction between the 'expediency' and 'justice' claims of suffragism in the US was made earlier in Aileen S. Kraditor, *The Ideas of the Woman Suffrage Movement* (New York: Columbia University Press, 1965).

[12] See Deborah Gorham, 'Flora MacDonald Denison: Canadian Feminist', in Linda Kealey, ed., *A Not Unreasonable Claim: Women and Reform in Canada* (Toronto: Women's Press, 1979), 47-70.

[13] J. Stanley Lemons, *The Woman Citizen: Social Feminism in the 1920s* (Urbana: University of Illinois Press, 1973), ix. For a comparative study of this phenomenon, see Naomi Black, *Social Feminism: Theory and Organization in England, France and the United States* (Ithaca: Cornell University Press, 1989).

[14] On the role of maternal feminism in Canada, see Linda Kealey, 'Introduction', to *A Not Unreasonable Claim*, 1-14.

[15] Bacchi, *Liberation Deferred*, 35.

[16] Cleverdon, *The Woman Suffrage Movement in Canada*, chaps 6 and 7.

[17] The pivotal role of these women's organizations is discussed in Veronica Strong-Boag, '"Setting the Stage": National Organization and the Women's Movement in the Late Nineteenth Century', in Susan Mann Trofimenkoff and Alison Prentice, eds., *The Neglected Majority* (Toronto: McClelland and Stewart, 1977), 87-103; and Wendy Mitchinson, 'The WCTU: "For God, Home and Native Land"', in Kealey, ed., *A Not Unreasonable Claim*, 151-67.

[18] See Cleverdon, *The Woman Suffrage Movement in Canada*, chaps 6 and 7.

[19] Allen Mills summarizes this position in his study of J.S. Woodsworth: 'In Woodsworth's view what was wrong with Parliament was the partisan system that destroyed the independence of the average Member of Parliament . . . Government, he felt, should not be party government but a committee of the best minds.' See Mills, 'The Later Thought of J.S. Woodsworth, 1918-1942', *Journal of Canadian Studies* 17 (Fall 1982), 80.

[20] W.L. Morton, *The Progressive Party in Canada* (Toronto: University of Toronto Press, 1967).

[21] Ibid., 16.

[22] Candace Savage, *Our Nell: A Scrapbook Biography of Nellie L. McClung* (Saskatoon: Western Producer Prairie Books, 1979), 26. See also Veronica Strong-Boag, '"Ever a Crusader": Nellie McClung, First-Wave Feminist', in Strong-Boag and Anita Clair Fellman, eds., *Rethinking Canada: The Promise of Women's History* (Toronto: Copp Clark Pitman, 1991), 308-21.

[23] Savage, *Our Nell*, 27.

[24] Ibid., 83.

[25] Ibid., 95.

[26] On the early debate over federal enfranchisement, see Cleverdon, *The Woman Suffrage Movement in Canada*, 105-18; and Bacchi, *Liberation Deferred*, 134-9.

[27] See Bacchi, *Liberation Deferred*, 139-43; and Gloria Geller, 'The Wartime Elections Act of 1917 and the Canadian Women's Movement', *Atlantis* 2 (Fall 1976), 88-106. On the background to this period, see Ceta Ramkhalawansingh, 'Women During the Great War', in *Women at Work* (Toronto: Women's Press, 1974), 261-307.

[28] Dr Margaret Gordon, as quoted in Geller, 'Wartime Elections', 104.

[29] Bacchi, *Liberation Deferred*, 141.

[30] See Savage, *Our Nell*; as well as Carol Bacchi, 'Race Regeneration and Social Purity: A Study of the Social Attitudes of Canada's English-Speaking Suffragists', *Histoire Sociale/Social History* 11 (November 1978), 460-74.

[31] Cleverdon, *The Woman Suffrage Movement in Canada*, 129.

[32] See Geller, 'Wartime Elections'.

[33] Savage, *Our Nell*, 171.

[34] See Bacchi, *Liberation Deferred*, 129-31.

[35] One major difference between the two cases, however, was that in the US the Woman's Party grew out of 'hard-core' feminist activities, while in English Canada it developed from the social feminist NEFU. On the American experience, see Susan D. Becker, *The Origins of the ERA: American Feminism betweeen the Wars* (Westport, Conn.: Greenwood, 1981).

[36] See Lemons, *The Woman Citizen*, chaps 2-9.

[37] See Savage, *Our Nell*.

[38] Elsie Gregory MacGill, *My Mother the Judge*, with an Introduction by Naomi Black (Toronto: Peter Martin, 1981).

[39] Ibid., 104.

[40] Diane Crossley, 'The BC Liberal Party and Women's Reforms, 1916-1928', in Barbara Latham and Cathy Kess, eds., *In Her Own Right: Selected Essays on Women's History in BC* (Victoria: Camosun College, 1980), 229-53.

[41] Smith was initially elected as an Independent in 1918, replacing her deceased husband who had sat both provincially and federally as a Liberal. She was re-elected in 1920 and 1924 as a Liberal.

[42] See Crossley, 'The BC Liberal Party and Women's Reforms', 234-5.

[43] Bacchi, *Liberation Deferred*, 32. On the reluctance to pursue public office among Western Canadian suffragists, see L.G. Thomas, *The Liberal Party in Alberta* (Toronto: University of Toronto Press, 1959), 177.

[44] See Liane Langevin, *Missing Persons: Women in Canadian Federal Politics* (Ottawa: Canadian Advisory Council on the Status of Women, 1977).

[45] According to one biography, the local UFO riding executive 'was besieged by protests' concerning its choice of Macphail as a candidate for the 1921 elections, and asked her to resign. See Margaret Stewart and Doris French, *Ask No Quarter* (Toronto: Longmans, Green, 1959), 56. Subsequent accounts of Macphail's career include Terry Crowley, *Agnes Macphail and the Politics of Equality* (Toronto: Lorimer, 1990); and Doris Pennington, *Agnes Macphail: Reformer, Canada's First Female M.P.* (Toronto: Simon and Pierre, 1989).

[46] Macphail, 'Men Want to Hog Everything', 72.

[47] See Stewart and French, *Ask No Quarter*.

[48] In the words of Stewart and French, *Ask No Quarter*, Macphail 'never took any part in the battle for votes for women . . . She was so absorbed in farm problems and cooperatives that the struggle seemed a long way off. She was never a formal feminist, nor even an informal one in the conduct of her life. She blamed women as much as men for the inferior position of the female citizen' (38-9).

[49] Macphail, 'Men Want to Hog Everything', 72.

[50] According to Stewart and French, *Ask No Quarter*, Macphail walked out of a CCF Women's luncheon with the words, 'I'm sick and tired of all this "woman" business. In all the time I've been in the House of Commons I've never asked for anything on the ground that I was a woman. If I didn't deserve it on my own merit I didn't want it! That's all I have to say' (170). See also Linda Rae Steward, 'A Woman of Courage: A Biography of Agnes Campbell Macphail' (unpublished Ph.D. dissertation, University of Toronto, 1991), 536.

[51] Macphail, 'Men Want to Hog Everything', 72. LaMarsh's memoirs were published in 1968 by McClelland and Stewart under the title *Memoirs of a Bird in a Gilded Cage*.

[52] See Doris French, 'Agnes Macphail, 1890-1954', in Mary Quayle Innis, ed., *The Clear Spirit* (Toronto: University of Toronto Press, 1966), 179-97.

[53] A major snowstorm on the day of the 1940 federal elections also damaged Macphail's chances for re-election. See Steward, *A Woman of Courage*, 469-71.

[54] See French, 'Agnes Macphail'.

[55] For details of this background, see Rudy G. Marchildon, 'The "Persons" Controversy', *Atlantis* 6:2 (Spring 1981), 99-113; A. Anne McLellan, 'Legal Implications of the Persons Case', *Constitutional Forum* 1:1 (October 1989), 11-14; and on Murphy in particular, Christine Mander, *Emily Murphy: Rebel* (Toronto: Simon and Pierre, 1985).

[56] See Marchildon, 'The "Persons" Controversy', 103ff.

[57] Rowell's activities as Ontario Opposition leader are summarized in Cleverdon, *The Woman Suffrage Movement in Canada*, 35-44. It is notable that Murphy learned of this provision through her brother, an insightful Ontario lawyer with Conservative political ties.

[58] Marchildon, 'The "Persons" Controversy', 106.

[59] Ibid., 111.

[60] John Leslie Scott, 'Our New Woman Senator, The Honourable Cairine Wilson', *Maclean's Magazine* 1 April 1930, 97. See also A.R. Way, 'From Time to Time in the Queen's Name: The Story of the Honourable Cairine Reay Wilson' (MA thesis, Carleton University, 1984); Valerie Knowles, *First Person: A Biography of Cairine Wilson* (Toronto: Dundurn Press, 1988); and Franca Iacovetta, '"A Respectable Feminist": The Political Career of Senator Cairine Wilson, 1921-1962', in Linda Kealey and Joan Sangster, eds., *Beyond the Vote* (Toronto: University of Toronto Press, 1989), 63-85.

[61] Scott, 'Our New Woman Senator', 98, 97. As of 1992, there were 13 female senators among 103 Senate members.

[62] Ibid., 97.

[63] Veronica Strong-Boag, *The New Day Recalled: Lives of Girls and Women in English Canada, 1919-1939* (Markham, Ont.: Penguin, 1988), 2. On developments in the US during this time, see Susan Ware, *Beyond Suffrage: Women in the New Deal* (Cambridge: Harvard University Press, 1981).

[64] Mary Vipond, 'The Image of Women in Mass Circulation Magazines in the 1920s', in *The Neglected Majority*, 118; emphasis in original. On the idea of educated motherhood in the US during this period, see Sheila M. Rothman, *Woman's Proper Place* (New York: Basic Books, 1978).

[65] See Vipond, 'The Image of Women'.

[66] Joan Sangster, *Dreams of Equality: Women on the Canadian Left, 1920-1950* (Toronto: McClelland and Stewart, 1989); Sangster, 'The Role of Women in the Early CCF, 1933-1940', in Kealey and Sangster, eds., *Beyond the Vote*, 118-38; and John Manley, 'Women and the Left in the 1930s: The Case of the Toronto CCF Women's Joint Committee', *Atlantis* 5:2 (Spring 1980), 100-19.

[67] See Sangster, *Dreams of Equality*, 111-14; and Manley, 'Women and the Left', 111-13.

[68] Ruth Pierson, 'Women's Emancipation and the Recruitment of Women into the Labour Force in World War II', in *The Neglected Majority*, 125-45; and Ruth Roach Pierson with Marjorie Cohen, *'They're Still Women After All': The Second World War and Canadian Womanhood* (Toronto: McClelland and Stewart, 1986).

[69] Pierson, 'Women's Emancipation', 142. Federal tax statutes were relaxed during the Second World War, permitting husbands to claim a married status exemption if their wives were employed for pay.

[70] Ibid., passim.

[71] Betty Friedan, *The Feminine Mystique* (New York: Dell, 1963).

[72] Sangster, *Dreams of Equality*, chap. 7; and Dean Beeby, 'Women in the Ontario CCF, 1940-1950', *Ontario History* 74:4 (December 1982), 258-83.

[73] See Sangster, *Dreams of Equality*, 215-22; and Beeby, 'Women in the Ontario CCF', 275-9.

[74] Kay Macpherson and Meg Sears, 'The Voice of Women: A History', in Gwen Matheson, ed., *Women in the Canadian Mosaic* (Toronto: Peter Martin, 1976), 71. See also Barbara Roberts, 'Women's Peace Activism in Canada', in Kealey and Sangster, eds., *Beyond the Vote*, 276-308; and Janice Williamson

and Deborah Gorham, eds., *Up and Doing: Canadian Women and Peace* (Toronto: Women's Press, 1989).

[75] Cerise Morris, '"Determination and Thoroughness": The Movement for a Royal Commission on the Status of Women in Canada', *Atlantis* 5:2 (Spring 1980), 6.

[76] Macpherson and Sears, 'The Voice of Women', 75.

[77] Barry Craig, 'Women's March May Back Call for Rights Probe', *Globe and Mail*, 5 January 1967, 1.

[78] See Lynne Teather, 'The Feminist Mosaic', in Matheson, ed., *Women in the Canadian Mosaic*, 308-10.

[79] Morris, '"Determination and Thoroughness"', 11. According to Laura Sabia, 'The CFUW generally worked on scholarship funds, white-glove tea parties and the like. They were a very proper and academic group . . . whose membership and executive frequently objected to my activities on behalf of the royal commission. One member even wrote to me and said that she was handing in her membership card because we were becoming too militantly feminist. Of course, when my statement about a march on Ottawa appeared in the *Globe and Mail*, the CFUW women were just appalled.' Interview with Laura Sabia, 15 March 1983.

[80] See Doris Anderson, 'Let's Find Out What's Happening to Women', *Chatelaine*, July 1966, 1. The CEW brief was compiled by a Toronto lawyer, Margaret Hyndman. On the chronology of this period, see Morris, '"Determination and Thoroughness"', 8-14.

[81] See Macphail, 'Men Want to Hog Everything', 72; as well as Susan Walsh, 'The Peacock and the Guinea Hen: Political Profiles of Dorothy Gretchen Steeves and Grace MacInnis', in Alison Prentice and Susan Mann Trofimenkoff, eds., *The Neglected Majority: Essays in Canadian Women's History*, vol. 2 (Toronto: McClelland and Stewart, 1985), 144-59.

[82] See Morris, '"Determination and Thoroughness"', 14.

[83] LaMarsh, *Memoirs of a Bird in a Gilded Cage*, 292.

[84] Bird's account of the royal commission is presented in *Anne Francis: An Autobiography* (Toronto: Clarke, Irwin, 1974), esp. 294ff.

[85] In her *Memoirs*, LaMarsh observed, 'There seems no one now within Government circles who is interested in seeing its recommendations take legislative form' (301).

[86] See *Report* of the Royal Commission on the Status of Women in Canada (Ottawa: Information Canada, 1970).

[87] One radical brief presented to the royal commission in June 1968 was prepared by Bonnie Kreps. See Kreps, 'Radical Feminism I', in *Women Unite! An Anthology of the Canadian Women's Movement* (Toronto: Canadian Women's Educational Press, 1972), 70-5.

[88] See Judy Bernstein, Peggy Morton, Linda Seese and Myrna Wood, 'Sisters, Brothers, Lovers . . . Listen . . . ', in *Women Unite!*, 31-9. For a more general account, see Nancy Adamson, Linda Briskin and Margaret McPhail, *Feminist Organizing for Change: The Contemporary Women's Movement in Canada* (Toronto: Oxford University Press, 1988).

[89] For a useful clarification of these various streams, written from a Marxist perspective during the same period, see Charnie Guettel, *Marxism and Feminism* (Toronto: Women's Press, 1974).

[90] The highlights of this conference are documented in a 1974 film by Moira Armour, entitled *The Status of Women: Strategy for Change*.

[91] See Sandra Burt, 'Women's Issues and the Women's Movement in Canada since 1970', in Alan Cairns and Cynthia Williams, eds., *The Politics of Gender, Ethnicity and Language in Canada*, Royal Commission Research Studies, vol. 34 (Toronto: University of Toronto Press for Supply and Services Canada, 1986), 111-69; and Sandra Burt, 'Organized Women's Groups and the State', in William D. Coleman and Grace Skogstad, eds., *Policy Communities and Public Policy in Canada* (Toronto: Copp Clark Pitman, 1990), 191-211.

[92] On NAC's development, see Jill Vickers, 'Bending the Iron Law of Oligarchy: Debates on the Feminization of Organization and Political Process in the English Canadian Women's Movement, 1970-1988', in Jeri Dawn Wine and Janice L. Ristock, eds., *Women and Social Change: Feminist Activism in Canada* (Toronto: Lorimer, 1991), 75-94; and Sylvia Bashevkin, 'Free Trade and Canadian Feminism: The Case of the National Action Committee on the Status of Women', *Canadian Public Policy* 15 (December 1989), 363-75.

[93] Christine Appelle, 'The New Parliament of Women: A Study of the National Action Committee on the Status of Women' (MA thesis, Carleton University, 1987), 55, 64. On the larger question of state dependence, see Sue Findlay, 'Facing the State: The Politics of the Women's Movement Reconsidered', in Heather Jon Maroney and Meg Luxton, eds., *Feminism and Political Economy* (Toronto: Methuen, 1987), 31-50; and Alicia Schreader, 'The State-Funded Women's Movement: A Case of Two Political Agendas', in Roxanna Ng, Gillian Walker and Jacob Muller, eds., *Community Organization and the Canadian State* (Toronto: Garamond Press, 1990), 184-99.

[94] See *Report* of the RCSW, chap. 7.

[95] Rosemary Brown, 'A New Kind of Power, 1973 Address to Women for Political Action', in Matheson, ed., *Women in the Canadian Mosaic*, 291. Brown's subsequent reflections on the subject include 'Women and Electoral Politics', in Sue Findlay and Melanie Randall, eds., *Feminist Perspectives on the Canadian State*, special issue of *Resources for Feminist Research* 17:3 (September 1988), 106-8; and *Being Brown: A Very Public Life* (Toronto: Random House of Canada, 1989).

[96] See '105 Potential Women MPs', *Chatelaine*, October 1971, 33ff.; and Barbara Frum, 'Insiders' Tips on How to Get Women Elected', *Chatelaine*, October 1971, 38.

[97] It should be noted that between 1968 and 1972, Grace MacInnis was the sole female MP in Canada.

[98] This idea was advanced by Kay Macpherson at the Strategy for Change conference in 1972, where 'Ms. for M.P.' buttons were sold. See Armour's film, *The Status of Women*.

[99] Interview with Margaret Bryce, 14 March 1983. Similar interpretations of the period following 1972 were presented in interviews with Kay Macpherson, 18 March 1983 and Helen Lafountaine, 25 February 1983.

[100] Interview with Margaret Bryce.

[101] An important exception to this trend was Laura Sabia, who ran as a Conservative candidate in the 1968 federal elections and 1981 Spadina by-election.

[102] In March 1971, for example, Prime Minister Trudeau appointed a three-woman task force 'to investigate and report on the priorities which Liberals and others gave to the Royal Commission recommendations'. See Report from Liberal Party Task Force on the Status of Women to LPC Consultative Council, dated October 1971.

[103] Interviews with Aideen Nicholson, 11 September 1982 and Lorna Marsden, 18 March 1983.

[104] Interviews with Kay Macpherson and Muriel Smith, 7 July 1982. See also Brown, *Being Brown*, chaps 8, 9.

[105] On the general absence of legislative progress, see *Ten Years Later: An Assessment of the Federal Government's Implementation of the Recommendations Made by the Royal Commission on the Status of Women* (Ottawa: Canadian Advisory Council on the Status of Women, October 1979). The recommendations of the LPC Task Force on the Status of Women were also shelved, according to at least two of its members. Interview with Esther Greenglass, 17 March 1983 and note from Jan Steele to Esther Greenglass, dated 30 July 1973.

[106] See Sandra Burt, 'Canadian Women's Groups in the 1980s: Organizational Development and Policy Influence', *Canadian Public Policy* 16:1 (March 1990), 17-28.

[107] Interviews with Laura Sabia, Lorna Marsden and Esther Greenglass.

[108]Feminist Party of Canada, 'Towards a Canadian Feminist Party', April 1979.

[109]Ibid. See also Dorothy Zaborszky, 'Feminist Politics: The Feminist Party of Canada', in Peta Tancred-Sheriff, ed., *Feminist Research: Prospect and Retrospect* (Kingston: McGill-Queen's University Press, 1988), 255-65.

[110]The 'Yvette' rally of about 15,000 women in Montreal and a series of smaller gatherings of federalist women during the referendum campaign were organized in response to statements by the PQ Minister of State for the Status of Women, Lise Payette. In March 1980, Payette stated that the period of the obedient little 'Yvette' of Quebec schoolbooks had passed, and compared women who voted against sovereignty-association to passive 'Yvettes'. Furthermore, she commented that the leader of the 'No' forces in the referendum campaign, Liberal Claude Ryan, was himself married to an 'Yvette'. See Evelyne Tardy, 'Les femmes et la campagne référendaire', in *Québec: Un pays uncertain* (Montreal: Québec-Amérique, 1980), 184-203; and Michèle Jean, Jacqueline Lamothe, Marie Lavigne and Jennifer Stoddart, 'Nationalism and Feminism in Quebec: The "Yvettes" Phenomenon', in Roberta Hamilton and Michèle Barrett, eds., *The Politics of Diversity* (Montreal: Book Center, 1986), 322-38.

[111]For analyses of the ERA defeat, see Mary Frances Berry, *Why ERA Failed: Politics, Women's Rights, and the Amending Process of the Constitution* (Bloomington: Indiana University Press, 1986); and Jane J. Mansbridge, *Why We Lost the ERA* (Chicago: University of Chicago Press, 1986).

[112]French/English differences among feminists in this period are reflected clearly in Audrey Doerr and Micheline Carrier, eds., *Women and the Constitution in Canada* (Ottawa: Canadian Advisory Council on the Status of Women, 1981).

[113]CACSW member Florence Ievers, as quoted in Marjorie Cohen, 'Editorial: The Need for Independent Feminism', *Canadian Forum*, March 1981, 4.

[114]According to most accounts, approximately 1,300 women attended the Ad Hoc Conference. See Anne Collins, 'Which Way to Ottawa?' *City Woman*, Holiday 1981, 12; and Chaviva Hosek, 'Women and the Constitutional Process', in Keith Banting and Richard Simeon, eds., *And No One Cheered* (Toronto: Methuen, 1983), 280-300. Additional studies of women and the 1981-82 round of constitutional debate include Penney Kome, *The Taking of Twenty-Eight* (Toronto: Women's Press, 1983); and Sandra D. Burt, 'The Charter of Rights and the Ad Hoc Lobby: The Limits of Success', *Atlantis* 14:1 (Fall 1988), 74-81.

[115]Interview with Lorna Marsden.

[116]See Collins, 'Which Way to Ottawa'; and Cohen, 'Editorial'.

[117]See Elizabeth Gray, 'Women's Fight to Get in from the Cold Political Wind', *Globe and Mail* 30 January 1981, 7.

[118]Lynn McDonald, 'The Charter of Rights and the Subjection of Women', *Canadian Forum*, June-July 1981, 18.

[119]See Sherene Razack, *Canadian Feminism and the Law: The Women's Legal Education and Action Fund and the Pursuit of Equality* (Toronto: Second Story Press, 1991).

[120]See Beverley Baines, 'Women and the Law', in Sandra Burt, Lorraine Code and Lindsay Dorney, eds., *Changing Patterns: Women in Canada* (Toronto: McClelland and Stewart, 1988), 157-83.

[121]Studies in this area include Anne F. Bayefsky and Mary Eberts, eds., *Equality Rights and the Canadian Charter of Rights and Freedoms* (Toronto: Carswell, 1985); Christine Boyle et al., *Charterwatch* (Toronto: Carswell, 1986); Karen Busby, Lisa Fainstein and Holly Penner, eds., *Equality Issues in Family Law* (Winnipeg: Legal Research Institute of the University of Manitoba, 1990); Kenneth Fogarty, *Equality Rights and their Limitations in the Charter* (Toronto: Carswell, 1987); Judy Fudge, 'The Public/Private Distinction: The Possibilities of and Limits to the Use of the Charter to Further Feminist Struggle', *Osgoode Hall Law Journal* 25:3 (Fall 1987); and Lise Gotell, *The Canadian Women's Movement, Equality Rights and the Charter* (Ottawa: Canadian Research Institute for the Advancement of Women, 1990).

[122]Gwen Brodsky and Shelagh Day, *Canadian Charter Equality Rights for Women: One Step Forward or Two Steps Back?* (Ottawa: Canadian Advisory Council on the Status of Women, 1989), 3. For an equally pessimistic view, see Margaret Buist, 'Elusive Equality: Women and the Charter of Rights and Freedoms', in Findlay and Randall, eds., *Feminist Perspectives on the Canadian State*, 103-5.

[123]These groups have adopted different names across the country and developed a communications network connecting the 52 Percent Solution in Newfoundland, Femmes regroupées pour l'accessibilité aux pouvoirs politique et économique in Montreal, Winning Women in Winnipeg and others. See Chantal Maillé with Valentina Pollon, *Primed for Power: Women in Canadian Politics* (Ottawa: Canadian Advisory Council on the Status of Women, 1990), 26-30.

[124]Materials produced include Association féminine d'éducation et d'action sociale (AFEAS), *L'accès des femmes au pouvoir politique* (Montreal: AFEAS, 1987); Josephine Payne-O'Connor, *Sharing Power: A Political Skills Handbook* (Victoria: Kachina Press, 1986) and a six-part television series by TVOntario based on a 1986 conference organized by the Committee for '94. This series is compiled in Carol Sevitt, ed., *Women and Politics, Transcripts of the Ryerson Conference* (Toronto: TVOntario, 1988).

Other publications that reflected an effort to increase female participation were Penney Kome, *Play from Strength: A Canadian Woman's Guide to Initiating Political Action* (Ottawa: Canadian Advisory Council on the Status of Women, 1983); Kome, *Every Voice Counts: A Guide to Personal and Political Action* (Ottawa: Canadian Advisory Council on the Status of Women, 1989); Maillé, *Primed for Power*; and *Resources for Research and Action* (Ottawa: Canadian Research Institute for the Advancement of Women, 1991).

[125]Committee for '94, 'Let Women Play Too! The Case for Public Funding of Canadian Elections', Brief presented to the Royal Commission on Electoral Reform and Party Financing (RCE-597/A), 7 May 1990.

[126]R.E.A.L. was an acronym for Realistic, Equal, Active, for Life. See Karen Dubinsky, *Lament for a Patriarchy Lost: Anti-Feminism, Anti-Abortion and R.E.A.L. Women in Canada* (Ottawa: Canadian Research Institute for the Advancement of Women, 1985); Margrit Eichler, *The Pro-Family Movement: Are They For or Against Families* (Ottawa: Canadian Research Institute for the Advancement of Women, 1985); Lorna Erwin, 'What Feminists Should Know About the Pro-Family Movement in Canada', in Tancred-Sheriff, ed., *Feminist Perspectives*, 266-78; Lorna Erwin, 'R.E.A.L. Women, Anti-Feminism and the Welfare State', in Findlay and Randall, eds., *Feminist Perspectives on the Canadian State*, 147-9; Joan Hannant, 'The Rise of the New Right in Canada: Implications for the Women's Movement' (Toronto: National Action Committee on the Status of Women, April 1988); and Danielle Crittenden, 'R.E.A.L. Women Don't Eat Crow', *Saturday Night* (May 1988), 27-35.

[127]R.E.A.L. Women received approximately $21,000 in federal funds from the Secretary of State Women's Program to support a conference held in Ottawa in April 1989.

[128]See Bashevkin, 'Free Trade and Canadian Feminism'.

[129]For assessments of Meech Lake vis-à-vis women, see Beverley Baines, 'Gender and the Meech Lake Committee', *Queen's Quarterly* 94:4 (Winter 1987), 807-16; *Brief to the Special Joint Committee of the Senate and House of Commons on the 1987 Constitutional Accord* (Ottawa: Canadian Advisory Council on the Status of Women, August 1987); Kathy Brock, 'Being Heard: Interest Representation in the Manitoba Constitutional Process', paper presented at Canadian Political Science Association meetings, Queen's University, June 1991; Katherine E. Swinton and Carol J. Rogerson, eds., *Competing Constitutional Visions: The Meech Lake Accord* (Toronto: Carswell, 1988); and Women's Economic Agenda, *Three Deals, One Game: BC Women Look at Free Trade, Meech Lake and Privatization* (Burnaby: Press Gang, July 1988).

[130]It should be emphasized that women's organizations in English Canada, notably the Ad Hoc Committee of Women on the Constitution, did *not* oppose the goal of bringing Quebec within the constitutional fold. Although proponents of Meech Lake suggested that feminist critics were anti-French and insensitive to the concerns of Quebec, the Ad Hoc Committee argued 'that notwithstanding anything we say, anything we have said, or anything we are reported to have said—

the women of Canada support the intent of the Meech Lake Constitutional Accord. We are in favour of bringing in the Government of Quebec as a signatory to the Canadian Constitution'. See Ad Hoc Committee of Women on the Constitution, 'We Can Afford a Better Accord: The Meech Lake Accord', in Findlay and Randall, eds., *Feminist Perspectives on the Canadian State*, 142.

[131] See Barbara Roberts, *Smooth Sailing or Storm Warning: Canadian and Quebec Women's Groups and the Meech Lake Accord* (Ottawa: Canadian Research Institute for the Advancement of Women, 1988).

[132] For one example, see Beverley Baines, 'After Meech Lake: The Ms/Representation of Gender in Scholarly Spaces', in David E. Smith, Peter MacKinnon and John C. Courtney, eds., *After Meech Lake* (Saskatoon: Fifth House, 1991), 205-18.

[133] See 'Why You Need to be at the Constitutional Table', pamphlet produced by Equality Eve, Toronto, November 1991.

[134] Not only did women's groups in English Canada take on the Conservatives over free trade and Meech Lake, but they also opposed government fiscal policy, decisions to cut back on VIA Rail service, the handling of the Oka crisis and other policies. See Louise Dulude, 'The Status of Women under the Mulroney Government', in Andrew B. Gollner and Daniel Salée, eds., *Canada Under Mulroney* (Montreal: Véhicule Press, 1988), 253-64.

[135] In the spring of 1989, the federal Conservatives announced a decision to reduce NAC's funding by more than 50 percent to approximately $300,000 by 1992, and refused to participate in the annual NAC lobby on Parliament Hill. A year later, in its February 1990 budget, the government eliminated a further $1.6 million from the Secretary of State Women's Program, much of which would have gone to women's centres and periodicals, and again refused to participate in the NAC lobby.

[136] For one account of internal tensions, see Lorraine Greaves, 'Reorganizing the National Action Committee on the Status of Women, 1986-1988', in Wine and Ristock, eds., *Women and Social Change*, 101-16.

[137] For an introduction to these issues, see Wine and Ristock, eds., *Women and Social Change*; Maroney and Luxton, eds., *Feminism and Political Economy*; Susan D. Phillips, 'Meaning and Structure in Social Movements', *Canadian Journal of Political Science* 24:4 (December 1991), 755-82; *Enough is Enough: Aboriginal Women Speak Out*, as told to Janet Silman (Toronto: Women's Press, 1987); and Jo-Anne Fiske, 'Native Women in Reserve Politics: Stategies and Struggles', in Ng, Walter and Muller, eds., *Community Organization and the Canadian State*, 131-46.

[138] On policy developments in this period, see Margaret Royal, 'Women's Issues and the Public Policy Process: The Tory Shape of Canada's Child Care Policy', paper presented at Canadian Political Science Association meetings, Queen's University, 1990; Susan D. Phillips, 'Rock-a-Bye, Brian: The National Strategy on Child Care', in Katherine A. Graham, ed., *How Ottawa Spends, 1989-90* (Ottawa: Carleton University Press, 1989), 165-208; and Sylvia Bashevkin, 'Building a Political Voice: Women's Participation and Policy Influence in Canada', in Barbara Nelson and Najma Chowdhury, eds., *Women and Politics Worldwide* (New Haven: Yale University Press, 1993).

CHAPTER TWO

Attitudes and Involvement in the General Public

Men are more likely than women to feel they can cope with the complexities of politics and to believe that their participation carries some weight in the political process . . . what has been less adequately transmitted to the women is a sense of some personal competence vis-a-vis the political world.

—Angus Campbell et al., *The American Voter*, 1960[1]

Writing in 1960, the authors of *The American Voter* identified fundamental differences in the ways in which women and men approached the formal political arena. Their finding of lower levels of political competence among women became part of the 'received wisdom' in this field, and remains relevant to discussions of Canada, the United States and other comparable political systems more than thirty years later.

What has continued to stir controversy in this literature is the interpretation of male/female variation. Survey data reveal that even though roughly equal proportions of women and men turn out to vote in most advanced industrial democracies, males and females tend to hold differing political orientations and issue positions, with the latter tending towards stronger support for centrist political parties, peace and social welfare programs. As well, women in many countries report lower levels of political interest and efficacy (that is, belief in their individual political influence) than men.[2]

Much of the debate over these patterns turns on questions of explanation and expectation. First, if women's political attitudes and approaches to participation differ from those of men, then do these disparities reflect a degree of 'deviance', or some unexplained 'lag' among females? Second, would increasing women's access to higher education and paid employment eliminate these differences, thus 'integrating' females within the political mainstream? That is, if women do not presently conform to masculine norms of either opinion or participation on the mass level, then how and when are they likely to do so?[3]

An alternative to this conventional view posits that women have different political experiences and, in fact, that they operate within a different political culture from that inhabited by men. This 'dual cultures' perspective, initially developed in a 1975 article by Thelma McCormack, challenges the deviance thesis in explaining disparate policy priorities and patterns of involvement with reference to two worlds of political life. Rather than viewing females as deficient vis-à-vis masculine norms of formal politics, McCormack argues that 'the experience of women ranges from total exclusion to selective inclusion, from discrimination to paternalism, from rejection to condescension'.[4]

The two cultures thesis addresses mass-level patterns in a manner that is congruent with the historical arguments presented in Chapter 1. As Jill Vickers describes this bridge, 'women's historic exclusion from the formal politics of the state has left its mark'.[5] The extent to which women in English Canada have been formally empowered yet effectively marginalized despite these formal rights is notable; it implies that different political orientations among women and men constitute realistic responses to disparate experiences.

The next section begins to untangle conceptual questions of explanation and expectation, suggesting that the two cultures thesis provides a more balanced starting point than do conventional assumptions regarding female deviance. This examination of interpretive frameworks sets the stage for a more detailed empirical discussion of attitudes and participation in the remainder of the chapter.

EXPLANATIONS AND EXPECTATIONS

Conventional interpretations of gender differences at the mass level borrow from one of the most powerful theoretical streams in modern social science: the modernization thesis. Viewing political systems and groups as gradually 'coming of age' through their adoption of urban, industrial norms, the modernization thesis is applied to marginal entities within a democratic electorate that do not reflect dominant attitudinal and participatory norms.[6]

Some North American and Western European survey research has relied heavily on the modernization approach. Descriptions through the 1970s of female voters as parochial, isolated, naïve and otherwise politically impaired drew their inspiration from this perspective; that is, women circulated less widely in society than men, based their political judgements on a narrower experiential base than men and, ultimately, failed to meet the criteria required for cosmopolitan or sophisticated political engagement.[7] This same explanatory approach can be identified in the small Canadian literature on sex differences in the general public. Books published in the 1960s by Peter Regenstreif and Mildred Schwartz, for example, situated female public opinion in the context of limitations imposed by conventional domestic roles. According to Regenstreif, women's political interest and participation were generally less than those of males; as well, women were 'disposed to favour the traditional [Liberal and Conservative] parties over the 'radical' ones', namely the New Democratic party.[8] These trends, along with impressionistic evidence that married women accepted political direction from their husbands, indicated to Regenstreif that female behaviour was governed by 'the cultural norm that the place of women is in the home and not in the world of politics'.[9]

A more explicitly domestic explanation of political attitudes is presented in Schwartz's 1965 study. *Public Opinion and Canadian Identity* quoted at length from a British study that attributed lower female support for the Labour party, described as 'women's political conservatism', to 'a greater social isolation which makes them slower than men to change their opinions and attitudes'.[10] Applying this argument in a Canadian context, Schwartz claimed that within the Conservative and Liberal electorates women 'appeared more parochial in their outlook' on national issues than men; therefore, 'like older respondents, women tend to be more traditional in their approach to national problems'.[11]

More explicit still in its link to the modernization thesis was Jean Laponce's 1969 identification of the bulk of 'political barbarians' as women, who have limited appreciation of the dominant symbols and issues that inform political discourse in Canada. Laponce's discussion of electoral behaviour in Vancouver-Burrard referred to the major constraints upon political awareness that, in his view, were imposed by conventional domestic roles.[12] Similarly, in 1970 Rick Van Loon claimed that the limited social contacts of housewives combined with traditional assumptions that politics was a masculine enterprise, produced lower levels of politicization among Canadian women than men.[13]

On a conceptual level, older arguments to the effect that isolation in the domestic household shapes women's political attitudes deserve careful scrutiny. Drawing upon an Aristotelian dichotomy between public (hence political) male and private (hence apolitical) female spheres, this argument suggests that, by definition, women are not equipped to be politically competent or active on a regular basis.[14] Their isolation in the home and child-rearing responsibilities, frequently accompanied by greater religiosity and lower educational attainment than among men, are seen as the source of attitudinal 'traditionalism' and 'parochialism'. The overall point of such conventional arguments is thus consistent with the idea that women's political outlook is impaired: lacking meaningful ties with political institutions or with political history, women's views remain static, changeless and, in the words of Thelma McCormack, 'deviant' features of Western public opinion.[15]

A useful way of understanding the main lines of this argument is provided in Figure 2.1, which presents a simplified version of the standard explanation. According to this perspective, women's political attitudes and participation are defined by the experience of domestic isolation, and by the absence of consistent political stimuli that motivate the presumably more active and aware lives of men in modern democracies.

On an empirical level, this approach is complicated by the absence of methodologically rigorous analyses. For example, if women's attitudes were indeed characterized by lower support for the NDP during the period considered by

Regenstreif, and if this phenomenon was related at the time to domestic isolation and its various demographic correlates (including greater religiosity and lower educational attainment), then one could expect to find systematic documentation of these patterns in the existing literature. Unfortunately, empirical evidence of this kind is generally not provided; neither Regenstreif nor Schwartz introduces tabular controls that could help to establish 'isolation' as the basis for women's views. Moreover, Regenstreif's discussion does not offer a basic male/female breakdown in partisan attitudes.

These conceptual and empirical problems have led at least one social scientist to challenge the relevance of modernization theory to sex differences in the mass public. According to Thelma McCormack, a more useful approach would begin with the premise that male/female variation is 'based in the reality of

FIGURE 2.1   CONVENTIONAL MODEL OF WOMEN AND POLITICS

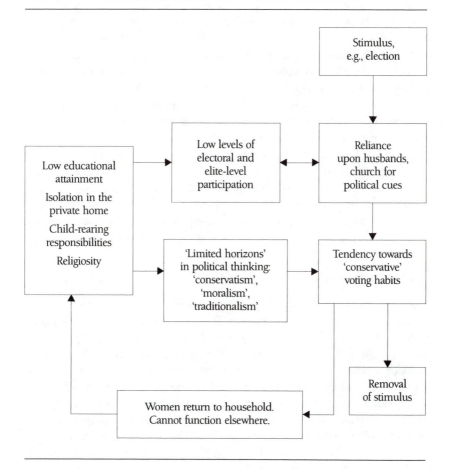

a gendered social system'.[16] Women and men operate in two separate but over-lapping political cultures; women have relatively low expectations of the primarily male realm of electoral politics, but are more optimistic about and likely to engage in extra-parliamentary political action.

When translated into the language of political behaviour, McCormack's thesis regarding dual cultures suggests that women would be more alienated from mainstream political activity than men for reasons other than the 'lag' posited by modernization theory. Because the dominant electoral and party institutions operate according to masculine norms of individual achievement, instrumental power and career success, McCormack argues, women learn that the dynamics of power are aggressive and, above all, exclusionary. Politics in a formal sense requires that females adjust to prevailing male standards rather than vice versa.

In applying McCormack's alternative thesis to research on nine Canadian wo-men's groups, Jill Vickers clarified the notion of a 'doubled vision'. According to Vickers, females have historically been passive spectators at a distance from what one respondent termed 'big P politics'.[17] Less formal, community-based political activity has therefore offered a more attractive and promising venue. Nevertheless, women recognize that 'the dominant political culture, its norms and rules are made legitimate by their longevity and the sanction of the law'.[18]

Vickers proposes that instead of a lag in political integration, there exists a well-embedded, systematic 'exclusion from the formal politics of the state'.[19] This 'historic exclusion' has encouraged women to pursue other kinds of informal participation, and has led to the development of attitudes and orientations dif-ferent from those of men. In short, according to both Vickers and McCormack, explanations of gender differences at the mass level need to address the realities of exclusion rather than the 'deviant' results of incomplete modernization. More-over, expectations of future trends include a continuation of 'doubled visions' rather than simple integration within dominant structures.

To what extent do mass-level data on public opinion and participation support either set of arguments? The following sections examine this question.

PARTISAN ATTITUDES

Conventional views of women's political attitudes suggest two empirical hypo-theses, one concerning the direction and the other the correlates of female public opinion. In terms of direction, studies by Regenstreif, Schwartz, Laponce and others maintain that Canadian women during the 1960s were politically more traditional, particularly in terms of partisan preferences, than men.[20] This position can be evaluated in a fairly straightforward manner, using survey data from the mid-1960s to ascertain whether females were in fact more likely to identify with the older Liberal and Conservative parties, and less likely to identify with the newer NDP, than males.

With reference to attitudinal correlates, older studies argue that the source of female 'traditionalism' or 'parochialism' rests in a condition of isolation within the domestic household. Given that female employment status was not ascertained in the 1965 study (it asked the occupation only of the main wage earner in each household), this analysis employs frequent church attendance and limited educational attainment as indicators of domestic 'isolation'.

To what extent were women's attitudes less radical and more 'traditional' than those of men in 1965? The figures in Table 2.1 indicate a 6.5 percent gender difference in levels of NDP identification, with 18.9 percent of men and 12.4 percent of women expressing New Democratic partisanship.[21] The Liberal party would appear to have benefited most directly from this difference, since 42.3 percent of women and 37.2 percent of men reported Liberal identification. Table 2.2 provides additional evidence of somewhat less support for the NDP among English Canadian women in 1965: 46.7 percent of men and only 38.4 percent of women gave favourable ratings to New Democratic members of parliament in that year.[22] As well, an additive measure of NDP support was constructed using seven items from the 1965 survey: Table 2.3 shows significant gender differences in mean scores, with men substantially more in favour of the party than women.[23] These findings suggest that, if defined in terms of party support, the attitudes of English Canadian women in 1965 were less leftist and more favourable toward the moderate centre (that is, the Liberals) than those of men.

When we turn to the correlates of partisanship in that year, however, the results fail to support conventional arguments. In Table 2.4, male and female respondents in 1965 are assigned to categories of cultural 'isolation' that represent high, medium and low levels of the phenomenon identified by the modernization

TABLE 2.1   PARTY IDENTIFICATION OF ANGLOPHONE CANADIANS, 1965 (%)[a]

	WOMEN	MEN
Liberal	42.3	37.2
New Democratic	12.4	18.9
Progressive Conservative	39.7	38.1
Social Credit	5.6	5.8
(N)	(804)	(728)

[a]Respondents were asked, 'Generally speaking, do you think of yourself as Conservative, Liberal, Social Credit, Créditiste, NDP, Union nationale, or what?' Non-identifiers were probed a second time: 'Well, do you generally think of yourself as a little closer to one of the parties than the others?' (If yes) 'Which one?' In this and the following tables, only English-speaking respondents from outside Quebec have been included (except where indicated), and all missing data are excluded.

SOURCE: 1965 Canadian Election Study.

thesis. Patterns of radical (defined as NDP) partisanship can then be compared across categories, with the expectation that secular, well-educated (or 'low isolate') respondents would express relatively similar levels of NDP identification, while religious, less-educated (or 'high isolate') ones would express more disparate views. Following the 'lag' argument, one would expect women in the 'high isolate' category (that is, with frequent church attendance and low educational attainment) to express particularly limited preference for the NDP.

Contrary to this hypothesis, the data in Table 2.4 show that the greatest sex difference in NDP support (7.5 percent) occurred among 'low isolates', who reported both advanced education and infrequent church attendance. By contrast,

TABLE 2.2   RATINGS OF NDP MEMBERS OF PARLIAMENT BY ANGLOPHONE
CANADIANS, 1965 (%)[a]

	WOMEN	MEN
Pretty good	38.4	46.7
So-so	45.6	35.5
Not good	16.0	17.8
(N)	(636)	(712)

[a]Respondents were asked their opinions regarding the MPs that each of the major parties had sent to Ottawa in the last few years.

SOURCE: 1965 Canadian Election Study.

TABLE 2.3   COMPARISON OF MEAN SCORES OF NDP SUPPORT AMONG
ANGLO-CANADIAN WOMEN AND MEN, 1965 and 1979[a]

	1965			1979		
	WOMEN	MEN	t	WOMEN	MEN	t
NDP support	0.659	0.967	-3.42[b]	0.607	0.810	-3.22[b]
(N)	(882)	(842)		(1010)	(898)	

[a]These additive measures were constructed by summing pro-NDP responses to the following 1965 items: party identification (weighted for strength of that identification); identification with a different party in the past; party identification on the federal or provincial levels if initial identification was not for both levels; party chosen in previous provincial and federal elections if respondent always votes for the same party; 1963 federal party choice; 1965 federal party choice; party choice in last provincial election. The items used for 1979 measure were federal party identification, federal vote were election held today, provincial identification, and provincial vote were election held today.

[b]Significant at the .01 level

SOURCES: 1965 Canadian Election Study; 1979 Social Change in Canada Study.

the disparity among 'high isolates', who had limited education and weekly church attendance, was less than half this figure (3.6 percent), while that in the intermediate category was virtually nil (0.1 percent).

Similarly, examining absolute levels of NDP support among both genders indicates that the 'isolation' argument was more applicable to males than to females. That is, the difference between 'high' and 'low isolates' was nearly 6 percent among men, compared with only 2 percent among women. Moreover, females in the 'high isolate' category, who were expected to identify least with the NDP, expressed slightly higher New Democratic partisanship than both men and women in the intermediate category. These results suggest that education and religious attendance had a less than profound impact upon the key group—women—to which the phenomenon of social isolation was assumed to be crucial.

Overall, then, the 1965 survey data show women's partisan attitudes to be less favourable towards the NDP than those of men, but they do not reflect any systematic relationship between the phenomenon of NDP identification and indicators of female cultural 'isolation'. Moreover, in reporting a number of empirical trends that are the reverse of those predicted by conventional arguments (notably, greater sex differences in partisanship among 'low' than 'high' isolates), this analysis fails to support the modernization thesis as an explanation of women's attitudes in 1965.

THE DISPARATE EXPERIENCES THESIS

If conventional explanations do not account for patterns of party support, how helpful are the alternative views suggested by McCormack and Vickers? This section employs the background presented in Chapter 1 as a basis from which to assess public opinion in English Canada.

TABLE 2.4   NDP IDENTIFICATION BY LEVEL OF CULTURAL 'ISOLATION' IN ENGLISH CANADA, 1965[a]

	HIGH		MEDIUM		LOW	
	WOMEN	MEN	WOMEN	MEN	WOMEN	MEN
NDP identification (%)	14.7	18.3	12.7	12.6	16.7	24.2
Difference (W – M)	–3.6		+0.1		–7.5	
(N)	(75)	(55)	(134)	(85)	(68)	(113)

[a]Categories of cultural 'isolation' were established as follows: high = elementary education, weekly church attendance; medium = secondary education, 1-3 times/month church attendance; low = university education, few times/year or no church attendance.

SOURCE: 1965 Canadian Election Study.

Historical approaches use the experiences of Canadian women since the suffrage period as a conceptual starting point, a foundation from which to generate propositions about subsequent attitudinal developments. At least three general hypotheses follow from such a process. First, the limitations on suffragism and feminism during the early decades of this century, particularly their wedging within the broader federal conflict over conscription, meant that women's formal political rights were granted as part of a larger legislative package rather than as the consequence of a national debate on the independent merits of enfranchisement. This pattern, combined with exclusionary party practices as well as organizational and ideological disunity in the suffrage movement, suggests that women may have entered the political system with a collective sense of hesitation or ambiguity.[24] Empirical data on political interest, efficacy and survey non-response can be used to explore the relationship between circumstances surrounding formal enfranchisement and subsequent patterns of female politicization.

Second, suffragism in Western Canada was associated with a larger progressive movement that developed close ties with provincial Liberal parties as well as with the agrarian and labour precursors of the CCF/NDP. This alliance could be reflected empirically in relatively high levels of CCF/NDP and Liberal identification among older women in Western Canada, particularly those who came of age politically during the suffrage period.

Third, contemporary feminism has been ideologically and organizationally closer to the federal New Democratic and Liberal (LPC) parties than to the Progressive Conservative (PC) organization. As was pointed out in Chapter 1, many younger feminists who sought to influence established parties during the 1970s and following joined the LPC and NDP organizations and worked to recruit additional support among other women for these parties. We hypothesize that younger women and those attaching a high priority to women's rights would express relatively strong preference for the federal NDP and Liberals during the 1970s. Moreover, we expect that the tense and often polarized relations between organized feminism and the Progressive Conservatives after 1984 would be reflected in less support among women not only for that party, but also for the issue positions associated with neo-conservatism in the 1980s.

PATTERNS OF FEMALE POLITICIZATION

To examine the impact of circumstances surrounding female enfranchisement on subsequent patterns of politicization, we begin with 1965 data on political interest (Table 2.5). Although these figures were gathered nearly fifty years after the granting of suffrage to most English Canadian women, they represent the earliest baseline year for which data are available.

Turning first to Table 2.5, we find that English Canadian women expressed considerably less political interest in 1965 than did men, with 23.1 percent of females and 33.3 percent of males reporting a 'good deal' of interest in politics. These results support the argument that circumstances surrounding female enfranchisement in English Canada tended to keep women outside the mainstream political process; as well, they indicate that gender differences in English Canada in 1965 were less than those in Francophone Quebec. As reported in Table 2.5, only 13.0 percent of Quebec Francophone females expressed a 'good deal' of interest, and a majority (50.6 percent) claimed to have 'not much' interest. The latter result, which differed by approximately 20 percent from both French-speaking males and English-speaking females, suggests that the exceptionally late date of provincial enfranchisement in Quebec (1940) influenced women's politicization through 1965. We therefore conclude that by the mid-1960s, gender differences in political interest in English Canada remained substantial but considerably less than those in Francophone Quebec.

Comparable figures from 1979, presented in Table 2.6, reflect continued sex differences in political interest among both Anglophone and Francophone respondents. In 1979, the male/female difference among Anglophones residing outside Quebec remained in the 9 percent range: 61.9 percent of women and 70.6 percent of men claimed to be 'very' or 'fairly' interested in politics. By way of comparison, figures from Francophone Quebec suggest an approximate doubling of gender differences over time, from slightly over 11 percent (13.0 percent versus 24.3 percent interested) in 1965 to about 23 percent (42.2 percent versus 64.9 percent interested) in 1979. Although these findings could result from divergent question wording in the 1965 and 1979 surveys, they seem to indicate a general continuity over time in patterns of male and female political interest in English Canada.

TABLE 2.5   POLITICAL INTEREST OF CANADIAN RESPONDENTS, 1965 (%)[a]

	ANGLOPHONES OUTSIDE QUEBEC		FRANCOPHONES IN QUEBEC	
	WOMEN	MEN	WOMEN	MEN
Good deal	23.1	33.3	13.0	24.3
Some	45.7	43.2	36.4	48.9
Not much	31.2	23.5	50.6	26.8
(N)	(880)	(839)	(324)	(317)

[a]Respondents were asked, 'How much interest do you generally have in what is going on in politics—a good deal, some, or not much?'

SOURCE: 1965 Canadian Election Study.

This continuation of sex differences in baseline measures of political engagement, rather than the disappearance of such disparities as predicted by the modernization thesis, is confirmed by subsequent research in the field. Data from the 1981 Quality of Life survey, for example, show levels of political interest similar to those found in 1979.[25] Moreover, the 1981 responses to one efficacy measure ('sometimes politics and government seem so complicated that a person like me can't really understand what's going on') indicate that 56 percent of males compared with 72 percent of females agreed.[26] As Sandra Burt observes: 'This pattern did not disappear when education and occupation controls were used. For women, the remoteness of politics goes beyond the sense that politicians don't pay much attention to them, to a more fundamental pattern in understanding how the process works . . . women are less involved psychologically and are more likely to find politics complicated.'[27]

Parallel conclusions follow from a longitudinal analysis that used data from six national election studies.[28] Barry Kay and his colleagues reported sustained sex differences across the years 1965-84 on measures of political interest, vote proselytizing and efficacy, a pattern that—like the results of Burt's analysis—casts doubt on the integration thesis as applied to mass-level orientations.

Another indicator of politicization, in addition to interest and efficacy, is survey non-response—particularly on party and issue items.[29] As reported in Table 2.7, Anglophone respondents residing outside Quebec had fairly similar levels of non-response in both 1965 and 1979, with neither men nor women evidencing consistently higher levels of this phenomenon. By contrast, Francophone females in Quebec had somewhat higher levels of non-response than Francophone males, suggesting once again that the delay in Quebec women's enfranchisement had important effects upon female politicization through the late 1970s.

TABLE 2.6   POLITICAL INTEREST OF CANADIAN RESPONDENTS, 1979 (%)[a]

	ANGLOPHONES OUTSIDE QUEBEC		FRANCOPHONES IN QUEBEC	
	WOMEN	MEN	WOMEN	MEN
Very, fairly interested	61.9	70.6	42.2	64.9
Not very interested	28.8	22.6	41.4	25.8
Not interested	9.3	6.8	16.4	9.3
(N)	(1,003)	(893)	(351)	(382)

[a]Respondents were asked, 'How interested are you in politics and political events? Would you say . . . very interested, fairly interested, not very interested, or not at all interested?'

SOURCE: 1979 Social Change in Canada Study.

Gender differences in non-response were clear in both cultures, however, on a large number of other survey items. In summarizing the results of field work during the late 1970s in Peterborough, Lethbridge and Trois Rivières, Joel Smith and his co-authors noted, 'Women were more likely than men either to be unable to answer or to say 'don't know' to many questions concerning political attitudes, opinions and behaviour.'[30]

This same pattern was very clear in April 1991 poll data on the dynamics of constitutional change. A CBC/*Globe and Mail* national survey, summarized in Table 2.8, showed that both Francophone women in Quebec and Anglophone women outside Quebec were consistently more likely than men in these same cultures to have no opinion or to refuse to answer constitutional probes. For example, when questioned about the likely effects of the Citizens' Forum headed by Keith Spicer, 19.3 percent of Quebec women and 14.4 percent of English Canadian women said 'don't know' or refused to answer, as compared with 8.9 percent of Quebec and 8.7 percent of English Canadian men. Similarly, when asked about the commitment of Premier Bourassa to federalism or sovereignty, the non-response levels for women in Quebec and English Canada were very high, more than 7 percent above the non-response levels for men in the same culture (16.8, 23.8, 9.5 and 15.2 percent, respectively).

Systematically higher levels of non-response suggest that many Canadian women during the early 1990s felt left out of the formalized realm of constitutional debate, which since the end of the Second World War has tended to operate

TABLE 2.7   SURVEY NON-RESPONSE OF CANADIAN RESPONDENTS, 1965 AND 1979 (%)

| | ANGLOPHONES OUTSIDE QUEBEC | | FRANCOPHONES IN QUEBEC | |
	WOMEN	MEN	WOMEN	MEN
1965 party identification	8.9	13.5	20.7	20.4
1965 federal vote	17.1	18.2	29.3	22.2
Last provincial vote	26.9	22.4	28.4	20.6
(N)	(882)	(842)	(324)	(319)
1979 federal identification	18.2	18.6	22.2	24.3
1979 provincial identification	18.4	16.8	17.4	11.6
1979 federal preference	20.8	18.9	25.0	25.5
1979 provincial preference	20.1	19.7	21.2	19.2
(N)	(1,007)	(897)	(353)	(384)

SOURCES: 1965 Canadian Election Study; 1979 Social Change in Canada Study.

in an elite-driven, government-to-government mode known as executive federalism. In this case, survey non-response could be a useful indicator of continued political marginalization, reflecting the gulf that seems to separate many women in the general public from opaque processes of constitutional bargaining.

To summarize this discussion, survey data through the early 1990s suggest that historical experiences continue to produce disparate patterns of political interest, efficacy and non-response among men and women. Integration, defined as the elimination of such differences, whereby female behaviour would converge toward male norms, is predicted by the terms of the modernization thesis but is generally *not* confirmed by the data presented thus far.

DIMENSIONS OF PARTY PREFERENCE IN 1965

A second hypothesis that follows from the history outlined in Chapter 1 concerns the relationship between early feminist alliances in Western Canada and subsequent patterns of female partisanship. The coalitions built by Western progressives, including mainstream social feminists, with provincial Liberal parties and with the agrarian and labour precursors of the CCF/NDP may have contributed to relatively high levels of both CCF/NDP and Liberal identification among older women in Western Canada—particularly those who came of age politically during the suffrage period. This proposition is based on a generational view of female

TABLE 2.8   SURVEY NON-RESPONSE OF CANADIAN RESPONDENTS, 1991 (%)[a]

	ANGLOPHONE NON-QUEBEC		FRANCOPHONE QUEBEC	
	WOMEN	MEN	WOMEN	MEN
Effects of Spicer Forum on national unity	14.4	8.7	19.3	8.9
Rest of Canada should negotiate with Quebec	9.2	4.0	6.1	2.4
Constitutional deal must resolve aboriginal issues	11.0	4.4	10.0	2.0
Bourassa prefers federalism or sovereignty	23.8	15.2	16.8	9.5
How Quebeckers will vote in a referendum on sovereignty	14.1	9.1	17.6	11.9
Effects of constitutional debate on Canadian economy	7.8	4.4	8.0	3.0
Effects of Quebec's relationship with rest of Canada on interests of Quebeckers	14.6	8.1	10.2	4.3

[a]Survey non-response includes both 'don't know' and 'refused to answer' categories.

SOURCE: CBC/Globe and Mail poll conducted in April 1991.

partisanship that links the political experiences of various demographic groups (termed 'cohorts') to their subsequent attitudinal development.[31]

The late beginnings of Canadian survey research complicate this analysis. Because the first major national election study was not conducted until 1965, a smaller cohort of pre-enfranchisement respondents exists than might have been available earlier. Nevertheless the number of older Western Canadian respondents represented in, Table 2.9 (N = 88) is sufficient to permit preliminary examination of the generational hypothesis.

Table 2.9 shows that Western Canadian women born before 1900, who came of age politically during the height of suffrage activism, reported considerably higher Liberal (28.2 percent versus 18.4 percent) and somewhat higher New Democratic (15.4 percent versus 10.2 percent) party identification than men of the same age. Notably, older men in Western Canada, particularly those residing in British Columbia, expressed substantially greater support for the Conservative party than did older women (81.0 percent versus 27.5 percent Conservative in BC).

Only among older respondents (those born before 1900) did women report higher levels of NDP identification than men. In all four other groups included in this table, male New Democratic partisanship exceeded female to the degree that men born since 1900 were between two and four times more likely than women born during this period to report NDP identification. Similarly, Western Canadian women in the enfranchisement cohort (born before 1900) had the highest level of NDP partisanship of any female cohort sampled.

This tendency for older Western Canadian women to report fairly high levels of identification with the Liberal and New Democratic parties could result from their enfranchisement-period experiences, notably the favourable treatment of women and women's rights by progressive political groups in the West during this period. But how did subsequent changes in Canadian politics and society, including changes in the status of women, shape patterns of female partisanship? In particular, how would a historical approach explain the aggregate differences in partisanship reported earlier in this chapter?

The evolution of the CCF/NDP sheds light on this broader development. Since the CCF emerged in a progressive 'social gospel' context, the party tended to emphasize social concerns—notably, in the words of the Regina Manifesto, the elimination of 'injustice and inhumanity'.[32] As Canadian society became more urban and industrialized, however, this ideological focus shifted so that the 1961 Draft Program of the New Party opened with a discussion of economic priorities under the heading 'planning for abundance'.[33] Thus while the CCF was formed in the Western provinces as an outgrowth of social initiatives that included a commitment to women's political rights, over time it moved in an increasingly economic and 'masculine' direction—in the sense that women's status received diminishing attention, while the concerns of paid, employed and, in particular, unionized men were elevated in prominence.[34]

TABLE 2.9 PARTY IDENTIFICATION OF WESTERN CANADIAN RESPONDENTS BY BIRTH COHORTS, 1965 (%)[a]

	1931-45		1916-30		1901-15		BEFORE 1900	
	WOMEN	MEN	WOMEN	MEN	WOMEN	MEN	WOMEN	MEN
Liberal	40.0	32.3	31.0	24.1	24.1	34.8	28.2	18.4
New Democratic	11.7	29.2	6.9	30.6	13.0	29.0	15.4	10.2
Progressive Conservative	36.6	30.2	43.7	28.7	44.4	26.1	33.3	59.2
Social Credit	11.7	8.3	18.4	16.6	18.5	10.1	23.1	12.2
(N)	(60)	(96)	(87)	(108)	(54)	(69)	(39)	(49)

[a]For exact question wording, see note to Table 2.1.

SOURCE: 1965 Canadian Election Study.

TABLE 2.10 PARTY IDENTIFICATION OF ANGLOPHONE CANADIAN RESPONDENTS BY BIRTH COHORTS, 1965 (%)[a]

	1931-45		1916-30		1901-15		BEFORE 1900	
	WOMEN	MEN	WOMEN	MEN	WOMEN	MEN	WOMEN	MEN
Liberal	48.5	42.8	42.0	36.3	37.6	35.7	36.2	27.4
New Democratic	14.9	18.3	9.1	22.7	14.8	19.1	10.9	10.3
Progressive Conservative	30.8	33.7	44.0	33.3	41.1	42.2	46.5	56.7
Social Credit	5.8	5.2	4.9	7.7	6.5	3.0	6.4	5.6
(N)	(259)	(218)	(268)	(250)	(159)	(166)	(110)	(88)

[a]For exact question wording, see note to Table 2.1.

SOURCE: 1965 Canadian Election Study.

In the same period post-war affluence led to an expansion of the Canadian welfare state. Conservatives and especially Liberals adopted many social initiatives first proposed by the CCF/NDP, including government-sponsored health and un-employment insurance.[35] Women may have been drawn toward the older parties as a result, since the initial social priorities of the early CCF became more and more blurred with the passage of time. As well, the CCF/NDP remained a political movement as well as a party, so that women who were socialized to the values of 'the feminine mystique' probably found it difficult to reconcile conventional role norms with the extensive involvement expected of participants in such a movement.[36] In short, the attention paid by the CCF/NDP to women's rights and social policy issues tended to decline over time, while the societal norms con-ducive to female involvement also receded. Women who came of age politically after the enfranchisement period but prior to the contemporary wave of English Canadian feminism might therefore report less support for the party than would both enfranchisement-cohort women and men in general.

Preliminary support for this hypothesis is presented in Table 2.10, which shows that New Democratic partisanship in 1965 was lowest (9.1 percent) among women who came of age politically during the period of the Second World War (born 1916-30). By contrast, identification with the NDP was highest (22.7 percent) among men in this same cohort, suggesting that gendered cues affected NDP support in the period between female enfranchisement and the renewal of organized feminism. Data in this same table also show that Liberal support grew system-atically among younger female cohorts, so that the increasingly economic and 'masculine' focus of the CCF/NDP, combined with the ability of the Liberals to 'pre-empt' many of the former's social programs, may have attenuated New Demo-cratic identification among women who came of age politically through 1950.[37]

The data in Table 2.11 also point towards the effects of a changing orientation in the CCF/NDP. Comparison of support for the New Democrats in unionized and non-unionized segments of the sample shows a 4.2 percent sex difference among the latter versus roughly three times that level among the former. About 30 percent of males and 18 percent of females residing in union households in 1965 were NDP identifiers. This pattern, which existed in all four regions outside Quebec in 1965, was accompanied by a related trend: whereas 24.6 percent of Anglophone men who stated they were members of the working or lower classes identified with the NDP, only 16.5 percent of women in the same group expressed such identification (compared with 13.0 percent and 10.9 percent of middle-class men and women, respectively).

In short, divergent patterns of party support emerged during the years between female enfranchisement and the development of contemporary feminism. Among respondents who came of age politically through 1950, as well as those residing in union households and identifying themselves as members of the working or lower classes, considerably fewer women than men were NDP supporters. These results, combined with data on Liberal and NDP partisanship among older women in Western Canada, provide important evidence that women's experiences vis-à-vis political organizations could constitute a key factor in attitude formation.

CONTEMPORARY ATTITUDES AND THE 'GENDER GAP'

Important changes occurred in the status of Canadian women after 1965. As described in Chapter 1, these developments were tied to the growth of contemporary feminism and, in turn, to the increasingly visible political role of women during and after the 1970s.

How these changes affected partisan attitudes is difficult to assess, in part because organized feminism remains enmeshed in an older tension between conventional partisanship and a more independent route toward political influence. Despite this tension, however, many English Canadian feminists who became active partisans joined the federal Liberal and New Democratic groupings in the 1970s and following. Younger women, whose political experiences included exposure to contemporary feminism at an early and thus impressionable age, as well as respondents committed to improved women's rights legislation, might therefore express relatively strong support for the NDP and Liberals during this period.

The discussion in Chapter 1 also demonstrated the other side of this process; that is, the distancing or political estrangement between organized feminism and the Progressive Conservative party, particularly after 1984. Much of the English Canadian women's movement identified the federal Tories with what was termed a neo-conservative political agenda, including a commitment to reduced social

TABLE 2.11   PARTY IDENTIFICATION AMONG RESIDENTS OF UNION AND NON-UNION HOUSEHOLDS, ENGLISH CANADA, 1965 (%)[a]

| | UNION | | NON-UNION | |
	WOMEN	MEN	WOMEN	MEN
Liberal	44.4	40.3	41.7	36.1
New Democratic	17.5	29.7	11.0	15.2
Progressive Conservative	31.5	24.5	41.9	42.8
Social Credit	6.5	5.6	5.4	6.0
(N)	(169)	(185)	(635)	(543)

[a]Respondents were asked, 'Do you (or does the head of this household) belong to any of the following groups . . . a labour union?' For exact question wording, see Table 2.1.

SOURCE: 1965 Canadian Election Study.

welfare but increased military spending, deficit reduction, unlimited foreign investment and Canada–US free trade.[38] As in the United States during the same period, where men were more supportive than women of Ronald Reagan and the priorities of his presidency, a parallel 'gender gap' may have unfolded in Canada during the Mulroney years.

Data from 1979 offer general support for the first proposition, although they also indicate the persistence of gender differences in New Democratic partisanship. As reported in Table 2.12, men were 3.8 percent more likely than women to express NDP identification on the federal level and 9.0 percent more so on the provincial level (the gender difference on a single measure of party identification in 1965 was 6.5 percent). This result confirms earlier findings (Table 2.3) that show a significant overall gender difference in 1979 using the additive measure of NDP support. With reference to Liberal partisanship, Table 2.12 also suggests that women were slightly more likely to be Liberal supporters than men at both the federal and provincial levels. In 1979, 37.6 percent of females in the national sample reported Liberal party identification at the federal level, compared with 36.9 percent of males.

The generational correlates of female party identification in 1979, summarized in Table 2.13, show that Liberal and New Democratic support was indeed highest in the youngest birth cohort. That is, women born since 1950, who came of age politically after 1970, were most likely to express preference for the federal Liberals (40.0 percent) and New Democrats (23.7 percent); at the same time,

TABLE 2.12 PARTY IDENTIFICATION OF ANGLOPHONE CANADIANS, 1979 (%)[a]

| | FEDERAL LEVEL | | PROVINCIAL LEVEL | |
	WOMEN	MEN	WOMEN	MEN
Liberal	37.6	36.9	28.6	24.2
New Democratic	17.4	21.2	18.9	27.9
Progressive Conservative	42.8	39.3	45.0	38.4
Social Credit	2.2	2.6	7.5	9.5
(N)	(827)	(730)	(825)	(746)

[a]Respondents were asked, 'Thinking of federal politics, do you usually think of yourself as a Liberal, Conservative, NDP, Social Credit, or what?' Non-identifiers were probed a second time: 'Still thinking of federal politics, do you generally think of yourself as being a little closer to one of the parties than to the others?' (If yes) 'Which party is that?' Similar probes, replacing 'federal' with 'provincial', were employed in order to ascertain provincial party identification.

SOURCE: 1979 Social Change in Canada Study.

Conservative support among both women and men was relatively low in this group. Indeed, the gender difference in NDP identification among respondents born after 1950 was less than 1 percent (0.4 percent)—the lowest gender difference in New Democratic partisanship of any cohort sampled.

What was the relationship between class and unionization factors and party identification in 1979? Data from the Social Change in Canada survey show that, as in 1965, gender differences in NDP support among respondents stating that they belonged to the working or lower classes exceeded differences among the middle class. Overall, 36.3 percent of working-class men and only 24.2 percent of working-class women stated that they identified provincially with the New Democrats, compared with 24.1 percent and 15.9 percent of middle-class men and women.

One plausible explanation of this finding, which follows from lower levels of unionization among women than men, is that working-class women were less likely to be exposed to partisan—specifically NDP—stimuli in the workplace than their male counterparts.[39] If we consider unionized respondents only, however, similar differentials remain, with 38.1 percent of unionized males and 28.5 percent of unionized females identifying with the New Democrats provincially, and 36.5 percent and 22.9 percent federally. In other words, both subjective social class and unionization appeared to have disparate influences on women and men in 1979, as in 1965, perhaps because of a continued masculine bias within trade unions as well as political parties.

As for the relationship between feminist beliefs and partisanship, 1979 data indicate that 26.7 percent of English Canadian females who endorsed much more government effort to eliminate discrimination against women identified federally with the New Democrats, while 30.8 percent did so provincially (comparable figures for men were 27.5 percent and 28.3 percent).[40] Given that aggregate levels of NDP support among women (reported in Table 2.12) were in the 18 percent range, these results confirm our expectation that feminist beliefs would be positively associated with New Democratic identification in 1979. In comparison, levels of Liberal partisanship among respondents endorsing much more government effort were very similar to those among the sample at large, while Conservative identification was generally lower among those wanting much more effort, relative to the overall sample.

Subsequent attitudinal research tends to confirm this relationship between feminism and left-of-centre partisanship; conversely, it also indicates a correlation between less progressive views regarding women's rights and right-of-centre politics. Studies by Janine Brodie, Joseph Fletcher and Marie-Christine Chalmers, and Roger Gibbins and Neil Nevitte demonstrate this linkage among members of the general public as well as among university students and party convention delegates.[41] Taken together, their findings parallel comparative data on the extent to which feminist consciousness often functions as an indicator of left/right beliefs.[42] As Gibbins and Nevitte reflect on the results of their Canadian and US

TABLE 2.13 FEDERAL PARTY IDENTIFICATION OF ANGLOPHONE CANADIANS BY BIRTH COHORTS, 1979 (%)[a]

	1950-61		1938-49		1926-37		1914-25		BEFORE 1914	
	WOMEN	MEN	WOMEN	MEN	WOMEN	MEN	WOMEN	MEN	WOMEN	MEN
Liberal	40.0	43.0	37.8	35.6	35.5	34.6	38.9	34.0	32.4	31.7
New Democratic	23.7	23.3	21.7	25.8	13.6	19.3	9.4	15.8	11.1	18.3
Progressive Conservative	33.3	31.9	39.0	36.7	50.5	44.3	49.5	47.6	52.7	42.8
Social Credit	3.0	1.8	1.5	1.9	0.4	1.8	2.2	2.6	3.8	7.2
(N)	(220)	(220)	(223)	(164)	(160)	(127)	(147)	(131)	(74)	(88)

[a]For exact question wording, see note to Table 2.12.

SOURCE: 1979 Social Change in Canada Study.

TABLE 2.14 MEN'S AND WOMEN'S PARTY VOTES, 1974-1988 (%)[a]

	1974		1979		1980		1984		1988	
	MALE	FEMALE	MALE	FEMALE	MALE	FEMALE	MALE	FEMALE	MALE	FEMALE
Liberal	48.0	56.8	38.2	46.0	43.0	52.1	23.3	26.7	22.4	29.0
PC	33.2	28.3	43.9	34.6	40.6	28.8	58.9	55.8	46.2	38.6
NDP	13.4	9.6	14.3	14.0	15.4	17.0	15.3	15.3	16.7	17.7

[a]Columns do not add to 100 percent because other parties, 'refused', and 'don't know' responses are excluded.

SOURCE: National Election Study data reported in Peter Wearing and Joseph Wearing, 'Does Gender Make a Difference in Voting Behaviour?' in Joseph Wearing, ed., The Ballot and Its Message (Toronto: Copp Clark Pitman, 1991), 343.

student surveys, 'feminism operates as a significant ideological optic' for both women and men in the two countries.[43]

This linkage between leftism and feminism can help to explain changing patterns of female partisanship. As summarized in Table 2.14, sex differences in reported NDP vote virtually disappeared in 1979 and following. Analyses of the 1984 elections report *no* gender differences in NDP support;[44] moreover, 'better educated women as well as men were more likely to perceive the NDP as the party most favorable to women's issues . . . and were significantly more likely to act upon this view by voting NDP'.[45] Survey research also showed slightly higher Liberal support among women than men, and less likelihood among women than men of shifting towards the Progressive Conservatives in 1979 and following.[46]

By 1988, when free trade constituted a major federal campaign issue, 46.2 percent of men versus 38.6 percent of women reported voting for the Progressive Conservatives. Contrary to integrationist predictions, gender differences in PC support were very clear among well-educated respondents, particularly in Ontario and Quebec.[47] This disparity was consistent with broader attitudinal patterns that showed lower support among women for free trade, a policy pursued by the Conservatives and opposed by the Liberals and New Democrats. As reflected in Table 2.15, females were less likely than men to endorse free trade as early as October 1987; sex differences in free trade views reached 20 percent in one October 1988 poll.

Women's lower support for free trade and the PCs in the late 1980s was part of an even larger attitudinal phenomenon, however. As in the US, where the liberal/feminist/anti-Reagan constellation of opinions was identified as 'gender gap' politics, women's views in Canada differed systematically from those of

TABLE 2.15   GENDER GAP IN FREE TRADE ATTITUDES, 1987-1988 (%)[a]

DATE OF POLL	FAVOUR FREE TRADE			UNDECIDED		
	MEN	WOMEN	DIFF.	MEN	WOMEN	DIFF.
October 1987	55	43	12	12	21	9
December 1987	47	34	13	16	26	10
June 1988	46	31	15	17	27	10
October 1988	53	33	20	11	18	7

[a]The question wording in 1987 was 'Do you strongly agree, somewhat agree, somewhat disagree, or strongly disagree that there should be free trade between Canada and the United States?" In 1988, the question was 'Do you strongly favour, somewhat favour, somewhat oppose or strongly oppose the free trade agreement that has been negotiated between Canada and the United States?'

SOURCE: Surveys were conducted by Environics Research Group and were reported in the *Globe and Mail* on 28 October 1987, 30 December 1987, 1 July 1988, and 14 October 1988.

men. Females tended to oppose Cruise missile testing and military spending in general; they also showed less support than men for foreign investment, and more for redistributive and social welfare policy. Paralleling these findings, men showed more concern with government deficits; women, with world peace.[48] This set of public opinion trends appeared to be a mass-level confirmation of the elite-level estrangement discussed in Chapter 1 between the organized women's movement and successive Conservative federal governments.

CONCLUSIONS

This chapter began by examining two interpretive perspectives, one drawn from the modernization thesis that predicted women's integration within established structures and patterns of political belief, and a second that focused on dual political cultures and the continuing impact of disparate experiences. Items from a variety of surveys conducted in 1965 and following measured political interest, efficacy and non-response as well as party and issue attitudes. Taken together, these data provide stronger evidence of continuing gender differences—and, by implication, the reality of distinctive orientations and cultures—than they do of political integration.

Even in the 1990s, more than seventy years after most Canadian women received formal rights to participate in the electoral process, considerable distance seems to separate many females at the mass level from that process. Except for their similar levels of voter turnout, women and men tended to differ on many fundamental measures of political engagement and policy choice. A 'gender gap' along the same guns/butter, right/left dimensions as in the United States had thus revealed itself in Canada.

NOTES

[1] Angus Campbell, Philip E. Converse, Warren E. Miller and Donald E. Stokes, *The American Voter* (New York: Wiley, 1960), 490.

[2] For a comparative treatment of these patterns, see Sandra Baxter and Marjorie Lansing, *Women and Politics: The Visible Majority* (revised ed.; Ann Arbor: University of Michigan Press, 1983).

[3] See Baxter and Lansing, *Women and Politics*; Carol A. Christy, 'American and German Trends in Sex Differences in Political Participation', *Comparative Political Studies* 18:1 (April 1985), 81-103; and Virginia Sapiro, *The Political Integration of Women: Roles, Socialization and Politics* (Urbana: University of Illinois Press, 1983).

[4] Thelma McCormack, 'Toward a Nonsexist Perspective on Social and Political Change', in Marcia Millman and Rosabeth Moss Kanter, eds., *Another Voice* (New York: Anchor, 1975), 25.

[5] Jill Vickers, ed., *Getting Things Done: Women's Views of their Involvement in Political Life* (Ottawa: Canadian Research Institute for the Advancement of Women, 1988), 6.

[6] For applications of this thesis to women, see, for example, Maurice Duverger, *The Political Role of Women* (New York: UNESCO, 1955); Robert E. Lane, *Political Life* (New York: Free Press, 1965); and Gabriel A. Almond and Sidney Verba, *The Civic Culture* (Boston: Little, Brown, 1965).

[7]For a more thorough review of these studies, see Thelma McCormack, 'Gender and the Polls', paper prepared for the Royal Commission on Electoral Reform and Party Financing, October 1990, 11.

[8]Peter Regenstreif, *The Diefenbaker Interlude* (Toronto: Longmans, 1965), 96.

[9]Ibid.

[10]M. Benney, A.P. Gray and R.H. Pear, *How People Vote*, as quoted in Mildred A. Schwartz, *Public Opinion and Canadian Identity* (Berkeley: University of California Press, 1967), 193-4.

[11]Schwartz, *Public Opinion*, 193.

[12]J.A. Laponce, *People vs Politics* (Toronto: University of Toronto Press, 1969), 37.

[13]Rick Van Loon, 'Political Participation in Canada: The 1965 Election', *Canadian Journal of Political Science* 3:3 (September 1970), 389.

[14]See Jean Bethke Elshtain, 'Moral Woman and Immoral Man: A Consideration of the Public-Private Split and its Political Ramifications', *Politics and Society* 4:4 (1974), 453-73; Susan Moller Okin, *Women in Western Political Thought* (Princeton: Princeton University Press, 1979); and Lorenne M.G. Clark and Lynda Lange, eds., *The Sexism of Social and Political Theory* (Toronto: University of Toronto Press, 1979).

[15]McCormack, 'Toward a Nonsexist Perspective on Social and Political Change', 12.

[16]Thelma McCormack, 'Examining the Election Entrails: Whatever Happened to the Gender Gap?' *This Magazine* 22:8 (March-April 1989), 32. McCormack's work is complementary to other female culture arguments presented in Jessie Bernard, *The Female World* (New York: Free Press, 1981); and Carol Gilligan, *In A Different Voice* (Cambridge: Harvard University Press, 1982).

[17]Vickers, *Getting Things Done*, 4.

[18]Ibid., 12.

[19]Ibid., 6.

[20]These additional sources include John C. Courtney and David E. Smith, 'Voting in a Provincial General Election and a Federal By-election: A Constituency Study of Saskatoon City', *Canadian Journal of Economics and Political Science* 32:3 (August 1966), 338-53; Pauline Jewett, 'Voting in the 1960 Federal By-elections at Peterborough and Niagara Falls', in John C. Courtney, ed., *Voting in Canada* (Scarborough: Prentice-Hall, 1967), 50-70; Richard Laskin and Richard Baird, 'Factors in Voter Turnout and Party Preference in a Saskatchewan Town', *Canadian Journal of Political Science* 3:3 (September 1970), 450-62; and John Meisel, *Working Papers on Canadian Politics* (Montreal: McGill-Queen's University Press, 1975), 12.

[21]Responses to an item regarding 1965 federal vote tended to parallel closely the party identification figures: 19.1 percent of men and 13.7 percent of women reported having voted for an NDP candidate in that election.

[22]Ratings of Liberal members of parliament were as follows: 43.3 percent of women and 37.9 percent of men rated them 'pretty good', 47.0 percent of women and 50.7 percent of men rated them 'so-so', and 9.7 percent of women and 11.5 percent of men said 'no good'. Ratings of Progressive Conservative MPs did not vary by gender.

[23]A similar result was obtained using 1979 survey data, as reported in Table 2.3.

[24]The circumstances surrounding female enfranchisement were described as follows by Charlotte Whitton, a prominent social welfare activist and mayor of Ottawa: 'Canadian women got the vote as a gift rather than as a reward. Moreover it was granted not as a conviction so much as a concession on the part of the major technicians within the parties.' See Whitton, 'Is the Canadian Woman a Flop in Politics?' (orig. pub. 1946), reprinted in Ramsay Cook and Wendy Mitchinson, eds., *The Proper Sphere* (Toronto: Oxford University Press, 1976), 329; and P.T. Rooke and R.L. Schnell, *No Bleeding Heart: Charlotte Whitton, A Feminist on the Right* (Vancouver: University of British Columbia Press, 1987).

[25]See Sandra Burt, 'Different Democracies? A Preliminary Examination of the Political Worlds of Canadian Men and Women', Women and Politics 6:4 (Winter 1986), 61; and Sandra Burt, 'Women's Issues and the Women's Movement in Canada since 1970', in Alan Cairns and Cynthia Williams, eds., The Politics of Gender, Ethnicity and Language in Canada, Royal Commission Research Studies, vol. 34 (Toronto: University of Toronto Press for Supply and Services Canada, 1986), 125.

[26]Burt, 'Women's Issues and the Women's Movement', Table 4-8, 126.

[27]Ibid., 126.

[28]See Barry J. Kay, Ronald D. Lambert, Steven D. Brown and James E. Curtis, 'Gender and Political Activity in Canada, 1965-1984', Canadian Journal of Political Science 20 (1987), 851-63.

[29]One problem in trying to interpret party data is that political independence (that is, non-partisanship) and non-voting, as well as refusals and 'don't know' replies, are grouped in a single category of non-response. Given that these are the only early data available, however, Table 2.7 provides a useful overview of the non-response phenomenon.

[30]Joel Smith, Allan Kornberg and Beth Rushing, 'The Changing Political Situation of Women in Canada', in Neil Nevitte and Allan Kornberg, eds., Minorities and the Canadian State (Oakville, Ont.: Mosaic Press, 1985), 224.

[31]This approach follows Karl Mannheim's work on the generational component of historical change, arguing that generations share a specific 'historico-social space—the same historical life community' (K.H. Wolfe, 'Introduction' to K. Wolfe, ed., From Karl Mannheim [New York: Oxford University Press, 1971], 1.) The chronological groups to be considered in this analysis are described as birth cohorts, who were born during a particular period in Canadian history and who matured to the point of formally entering the electorate as adulthood cohorts approximately twenty years later. See Norval D. Glenn, 'Cohort Analysis', Sage University Papers on Quantitative Applications in the Social Sciences (Beverly Hills: Sage, 1977).

[32]Regina Manifesto, as reprinted in Appendix A to Walter D. Young, The Anatomy of a Party: The National CCF, 1932-61 (Toronto: University of Toronto Press, 1969), 304. For a history of the Canadian social gospel phenomenon, see Richard Allen, The Social Passion (Toronto: University of Toronto Press, 1971) and, on its linkages with social feminism, see Beatrice Brigden, 'One Woman's Campaign for Social Purity and Social Reform', in Richard Allen, ed., The Social Gospel in Canada (Ottawa: National Museums of Canada, 1975), 36-62.

[33]Title of Part I of Draft Program of the New Party, as appended to Stanley Knowles, The New Party (Toronto: McClelland and Stewart, 1961), 9.

[34]For data on comparative levels of paid employment and unionization among males and females, see Julie White, Women and Unions (Ottawa: Canadian Advisory Council on the Status of Women, 1980).

[35]See Leo Zakuta, A Protest Movement Becalmed: A Study of Change in the CCF (Toronto: University of Toronto Press, 1964), 88ff.; and Gad Horowitz, Canadian Labour in Politics (Toronto: University of Toronto Press, 1968), 37ff.

[36]Betty Friedan, The Feminine Mystique (New York: Dell, 1963).

[37]Gary Teeple, '"Liberals in a Hurry": Socialism and the CCF/NDP', in Teeple, ed., Capitalism and the National Question in Canada (Toronto: University of Toronto Press, 1972), 237.

[38]See Louise Dulude, 'The Status of Women Under the Mulroney Government', in Andrew B. Gollner and Daniel Salée, eds., Canada Under Mulroney (Montreal: Véhicule Press, 1988), 253-64.

[39]On differential patterns of male and female employment and unionization, see White, Women and Unions.

[40]In the English Canadian sample overall, 17 percent of women (171) and 9 percent of men (78) stated that much more government effort should be devoted to eliminating discrimination against women.

[41]Janine Brodie, 'The Gender Factor and National Leadership Conventions in Canada', in George Perlin, ed., *Party Democracy in Canada* (Scarborough: Prentice-Hall, 1988), 172-87; Joseph F. Fletcher and Marie-Christine Chalmers, 'Attitudes of Canadians Toward Affirmative Action: Opposition, Value Pluralism and Nonattitudes', *Political Behavior* 13:1 (1991), 67-95; and Roger Gibbins and Neil Nevitte, 'The Ideology of Gender: A Cross-National Analysis', *Research in Political Sociology* 4 (1989), 89-113.

[42]See Neil Nevitte and Roger Gibbins, *New Elites in Old States: Ideologies in the Anglo-American Democracies* (Toronto: Oxford University Press, 1990), chap. 3.

[43]Gibbins and Nevitte, 'The Ideology of Gender', 103.

[44]Peter Wearing and Joseph Wearing, 'Does Gender Make a Difference in Voting Behaviour?' in Joseph Wearing, ed., *The Ballot and its Message: Voting in Canada* (Toronto: Copp Clark Pitman, 1991), 344.

[45]Barry J. Kay, Ronald D. Lambert, Steven D. Brown and James E. Curtis, 'Feminist Consciousness and the Canadian Electorate: A Review of National Election Studies', *Women and Politics* 8:2 (1988), 1-21.

[46]See Wearing and Wearing, 'Does Gender Make a Difference'; Brodie, 'The Gender Factor and National Leadership Conventions'; and John Terry, 'The Gender Gap: Women's Political Power', *Current Issue Review* 84-17E (Ottawa: Library of Parliament, May 1984).

[47]See Wearing and Wearing, 'Does Gender Make a Difference', 345.

[48]See ibid., 346-8; Brodie, 'The Gender Factor and National Leadership Conventions', 179-83; Terry, 'The Gender Gap;' and Kathryn Kopinak, 'Gender Differences in Political Ideology in Canada', *Canadian Review of Sociology and Anthropology* 24:1 (1987), 23-38.

CHAPTER THREE

The Higher the Fewer: Women's Participation in Major Party Organizations

She has been working in the trenches of this party for years . . . and particularly around the kitchen tables of this party.

—Ontario PC Association nomination speech, 1982[1]

Writing in 1950, historian Catherine Cleverdon suggested that a brighter future would await Canadian women who sought to become active in partisan politics. Cleverdon believed that political parties 'are becoming increasingly aware of the need to offer women something more in the way of political activity than to do party chores and to vote for their candidates (male, of course) on election days'.[2] Cleverdon's optimism grew out of a sense that the increasing educational and employment opportunities available to women after the Second World War would promote greater elite-level political participation.

Despite these trends, however, the involvement of Canadian women in the post-war years bore a close resemblance to that of previous decades. As Rosamonde Boyd observed in a comparative Canada-US study, 'women's rise to responsible positions of decision-making and administrative leadership has been slow and sporadic.'[3] The impact of traditional role constraints, combined with what Boyd termed 'an underestimation of their political potential' by North American women generally, helped to ensure that females were less numerous than males in positions of visible political influence.[4] As legislators, cabinet ministers and party leaders, women were simply few and far between.

A growing recognition of this weak numerical representation in North American political elites helped to fuel the feminist movement of the late 1960s and following. As was argued in Chapter 1, feminists responded to their lack of representation in diverse ways, including the fielding of independent candidates in federal elections and the establishment of assertive women's groups inside major party organizations. Overall, the objective of these activities was fairly consistent across time and across party ideologies: namely, to elevate both the numerical and the policy impact of women in Canadian politics.

One approach to this goal began with a focus on problems of political candidacy. Following early research in the field by Jill Vickers and Janine Brodie, activists tried to determine how the numbers of female candidates in winnable ridings could be increased and, concomitantly, how the policy priority accorded to women's issues could be improved.[5]

From an analytic perspective, this approach was weakened by its failure to situate women's participation in the broader context of party life at all levels. Although political candidacy remains an important and highly visible form of elite-level involvement, it hardly captures many less visible activities that generate and regenerate party organization in a modern democracy.[6] Local constituency-level work, campaign activity other than candidacy for public office, participation in party women's groups, internal party office-holding, delegation to party conventions and many other types of party involvement can be overlooked when overriding emphasis is placed on female candidacy.

This chapter extends research on women's participation by examining four other types of party work: local constituency activity, delegation to party conventions, party office-holding on the provincial and federal levels, and campaign management. We then introduce data on political candidacies, legislative office-holding and cabinet appointments in order to update existing research and to compare the problems of candidacy with the constraints facing women at other levels of party activity. This discussion forms the empirical background for a more speculative examination in Chapter 4 of responses to under-representation, including internal party affirmative action programs.

The main purpose of this chapter is to expand the study of women's political participation in Canada beyond questions of candidacy for public office and thus to situate female involvement in the broader context of party life at all levels. In so doing, we point toward constraints that influence party work at these various levels, and illustrate the extent to which women have been, and are, active and valuable partisans despite their numerical scarcity as candidates and elected legislators. In the words of former Liberal MP Judy LaMarsh: 'All political parties in Canada operate by and through women. Look into any committee room and you will find perhaps a man or two but dozens of women . . . My own nomination was secured because, as well as the group of men active in the party's inner circles, I gathered about me a group of women who had done the real donkey work in past elections.'[7] Like the Conservative activist referred to in the epigraph to this chapter, Liberal and New Democratic women have also laboured long and hard in the 'trenches' of their parties. Although relatively few have advanced beyond the point of routine 'donkey work', their contributions at each level of party activity must be acknowledged.

A second purpose of this chapter is to document from a Canadian perspective the phenomenon that Robert Putnam refers to as 'the law of increasing disproportion': the higher one goes in party elites, the fewer women are to be found.[8] As summarized in Figure 3.1, this law is clearly applicable to political party activity by women in Canada, where the percentage of female participants declines from a peak of approximately 70 percent, in the case of local constituency association secretaries, to a tiny handful in the case of major party leaders.[9] In addition, the following sections suggest a corollary to Putnam's argument: the more competitive the political position of any given provincial or federal party— and thus the higher the power stakes within that organization—the fewer women are to be found.

Before turning to data on women's involvement in party organizations, it is important to address the linkage between these numbers and feminist policy directions. Study after study of political elites in Canada, the US and other liberal democratic systems demonstrates that *women's numerical presence does make a substantive difference.* Whether measured with reference to the content of women's speeches in a legislature, their roll call behaviour on legislative bills or their policy preferences for future legislative action, the evidence of a policy differential

FIGURE 3.1   WOMEN'S PARTICIPATION IN MAJOR CANADIAN PARTY
ORGANIZATIONS, 1992

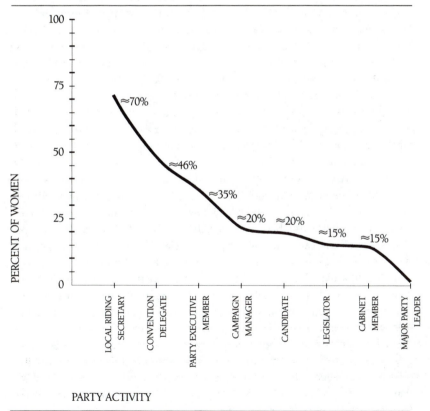

vis-à-vis men is sustained across a considerable body of empirical literature.[10] This literature does not suggest that all politically active women are feminists, nor does it posit that feminist women can achieve all of their goals through the established party system. What comparative studies do consistently show is the virtual impossibility of achieving important legislative reforms in the absence of numbers. In short, women's representation in party organizations is directly relevant to public policy outcomes.

LOCAL CONSTITUENCY ACTIVITY

Local riding associations serve as key political foundations for major provincial- and federal-level parties. Although many exist only on paper between elections, their mere presence at the constituency level helps to ensure a credible image of province- or nation-wide organization for the larger party grouping. In addition, by providing a core of real or potential political activists, and by functioning as a recruitment and mobilization arm for their parent parties, local riding as-sociations play a valuable but often neglected role in the party system.

The participation of women in local riding associations has received limited attention in the Canadian literature. One study of urban party organizations con-cludes that women form a disproportionately small segment of the party insider (intermediate level) and elite (top organizational) strata, while they are relatively over represented in the party stalwart (routine functionary) category.[11] According to Harold D. Clarke and Allan Kornberg, the few Canadian women who are involved in urban party activities tend to work harder than their male colleagues and, at the same time, expect fewer tangible rewards for their commitment. Clarke and Kornberg suggest that these females 'are in a very real sense "survivors"', who have reconciled themselves to the 'law of increasing disproportion' in urban party organizations.[12]

What activities do women perform in local constituency associations? Data collected by Kornberg, Smith and Clarke during the 1970s suggested that 'relatively similar proportions of men and women were members of their constituency executive committees or held poll captain and miscellaneous lower level po-sitions'.[13] Yet the research on federal and provincial ridings detailed in this section demonstrates considerable gender differences in both the *extent* and the *type* of local party activity. It suggests, first, that women perform stereotypically feminine types of party work at the local level; and second, that the competitive position of party organizations has had a direct impact upon female participation, limiting women's mobility in cases where the power stakes are high.

An appropriate place to begin this study of local constituency association ac-tivity is the province of Ontario, where approximately 45 percent of the An-glophone population of Canada reside.[14] With 99 (or about one-third) of the nation's federal ridings, and 130 (18.0 percent) of its provincial seats, Ontario has developed a fairly competitive three-party system at both levels. Consistent efforts by party women to monitor female involvement have provided a useful data base that extends back to the 1970s.

Figures on local riding participation at the provincial level in Ontario, presented in Table 3.1, document women's involvement in constituency associations in each of the three major parties. In terms of riding executive positions, the data indicate that, as expected, women in all three provincial parties were considerably less likely than men to serve as local riding presidents. In 1990, women comprised 22.3 percent of Conservative riding presidents (N = 29), 28.5 percent of Liberal riding presidents (37), and 34.6 percent of NDP riding presidents (45), so that overall in Ontario there were 111 female riding presidents out of a possible

TABLE 3.1   LOCAL PARTY PARTICIPATION BY WOMEN IN ONTARIO, PROVINCIAL LEVEL, 1973-1990[a]

YEAR	PRESIDENT %	PRESIDENT N	TREASURER/CFO %	TREASURER/CFO N	SECRETARY %	SECRETARY N
Liberal						
1981	20.0	(25)	29.6	(37)	76.8	(96)
1985	29.6	(37)	39.2	(49)	70.4	(88)
1988	20.0	(26)	23.8	(31)	65.4	(85)
1990	28.5	(37)	26.2	(34)	75.4	(98)
NDP						
1973	8.5	(10)	n.a.		n.a.	
1981	28.8	(36)	41.6	(52)	67.2	(84)
1985	30.4	(38)	36.8	(46)	69.3	(79)[c]
1988	26.2	(33)[b]	35.4	(46)	64.8	(70)[d]
1990	34.6	(45)	29.2	(38)	48.5	(63)
Progressive Conservative						
1977	9.6	(12)	5.6	(7)	62.4	(78)
1981	14.4	(18)	12.0	(15)	66.4	(83)
1985	19.2	(24)	24.0	(30)	69.6	(87)
1988	20.0	(26)	16.9	(22)	62.3	(81)
1990	22.3	(29)	16.9	(22)	64.6	(84)

[a]Cell entries in this and the following tables represent the percentage of local constituency positions held by women in the years and parties indicated, while figures in parentheses represent the actual number of women holding these positions. Note that percentages for 1973 are based on a total of 117 provincial ridings; for 1977, 1981 and 1985 on a total of 125 ridings; and for 1988 and 1990 on a total of 130 ridings.

[b]Since the position was vacant in 4 ridings, this percentage is calculated on a base of 126.

[c]Since the position was vacant in some ridings, this percentage is calculated on a base of 114.

[d]Since the position was vacant in 22 ridings, this percentage is calculated on a base of 108.

n.a. = not available.

SOURCE: Figures from 1973 and 1977 are based on internal party studies, while those for subsequent years are drawn from party records made available to the author.

390 in the three provincial parties, or 28.5 percent. The level of female representation in 1990 riding treasurerships was similar.

Comparing riding secretary data with these figures points towards the existence of a 'pink-collar' sector in local constituency organizations in Ontario. In 1981, between two-thirds and three-quarters of riding secretaries in the three parties were female (notably, 76.8 percent in the provincial Liberal organization); in 1990, between one-half and three-quarters were women. The same types of executive and financial positions usually held by men in the Canadian labour force, therefore, also tended to be held by men in the Ontario provincial ridings. At the same time, the more clerical and generally less prestigious positions in which women were clustered in the work force were also the ones in which they seemed ghettoized in Ontario riding associations. This clustering was least pronounced in NDP riding associations, however, where women were better represented as presidents and were less likely to serve as secretaries than in Liberal and Conservative executives.

What other conclusions can be drawn from riding-level data? First, with reference to their decision-making implications, these figures initially suggest that relatively few women wield effective power in local party organizations. However, closer inspection of internal riding activity in all three cases indicates that large numbers of women performed critical human relations, and especially communications, functions at the local level. As secretaries, they helped to ensure organizational continuity by keeping local riding minutes, recruiting new members and maintaining older memberships. In cases where the riding president or treasurer was not active, these women also provided the only visible evidence of their party's presence in the riding. Although it is important to recognize the implicit and often indirect nature of 'pink-collar' power in Ontario riding executives, the significance of women's contributions should not be overlooked.

The second point to be noted parallels the first: Ontario women who avoided the 'pink-collar' ghetto in the early 1980s did so in ridings where their party was generally inactive and had little chance of electoral success. Considerable numbers of female riding presidents in all three parties thus held only symbolic power in that period, since they had little opportunity to elect members to their legislative caucuses and could not attract resources from the central provincial organizations that supported party activity on the local level. For example, female NDP riding presidents in 1981 were clustered in rural Liberal and suburban Conservative-held seats, while Liberal women were frequently presiding in strong Tory and New Democratic areas. Over time, with growing numbers of women active in all provincial parties and Ontario's shift away from a one-party dominant to a three-party competitive system, this clustering has become less discernible.

A third conclusion from Table 3.1 concerns change over time in female riding involvement. Longitudinal figures suggest a significant increase in women's participation since the beginnings of data-gathering in the 1970s, which corresponds with the growth of feminist activism in Ontario, and in Canada generally. In the provincial NDP, for example, the number of women holding riding presidencies increased more than four fold over 17 years, from 10 in 1973 to 45 in 1990. Data from Conservative ridings suggest increased involvement as well, since 12 women were presidents in 1977, and 29 held these positions in 1990. However, during this same period women also became more numerous as Conservative riding secretaries (from 78 to 84), indicating that women continue to fill 'pink-collar' positions in many Ontario riding associations.

Comparable participation data from Manitoba, presented in Table 3.2, indicate fairly similar patterns in a smaller provincial political system. In 1992, three parties were represented in the 57-seat Manitoba legislature. Ten years earlier, when the system was a two-party one, women comprised less than 15 percent of NDP and Conservative riding presidents, and the figures for riding association vice-presidents were only slightly higher. As was the case in Ontario, female office-holding at these levels was greater in the New Democratic than the Conservative party, but only marginally so. Once again the heavy clustering of women in 'pink-collar' or clerical riding work was pronounced, with females comprising 69.6 percent of NDP secretaries and 69.8 percent of PC membership secretaries at the constituency level.[15]

By 1992 the differences between the NDP and the two other parties in Manitoba had become clearer. Women held 47.4 percent of riding presidencies in the NDP, 42.9 percent in the Liberal organization (where only 14 active riding associations existed) and 14.0 percent in the Progressive Conservative organization. More than 30 percent of riding treasurers in the Manitoba NDP were women, compared with 22.8 percent in the Conservative party. Conversely, traditional secretarial positions were more likely to be held by women in the Liberal and PC parties than in the NDP, as reported in Table 3.2. Overall, however, far more

TABLE 3.2   LOCAL PARTY PARTICIPATION BY WOMEN IN MANITOBA, PROVINCIAL LEVEL, 1982 AND 1992[a]

	PRESIDENT	VICE-PRESIDENT	TREASURER	SECRETARY
Liberal				
1992	42.9 (6/14)	n.a.	n.a.	71.4 (10/14)
NDP				
1982	14.3 (8/56)	16.1 (9/56)	41.1 (23/56)	69.6 (39/56)
1992	47.4 (27/57)	n.a.	31.6 (18/57)	42.1 (24/57)
Progressive Conservative				
1982	12.7 (7/55)	15.1 (8/53)	43.6 (24/55)	69.8 (37/53)
1992	14.0 (8/57)	36.8 (21/57)	22.8 (13/57)	66.7 (38/57)

[a]Cell entries represent percentages; fractions represent numbers of women out of total numbers holding position.

SOURCE: Party records made available to the author.

women were active at the local constituency level in Manitoba provincial politics in 1992 than in 1982.

Figures from the three major federal parties, gathered in 1990 (Table 3.3), indicate that large numbers of Canadian women in all provinces continued to fulfil primarily secretarial functions in local party executives. Across Canada, an average of 66.0 percent of federal Liberal, 48.2 percent of federal New Democratic and 64.9 percent of federal Conservative riding secretary positions were held by women. Conversely, the numbers and percentages of women who held local president and treasurer/chief financial officer (CFO) positions in 1990 were generally lower than those for constituency secretary. As one federal organizer reflected on her party's development, 'We have far more opportunity now for women to do what used to be the men's jobs in the ridings, but little change in the willingness of men to do what have traditionally been the women's jobs.'[16]

TABLE 3.3   LOCAL PARTY PARTICIPATION BY WOMEN IN CANADA, FEDERAL LEVEL, 1990[a]

PROVINCE/TERRITORY AND NUMBER OF RIDINGS	RIDING POSITION	LIBERAL	NDP	PROGRESSIVE CONSERVATIVE
Alberta				
26	President	26.9 (7)	23.1 (6)	11.5 (3)
	Treasurer/CFO	23.1 (6)	38.5 (10)	15.4 (4)
	Secretary	50.0 (13)	26.9 (7)	61.5 (16)
British Columbia				
32	President	18.8 (6)	34.4 (11)	9.4 (3)
	Treasurer/CFO	34.4 (11)	56.3 (18)	28.1 (9)
	Secretary	68.8 (22)	68.8 (22)	50.0 (16)
Manitoba				
14	President	28.6 (4)	14.3 (2)	7.1 (1)
	Treasurer/CFO	28.6 (4)	28.6 (4)	21.4 (3)
	Secretary	42.9 (6)	64.3 (9)	64.3 (9)
New Brunswick				
10	President	20.0 (2)	40.0 (4)	30.0 (3)
	Treasurer/CFO	30.0 (3)	40.0 (4)	20.0 (2)
	Secretary	80.0 (8)	50.0 (5)	90.0 (9)
Newfoundland				
7	President	14.3 (1)	14.3 (1)	n.a.
	Treasurer/CFO	n.a.	0.0 (0)	57.1 (4)
	Secretary	n.a.	28.6 (2)	n.a.

PROVINCE/TERRITORY AND NUMBER OF RIDINGS	RIDING POSITION	LIBERAL	NDP	PROGRESSIVE CONSERVATIVE
Nova Scotia				
11	President	27.3 (3)	27.3 (3)	9.1 (1)
	Treasurer/CFO	n.a.	45.5 (5)	9.1 (1)
	Secretary	n.a.	36.4 (4)	54.6 (6)
Ontario				
99	President	28.3 (28)	30.3 (30)	22.2 (22)
	Treasurer/CFO	n.a.	29.3 (29)	14.1 (14)
	Secretary	n.a.	46.5 (46)	65.7 (65)
Prince Edward Island				
4	President	0.0 (0)	0.0 (0)	0.0 (0)
	Treasurer/CFO	50.0 (2)	25.0 (1)	25.0 (1)
	Secretary	75.0 (3)	75.0 (3)	100.0 (4)
Quebec				
75	President	22.7 (17)	14.7 (11)	8.0 (6)
	Treasurer/CFO	n.a.	n.a.	30.7 (23)
	Secretary	n.a.	n.a.	64.0 (48)
Saskatchewan				
14	President	14.3 (2)	14.3 (2)	14.3 (2)
	Treasurer/CFO	0.0 (0)	42.9 (6)	7.1 (1)
	Secretary	100.0 (14)	50.0 (7)	85.7 (12)
Yukon & NWT				
3	President	0.0 (0)	33.3 (1)	0.0 (0)
	Treasurer/CFO	0.0 (0)	33.3 (1)	66.7 (2)
	Secretary	66.7 (2)	33.3 (1)	66.7 (2)
Totals				
295	President	23.7 (70)	24.1 (71)	14.2 (41/288)
	Treasurer/CFO	25.2 (26/103)	35.5 (78/220)	21.7 (64/295)
	Secretary	66.0 (68/103)	48.2 (106/220)	64.9 (187/288)

aCell entries represent percentages; figures in parentheses represent numbers of women.

n.a. = not available.

SOURCE: Party records made available to the author.

Are patterns of federal involvement related to a party's competitive position? In the past, it was far easier both at the national level and in many provinces, including Ontario and Manitoba, to identify what constituted a competitive political party—that is, one that held the reins of government or was likely to do so in the near future. Because the parties were generally able to classify their local bases as marginal, potentially winnable or safe, it was relatively easy to discern the patterns by which female activists were clustered in particular types of jobs in specific kinds of ridings.

However, with the rise of new parties federally and provincially, and the sustained volatility of the Canadian electorate, it has become increasingly difficult to tell whether female party presidents are clustered in weak or marginal ridings where their organization has little chance of electoral success. In general, the distribution of women appears less skewed than in the past, since there is no longer the very clear concentration of female presidents and CFOs in marginal constituencies. Part of this change may be due to shifts in voter mood that make it difficult for parties to identify their strong versus weak ridings, and part of it is likely due to growing demands from party women and growing awareness among party elites generally of the need to give *all* activists a fair chance at holding local executive positions.

Increases in female participation at the local level may also be attributable to the increasing numbers of organizations competing for volunteer time, especially interest groups. Some observers have suggested that partisan opportunities for women widened during the 1980s because local gate-keepers could no longer afford to block new talent. If women did not believe that the structure of opportunity in the local party organization was fair, according to this explanation, then there were plenty of other political groups to which they could devote time and effort. This view is particularly relevant to party women who could turn to non-partisan women's interest groups, in which organizational mobility patterns were more fluid than in local ridings with their 'pink-collar' sectors.

Since much political activity occurs outside of local riding associations, particularly at party conventions and in provincial-level and campaign organizations, we now examine these other participatory arenas.

CONVENTION DELEGATION

Conventions of the major Canadian political parties provide an important setting for both formal and informal decision-making. Whether organized as leadership or policy forums, conventions are designed to bring together delegates in a manner that renews or revitalizes the party organization.

Much of the literature on conventions assumes that they are socially representative.[17] Yet the few studies published in the early 1970s that considered female involvement reported clear evidence of under-representation.[18] These patterns and the subsequent growth in women's convention delegation—from less than 20 percent in both the United States and Canada in 1968 to more than double that figure by the 1980s—elicited barely a nod from Canadian political scientists.[19]

In historical terms, the participation of women in Canadian party conventions has been generally viewed as slight or at best episodic. One source notes that at least two women, including social feminist Nellie McClung, attended the 1914

Manitoba Liberal convention that endorsed woman suffrage.[20] Catherine Cleverdon's research shows that the pressure applied subsequently by suffragists in British Columbia and Quebec helped to ensure the adoption of proenfranchisement platforms—and, ultimately, the successful sponsorship of suffrage legislation—by both provincial Liberal parties. Overall, however, women were more frequently viewed as the spouses of male convention delegates and as alternates or observers who played only marginal political roles at major party meetings.

This impression is generally confirmed by data from the early 1950s through the late 1960s, presented in Table 3.4. In the United States in 1952, by comparison, women comprised less than 13 percent of delegates to the two major presidential conventions, while in 1968 the percentage of female delegates at the Republican convention rose to approximately 17 percent. Female delegation to the Democratic party convention in 1968 was 12.9 percent, only marginally higher than the 12.5 percent level established nearly fifteen years earlier.

The percentages of women delegates in this period were slightly higher for major Canadian party conventions. For example, comparison of 1967 Progressive Conservative and 1968 Republican figures indicates that the level of female delegation was 2.3 percent higher for the PCs, while the rate for the Liberals in this same period was 5.1 percent higher than for Democrats.

This edge in Canadian party delegation was reversed by US party reforms of the 1970s, especially the equal representation or affirmative action terms

TABLE 3.4   WOMEN DELEGATES AT CANADIAN PARTY CONVENTIONS,
1967-1990 (%)

PARTY	YEAR	WOMEN DELEGATES
Federal Progressive Conservative	1967	19.0
Federal Liberal	1968	18.0
Federal NDP	1981	34.7
Federal Progressive Conservative	1981	33.0
Ontario Liberal	1982	39.2
Ontario NDP	1982	40.0
Federal Liberal	1982	37.6
Federal Progressive Conservative	1983 (Winnipeg)	41.4
Federal Progressive Conservative	1983 (Ottawa)	28.0
Federal Progressive Conservative	1989	46.0
Federal Liberal	1990	47.0

SOURCES: Sylvia B. Bashevkin, *Toeing the Lines: Women and Party Politics in English Canada* (1st ed.; Toronto: University of Toronto Press, 1985), Table 3.3; and party records made available to the author.

adopted at the 1972 Democratic convention (see Chapter 4). As female representation among Democratic delegates reached the 50 percent target in 1976, women's involvement in comparable Canadian parties remained close to older pre-affirmative action levels in the United States. Perhaps most notably, the percentages of female party delegates to the 1982 Ontario Liberal and NDP conventions closely resembled the figures for Democratic presidential conventions held ten years earlier. In subsequent years, however, Canadian party delegation levels more closely approximated the point of parity, with just under 50 percent female representation at major party conventions since 1989.[21]

PARTY OFFICE-HOLDING

Most of the important decision-making in Canadian party organizations, both between and during election campaigns, takes place among small groups of official and unofficial party elites. Whether these elites gather at specifically designated executive meetings or in informal backroom settings, their discussions frequently determine party campaign strategies, leadership politics and the overall deployment of human and financial resources within the larger organization.

One study of urban activists characterizes party elites as primarily male, middle-aged, politicized and well-educated members of the Canadian middle class.[22] In proportional terms, the authors of *Citizen Politicians* acknowledge that few decision-makers are female, particularly when those women who automatically hold provincial- or federal-level party office by virtue of their position in affiliated women's associations are removed from consideration.

Few other systematic efforts have been made to document female representation in elite party office. Such research is complicated by structural variations: the names and functions of official decision-making bodies vary widely across parties, across levels of government and, with frequent re-organizations of party structures, across single parties over time. Moreover, data on female representation in party officialdom can present a distorted view of actual participation and influence, since 'token' women on figurehead boards or committees are unlikely to have much meaningful input into decision-making.

Bearing in mind these problems, we can begin to evaluate formal representation in party elites using provincial-level data from Ontario and Manitoba. Briefly, the constitutionally recognized structures of the three Ontario parties are as follows. The provincial NDP is formally administered by the party leader and nine provincial officers who, in conjunction with sixteen members-at-large, two delegates to the NDP Federal Council, two youth delegates and one delegate to the Participation of Women (POW) Committee of the Federal Council, form the provincial executive. However, the party constitution states that 'the Provincial Council shall be the governing body between conventions'. This council usually meets four times a year. In 1982, the provincial NDP adopted an affirmative action resolution that urges ridings 'to adopt by-laws requiring equal (at least 50 percent) representation of women in their executives and convention delegations', and that requires equal representation in the provincial executive and all party committees.

The Ontario Liberal Party (OLP) is administered by nine table officers who— in conjunction with the party leader, one representative from the legislative caucus at Queen's Park, eight representatives from the youth committee and 24 area co-ordinators—form the OLP executive committee. Along with a number of other *ex-officio* members, the executive committee is responsible for appointing provincial committees, calling and presiding over annual meetings and generally administering party affairs.

The provincial organization of the Ontario Progressive Conservative Party is similar to that of the OLP in that it is governed by officers who constitute the executive of the Ontario PC Association. The executive consists of 21 members: the party president, the past president, nine vice-presidents (two designated as men, two as women, and two as youth), five regional vice-presidents, a secretary and a treasurer, and the presidents of affiliated women's, youth and campus party groups.[23]

In light of these differing constitutional arrangements in the three Ontario political parties, what generalizations can be made about provincial-level participation? The data in Table 3.5 indicate that it is in the relatively complex and decentralized NDP organization that women's representation is highest at the provincial level. Comparison of 1990 figures in all three provincial parties shows that females comprised 40.0 percent of the Liberal executive, 31.3 percent of the Conservative, and 50.0 percent of the New Democratic. Most of the data

TABLE 3.5   PROVINCIAL-LEVEL PARTICIPATION BY WOMEN IN ONTARIO, 1981-1990 (%)[a]

| YEAR | LIBERAL | | NDP | | PROGRESSIVE CONSERVATIVE |
	TABLE OFFICERS	EXECUTIVE COMMITTEE	PROVINCIAL EXECUTIVE	PROVINCIAL COUNCIL	EXECUTIVE COMMITTEE
1981	12.5 (1/8)	8.3 (1/12)	39.3 (11/28)	27.9 (41/147)	16.7 (3/18)
1985	37.5 (3/8)	33.3 (8/24)	50.0 (14/28)	34.9 (37/106)	38.9 (7/18)
1988	22.2 (2/9)	34.0 (16/47)[b]	48.3 (15/31)	37.1 (63/170)	28.6 (6/21)
1990	n.a.	40.0 (6/15)	50.0 (15/30)	26.3 (91/346)	31.3 (5/16)

[a]Cell entries represent percentages; figures in parentheses represent the proportion of women holding positions.

[b]Three positions on the Liberal executive committee were vacant.

n.a. = not available.

SOURCE: Data are drawn from party records made available to the author.

in Table 3.5 show an increase between 1981 and 1990 in women's participation in party executives in Ontario.

Turning to data on provincial elites in Manitoba, presented in Table 3.6, we find that the structures of the two major parties parallel closely their counterparts in Ontario. That is, the responsibilities of executive committee table officers in the Manitoba PC organization, and of provincial executive members in the Manitoba NDP, are similar to those assigned to comparable elites in Ontario. Manitoba Liberals had a party executive in 1992 that included the party leader, table officers, director of organization, and presidents of the women's and aboriginal commissions.

However, cross-party differences in Manitoba bore little similarity to those in Ontario. Executive officers in both the provincial NDP and PC organizations were approximately 40 percent female in 1982, while riding delegates to the NDP provincial Council were less than 20 percent female in that year (see Table 3.6). In Manitoba, therefore, the smaller PC executive had a considerably higher proportion of women than did the larger Ontario one (40.0 percent versus 16.7 percent), while the smaller NDP provincial council had a substantially lower percentage of women than its Ontario counterpart (17.5 percent versus 27.9 percent). Speculating on possible reasons for these results, we would suggest that the governing position of the Manitoba NDP and Ontario PC organizations in 1982 may have created a relatively competitive internal environment that was not conducive to elevated levels of female involvement. By contrast, the opposition status of the Manitoba PCs and Ontario NDP may have generated a less competitive atmosphere, permitting higher levels of female participation.

In 1992, when three parties held seats in the Manitoba legislature and the Conservatives held power, women were best represented in numerical terms in the NDP executive (52.2 percent), followed by the Conservative (39.1 percent)

TABLE 3.6   PROVINCIAL-LEVEL PARTICIPATION BY WOMEN IN MANITOBA, 1982 AND 1992[a]

	LIBERAL		NDP		PROGRESSIVE CONSERVATIVE
YEAR	PARTY EXECUTIVE	COMMITTEE CHAIRS	PROVINCIAL EXECUTIVE	PROVINCIAL COMMITTEES	PARTY EXECUTIVE
1982	n.a.	n.a.	42.9 (6/14)	25.7[b]	40.0 (4/10)
1992	31.8 (7/22)	20.0 (1/5)	52.2 (12/23)	46.8[c]	39.1 (9/23)

[a]Cell entries represent percentages; figures in parentheses represent proportion of women holding position.

[b]Represent average percentage of women in 11 provincial NDP committees.

[c]Represents proportion of 80 women out of 171 committee members.

SOURCE: Party records made available to the author.

and Liberal (31.8 percent) executives. Women also filled nearly half (46.8 percent) of the 171 standing committee memberships in the Manitoba NDP in 1992.

Data on federal party office-holding, presented in Table 3.7, indicate that women were proportionately less well represented in the national elites of the Liberal and Conservative parties than of the NDP. The percentage of females in the Conservative national executive was 43.1 percent, about 20 percent higher than seven years earlier. Within the federal Liberal elite, women were not as well represented in 1990 as in 1983 on either the national executive (38.1 versus 43.3 percent) or the Standing Committee on Policy (21.1 versus 28.6 percent).

In the third federal party, the NDP, an affirmative action resolution that was adopted and implemented in 1983 ensured that female representation in elite bodies would be at or above parity. As reported in Table 3.7, women constituted 58.1 percent of NDP federal executive members in 1990. Data on a new right-of-centre federal formation, the Reform party, indicate exceedingly low numbers of women in that party's executive council. Only one of the 17 members in 1992 was female, for a rate of less than 6 percent.[24]

Cross-party comparison of these results suggests the effects of affirmative action in both federal and provincial NDP organizations. It is worth noting that only in the federal, Manitoba and Ontario NDP cases did women attain or, in the first two cases, exceed the 50 percent level in party executive positions. This pattern is consistent with the local riding data presented in Tables 3.1 through 3.3. They indicate that women in the NDP have generally been more likely than their Liberal and Conservative counterparts to break out of the pink-collar sector within constituency organizations and to obtain party president and treasurer positions.

TABLE 3.7   FEDERAL PARTY OFFICE-HOLDING BY WOMEN IN CANADA, 1983 AND 1990 (%)[a]

PARTY	ORGANIZATION	1983	1990
Liberal	National executive	43.3 (13/30)	38.1 (8/21)
	Policy committee	28.6 (6/21)	21.1 (4/19)
NDP	Federal executive	50.0 (6/12)	58.1 (18/31)
	Federal council	60.0 (12/20)	n.a.
Progressive Conservative	National executive	23.8 (35/147)	43.1 (25/58)

[a]Cell entries represent percentages; figures in parentheses represent the proportion of women holding positions.

n.a. = not available.

SOURCE: See Table 3.4.

The impact of a party's competitive position on women's representation at elite levels is also reflected in the experience of backroom political strategists. Although this type of party involvement is generally shielded from public view and remains difficult to assess directly, the experiences of women who have held backroom positions suggest that under-representation is most pronounced in competitive (usually governing) parties, and in organizations where the party leader has a long history of reliance on a tightly-knit male strategy network.

Participation often drops to zero or possibly one in ten in these cases, and may differ little from women's representation in opposition backrooms. As one veteran of backroom politics on the federal level observed, 'We were clearly the third party in national politics, yet the circle around the federal leader remained a real male network . . . It was extremely difficult to break through that network and, above all, I found that once inside it, people would raise their eyebrows if I pushed issues—and particularly what they viewed as "women's issues", too hard.' This opposition experience during the Broadbent years in the federal NDP has much in common with women's accounts of the Mulroney era in the Conservative organization.[25] In general, these observations support the view that women remain under-represented in positions (whether formal or informal) of major party responsibility, particularly where such positions are synonymous with political or governmental power.

Ultimately, the focus of activity for most party elites is provincial or federal election day. It is to women's involvement as campaign managers and candidates that we now turn our attention.

CAMPAIGN MANAGEMENT

Although the operation and administration of local election campaigns is generally overlooked in studies of Canadian parties, experience as a campaign manager likely offers valuable organizational training and visibility for aspiring activists. In particular, partisans who want to become candidates themselves can 'learn the ropes' regarding nomination and campaign organization, and can cultivate media, party and external fund-raising contacts.

The extent of women's involvement as campaign managers, summarized in Tables 3.8 through 3.10, has varied widely across time, region and party. For example, longitudinal data from Ontario (Table 3.8) suggest that female participation generally increased between 1981 and 1990, reaching as high as 37.7 percent in the case of NDP managers for the 1990 provincial campaign. By way of comparison, there were 30.8 percent female managers in the provincial Liberal and 23.9 percent in the provincial Conservative organizations in 1990. These data represent considerable improvement over figures from the 1970s (Table 3.9): only 19 women (or 16.2 percent) were NDP managers in the 1971 campaign (versus 41 or 32.8 percent in 1981), and only 9 (or 7.2 percent) were Conservative managers in the 1977 election (versus 16 or 12.8 percent in 1981).

TABLE 3.8 CAMPAIGN PARTICIPATION BY WOMEN IN ONTARIO, PROVINCIAL LEVEL, 1981, 1987, 1990[a]

	LIBERAL			NDP			PROGRESSIVE CONSERVATIVE		
	1981	1987	1990	1981	1987	1990	1981	1987	1990
Candidates	6.4 (8)	20.8 (27)	20.0 (26)	19.2 (24)	35.4 (46)	30.0 (39)	10.4 (13)	16.9 (22)	15.4 (20)
Campaign managers	22.4 (28)	23.8 (31)	30.8 (40)	32.8 (41)	36.9 (48)	37.7 (49)	12.8 (16)	28.5 (37)	23.9 (31)
Total (N)	(36)	(58)	(66)	(65)	(94)	(88)	(29)	(59)	(51)

[a]Cell entries represent the percentage of women participating; figures in parentheses represent the number. Note that a total of 125 provincial ridings existed in 1981, and 130 in 1987 and 1990.

SOURCE: Data are drawn from Ontario Official Election Returns and from party records.

TABLE 3.9   CAMPAIGN PARTICIPATION OF WOMEN IN ONTARIO BY PROVINCIAL PARTY AND PROVINCIAL ELECTION, 1971-1990[a]

		CANDIDATES	ELECTED MPPS	PLACED 2ND	PLACED 3RD	CAMPAIGN MANAGERS
1971	Liberal	4	0	0	4	n.a.
	NDP	7	0	3	4	19
	PC	6	2	2	2	n.a.
	Total	17	2	5	10	n.a.
1975	Liberal	18	1	8	9	n.a.
	NDP	13	3	2	8	n.a.
	PC	8	3	1	4	n.a.
	Total	39	7	11	21	n.a.
1977	Liberal	15	1	8	6	n.a.
	NDP	19	2	5	12	n.a.
	PC	10	3	6	1	9
	Total	44	6	19	19	n.a.
1981	Liberal	8	1	5	2	28
	NDP	24	1	1	22	41
	PC	13	4	6	3	16
	Total	45	6	12	27	85
1985	Liberal	15	3	8	4	n.a.
	NDP	28	3	6	19	n.a.
	PC	18	3	11	4	n.a.
	Total	61	9	25	27	n.a.
1987	Liberal	27	16	11	0	31
	NDP	46	3	16	27	48
	PC	22	1	6	15	37
	Total	95	20	33	42	116
1990	Liberal	26	6	18	2	40
	NDP	39	20	13	7	49
	PC	20	3	3	12	31
	Total	85	29	34	21	120

[a]All cell entries represent the number of women involved. Most data on campaign management other than for the 1981 and 1987 provincial elections were not available. One Conservative candidate in 1990 placed fourth.

n.a. = not available.

SOURCE: Cell entries for the first four columns are drawn from Ontario Official Election Returns, while figures on campaign management are from party records.

In Manitoba, women were 15.8 percent of NDP and 8.8 percent of Conservative campaign managers in the 1981 provincial elections, for a total of 14 female managers in the two major parties that year. For the 1990 provincial elections, the Liberals recruited 20 women campaign managers (35.1 percent), the NDP had 12 in 30 ridings (40.0 percent) and the Conservatives reported 22 (38.6 percent). In short, the number of women managers in major provincial party campaigns reached 54 by 1990.

Contemporary federal data in Table 3.10 indicate that women's involvement as managers in the 1988 campaign was somewhat lower than at the provincial level in either Manitoba or Ontario in 1990.[26] As in the case of party executive positions, cross-party patterns once again showed the highest involvement in the federal NDP and, where comparisons were possible, a general increase in most parties over time. Just as federal party executive data showed a decline over time in a long-governing party no longer in office (the federal Liberals), so too Ontario provincial data on campaign management indicated a decrease in the party that had long ruled the province (the Progressive Conservatives). Taken together, these data point towards fairly consistent increases over time in female numerical representation in the NDP as compared with less consistent and, in some cases, downward patterns of representation in ex-governing parties.

One generalization that follows from these data on local and intermediate-level involvement concerns the rough ordering among parties of female participation. Women in the NDP seem most engaged at the point of riding president, riding treasurer/CFO, provincial and federal party executive member and campaign manager, usually followed by Liberal and then Progressive Conservative organizations in that order. This pattern is helpful to bear in mind as we turn to elite-level involvement, including candidacy for public office, legislative office-holding, cabinet appointments and party leadership.[27]

TABLE 3.10   FEDERAL CAMPAIGN PARTICIPATION BY CANADIAN WOMEN, 1984 AND 1988

	1984 CANDIDATES		1988 CANDIDATES		1988 CAMPAIGN MANAGERS	
	%	N	%	N	%	N
Liberal	15.2	(43)	17.0	(50)	21.4	(63)
NDP	23.0	(65)	28.8	(85)	30.5	(90)
Progressive Conservative	8.1	(23)	12.5	(37)	18.6	(55)
Totals	15.5 (131)		19.4 (172)		23.5 (208)	

SOURCE: Party records made available to the author.

CANDIDACY FOR PUBLIC OFFICE

Much of the existing research on women's participation in Canadian politics has focused on election to public office. Studies that consider the dynamics of political nomination, candidacy and election generally conclude that role norms, a lack of money, discrimination by political organizations, and the responsibilities of family life, especially child-rearing, militated against female involvement in the campaign process. These same factors have also been linked with the proliferation of women candidates in no-win or long-shot constituencies.[28]

This literature points toward two main generalizations. First, women candidates and office-holders have been most common at the municipal level of government. According to Vickers, this pattern is attributable to the lower financial and personal costs incurred by local activists, and to 'the relatively low level of power and influence which has the effect of reducing competition [and of weakening] structures such as political parties' that tend to limit access to recruitment channels.[29] Second, on the basis of this finding and of data showing a concentration of women candidates in weak or marginal seats, Brodie and Vickers suggest that party control over elite recruitment constitutes a critical barrier to increased participation by women in Canadian politics.[30]

Although the relative absence of women in elected legislative office in Canada helps to support this view, the repeated occurrence of 'dirty tricks' in party nomination proceedings offers more direct evidence of bias at the level of public candidacy. According to Brodie, 50 percent of female candidates in competitive ridings experienced 'at least one negative incident', compared with 32 percent among the overall sample of women candidates.[31] Interviews with legislators and candidates also indicate that 'dirty tricks' continue to occur at the riding level, particularly in constituencies where the female nominee has a reasonable chance of winning election. Otherwise, as one candidate in a very weak seat observed, 'the riding executive begs you to run, welcomes you with open arms, and implicitly recognizes that no man with similar qualifications would consider such a "nomination".'

Two crucial questions that relate to candidacy are the following. First, to what extent did women candidates contest federal and provincial elections during recent campaigns? And second, how can parties address the clustering of women in weak seats? Data in Tables 3.9 and 3.10 indicate that although more women are legislative nominees now than in the past, they continue to be under-represented as candidates on both the federal and provincial levels. The total number of federal candidates for major parties increased from 131 or 15.5 percent in 1984 to 172 or 19.4 percent in 1988. At the provincial level in Ontario, 85 women candidates contested office for the three major parties in 1990 (21.8 percent), as compared with 45 (12.0 percent) in 1981. In Manitoba in 1990, 15 Liberal women, 16 NDP women and 9 Conservative women ran for office, for a total of 23.4 percent (40/171) of major provincial party candidates.

One major criticism of the candidacy situation is that female nominees at both federal and provincial levels tend to run in ridings where their parties are not in a competitive position. The tendency for parties to nominate women in constituencies held by the leader of another party, or in other presumably marginal seats, has been viewed as evidence that women face considerable hurdles at the elite level. It is argued, in short, that few women run in their parties' competitive constituencies where the political stakes are high.[32]

In part as a reaction to this criticism, some political parties have made a conscious decision to field more women candidates in competitive seats, even if fewer female candidates are nominated in total. Such a decline can be attributed to a qualitative as opposed to quantitative approach to candidacy; fewer women are fielded overall, but the ridings where they do run are more politically promising than in the past. In 1990 in Ontario, for example, the provincial NDP purposefully ran women in all three Metropolitan Toronto seats that had been vacated by NDP incumbents. Overall, the party fielded fewer female candidates in 1990 (39, or 30.0 percent) than it had in 1987 (46, or 35.4 percent).[33]

This response suggests that party ideology combined with feminist pressure inside the party organization can directly shape patterns of female candidacy.

LEGISLATIVE OFFICE-HOLDING

The paucity of women as elected legislators in Canada has long been a source of frustration and challenge to observers both inside and outside the chambers of government. In the sixty years following the election of Louise McKinney and Roberta Macadams as the first female provincial lawmakers (in Alberta) in 1917, and of Agnes Macphail as the first federal MP in 1921, approximately 100 women won legislative office in Canada. This record would probably have disappointed even the optimistic Macphail, whose biographers describe her initial entrance to the House of Commons as follows: 'She thought of the women who would surely walk this corridor too. 'I could almost hear them coming,' she said later. Her ear must have been tuned to a still remote time, for in the next quarter century only four other Canadian women were elected to the federal House of Commons.'[34]

A number of structural and psychological explanations have been proposed to account for this scarcity of women in elected legislative office.[35] Perhaps the most compelling reason follows from the interplay of gender role socialization and organizational processes in party politics; that is, the practice and/or expectation of male assertiveness, combined with the practice and/or expectation of female docility, have served to produce (and reproduce) a predominantly male party elite structure and a predominantly female party support base. Because they are essentially organizations of volunteers, with some careerists in their higher echelons, political parties are very dependent upon the initiative of individual activists—generally men—who until recently had little reason to seek out or encourage women elites. These organizational factors, combined with the impact of gender role socialization, dealt an especially hard blow to efforts toward increasing female representation within Canadian legislatures.

Many of the women who succeeded Agnes Macphail in the House of Commons shared important personal characteristics and political experiences with her: as a group, female legislators have tended to be unmarried; either childless or with children older than those of their male counterparts; and older than men upon their first election to public office. Like Macphail, as well, many have represented Ontario ridings; worked as teachers, journalists or social workers (unlike their male colleagues who often have legal and business backgrounds); and had pre-election political backgrounds.[36] While the specific experiences of these women within the House of Commons have varied, it seems fair to say that all confronted a predominantly masculine environment upon their entrance to Parliament. In the words of Liane Langevin: 'Legislatures are often compared to a men's club in that their membership is predominantly male and consequently so are their traditions and atmosphere. A woman who enters a legislature as a member is an anomaly, a deviant in the sense that she is defying traditional limits on acceptable feminine behaviour.'[37]

Nevertheless, the degree of gender role defiance implied by women's legislative participation has declined with the passage of time. Since the fourteen-year tenure of Agnes Macphail as the sole female MP, and the subsequent election of at least seven women who inherited federal seats from their husbands, the social limitations upon independent political involvement by Canadian women have generally subsided. One important barometer of change has been the growing numbers of females in federal cabinet positions, beginning in 1957 with the appointment of Hamilton accountant Ellen Fairclough to the secretary of state portfolio.

Despite these notable advances, however, women continue to be vastly underrepresented in both federal and provincial legislatures in Canada. The percentage of females holding elective parliamentary office remains far below their 52 percent level in the general population, with an overall provincial figure of 13.8 percent and a federal figure of 13.5 percent in 1989.[38]

One of the highest levels of numerical representation for Canadian women obtained in Ontario in 1990. The electoral decline of the Ontario Conservatives led to a provincial Liberal landslide in 1985, when 16 women were elected to the government caucus, followed by an NDP majority government in 1990. The conscious decision of the provincial NDP to field women candidates in more promising ridings, together with a history in the NDP of running relatively large numbers of women and a major electoral shift in the province, produced obvious legislative results. In 1990, the Ontario NDP elected 20 women MPPs as compared with only 3 in 1987. The NDP government caucus at Queen's Park was thus comprised of 27.0 percent women (20 out of 74) and the 1990 Ontario cabinet included 11 female ministers out of 26 members (42.3 percent). Much like previous increases in elite-level participation, these record numbers in Ontario may serve as new benchmarks against which future provincial and federal governments will be measured.

Major electoral shifts also produced substantial change in women's representation at the federal level. The 1984 Progressive Conservative landslide helped to elect many women in areas, including Quebec, that had traditionally been considered weak for that party, and meant that the number of female MPs nearly doubled from 14 (5.0 percent) in 1980 to 27 (9.6 percent) in 1984. This number increased once again to 39 (13.2 percent) in 1988.

CABINET AND LEADERSHIP POSITIONS

Increased participation can also be seen in data on cabinet office and party leadership. In contrast to the situation that prevailed through the 1960s, when one woman was seen as the limit in federal cabinets, 1992 figures show 6 out of 36 (16.7 percent) women in the federal cabinet. This quantitative shift was accompanied by a qualitative one as well: after the mid-1980s, female ministers were appointed to senior justice and economic portfolios rather than strictly to health, education, status of women and other less prestigious departments.

The experiences of the first female cabinet ministers on the federal level in Canada provide a useful contrast to current patterns. Appointed initially to the secretary of state portfolio in 1957, Ellen Fairclough served most of her term in the Diefenbaker cabinet as minister of citizenship and immigration (1958-62) and subsequently as postmaster general (1962-63). Fairclough described her appointment and problem-solving orientation toward cabinet responsibilities as follows:

> I hadn't expected the Secretary of State portfolio, but rather Labour, but it often happens that the ministerial assignment differs from the earlier shadow cabinet responsibility. Anyway, I was appointed to Citizenship and Immigration shortly thereafter, which proved to be very challenging because I had two citizenship branches plus the one immigration branch under me. I was also superintendant of Indian Affairs, and had a deputy minister in that area. I also had four agencies under me, headed by the Dominion Archivist, and the heads of the National Library, the National Gallery, and the National Film Board . . . I worked from dawn to dusk, often on administrative and technical matters which had to do with the establishment of a citizenship courts system, and the coordination of various agencies and ministerial branches under Citizenship and Immigration. People recognized that administration was my strong point, and I imagine this robbed me of some colour.[39]

Fairclough's experiences in cabinet thus indicate fairly early appointment to an administratively complex portfolio that challenged her problem-solving abilities, but made little direct impact on the broader policy directions of the Conservative government.

If Fairclough's administrative orientation 'robbed some colour' from her cabinet career, this was not the case with the subsequent appointment of Judy LaMarsh to the Pearson cabinet. LaMarsh entered the Liberal cabinet in 1963 as Minister of National Health and Welfare, a portfolio later assumed by Monique Bégin; later she became Secretary of State and organized the Canadian centennial celebrations of 1967. During her five years in cabinet, LaMarsh was frequently embroiled in conflicts over the new Canada Pension Plan, revisions to the Canada Broadcasting Act and, probably most important, the establishment of the Royal Commission on the Status of Women. Her perceptions of discrimination in the Pearson cabinet and party politics more generally were deep-seated, as reflected in the text of her 1969 autobiography, *Memoirs of a Bird in a Gilded Cage*: 'Throughout my years in the Liberal Party, I never saw evidence that any real attention was paid to seeking out and grooming women as part of the party machinery, or as parliamentary material, except in one area and that was the importuning of fresh widows of MP's to seek their husbands' unexpired terms.'[40]

LaMarsh's belief that gender tended to limit the political roles of female legislators was often confirmed by later developments. Although Flora MacDonald assumed the external affairs portfolio in the 1979 Clark government, and Jeanne Sauvé became Speaker of the House of Commons and later Governor General, many women who reached the elite level continued to hold conventional health, education, human resource and social development portfolios, or newer status of women responsibilities.[41] This clustering of female cabinet and shadow cabinet members was challenged most visibly at the federal level by the appointments of Pat Carney to international trade, Barbara McDougall to junior finance, and Kim Campbell to justice portfolios in Conservative governments after 1984.

Finally, some changes have occurred at the level of party leadership. In the past, women obtained party leadership in organizations that did not hold the reins of power at the time, and were viewed as unlikely to do so in the near future. Typified by the case of Thérèse Casgrain, who headed the Quebec CCF during the 1950s, Canadian women have tended to lead provincial parties, including the British Columbia Liberals, Nova Scotia New Democrats and New Brunswick Conservatives, during periods when those parties were relatively uncompetitive.[42]

A number of instances exist in which a woman has won the leadership of a party that at the time of her selection was not competitive, but that under her leadership improved its position. At the provincial level, the example of Sharon Carstairs is illustrative: the Manitoba Liberals were in a weak position in 1984 when she was selected as provincial leader, but subsequently obtained official opposition status (1988-90). At the federal level, Audrey McLaughlin won the leadership of the New Democrats in 1989, when the party was relatively low in the polls;[43] the NDP went on to improve its standing in national public opinion surveys.

Women have increasingly broken out of the earlier mould to contest the leadership of competitive parties. For example, Flora MacDonald ran in 1976 for the leadership of the federal Progressive Conservatives; Muriel Smith in 1979 for the Manitoba NDP; Grace McCarthy and Kim Campbell in 1986 for the British Columbia Social Credit party; Sheila Copps in 1982 and 1990 for the Ontario and federal Liberal parties, respectively;[44] Grace McCarthy and Rita Johnston in 1991 for the BC Social Credit party; and Lyn McLeod in 1992 for the Ontario Liberal party.

In each instance except the last two (Johnston and McLeod), these campaigns failed in the sense that the candidates lost, but they were successful to the extent that women's claims to competitive party leadership were taken increasingly seriously. Johnston went on to become Canada's first female premier. She led a right-of-centre party, however, that was not sympathetic to feminist issue positions, and lost the subsequent provincial election after less than six months in power.[45]

CONCLUSIONS

This chapter has considered data on provincial and federal political activity at many levels, including those of party executive, convention delegate and campaign manager. Combined with patterns of political candidacy, legislative office-holding and cabinet appointment, these figures offer strong evidence that the higher, more powerful and more competitive political positions remain overwhelmingly in the hands of men.

Contemporary efforts to increase female involvement in many phases of party activity have clearly had some impact. As well, patterns of electoral volatility have helped to elect female candidates in otherwise marginal seats. Yet our initial generalizations regarding 'the higher the fewer' and 'the more competitive the fewer' remain empirically valid in the early 1990s. In the following chapter we shall consider in greater detail the attempts that have been made to improve female political representation.

NOTES

[1] Ontario cabinet minister Robert Welch, nomination speech for Marg Lyon, candidate for Eighth Vice-President of Ontario Progressive Conservative Association, September 1982.

[2] Catherine L. Cleverdon, *The Woman Suffrage Movement in Canada* (Toronto: University of Toronto Press, 1950), 281.

[3] Rosamonde Ramsay Boyd, 'Women and Politics in the United States and Canada', *Annals of the American Academy of Political and Social Science* 375 (January 1968), 53.

[4] Ibid., 57.

[5] See M. Janine Brodie, 'The Recruitment of Canadian Women Provincial Legislators, 1950-1975', *Atlantis* 2:2 (part 1, Spring 1977), 6-17; Jill McCalla Vickers, 'Where Are the Women in Canadian

Politics?' *Atlantis* 3:2 (part 2, Spring 1978), 40-51; and Janine Brodie, *Women and Politics in Canada* (Toronto: McGraw-Hill Ryerson, 1985).

[6] Existing studies of Canadian parties, particularly those that address activity at the local level, tend to support this position. See Frederick C. Engelmann and Mildred A. Schwartz, *Canadian Political Parties: Origin, Character, Impact* (Scarborough, Ont.: Prentice-Hall, 1975); Conrad Winn and John McMenemy, *Political Parties in Canada* (Toronto: McGraw-Hill Ryerson, 1976); Allan Kornberg, Joel Smith and Harold D. Clarke, *Citizen Politicians—Canada* (Durham, NC: Carolina Academic Press, 1979); and Henry Jacek, John McDonough, Ronald Shimizu and Patrick Smith, 'The Congruence of Federal-Provincial Campaign Activity in Party Organizations', *Canadian Journal of Political Science* 5:2 (June 1972), 190-205.

[7] Judy LaMarsh, *Memoirs of a Bird in a Gilded Cage* (Toronto: McClelland and Stewart, 1969), 281-2.

[8] Robert D. Putnam, *The Comparative Study of Political Elites* (Englewood Cliffs, NJ: Prentice-Hall, 1976), 33.

[9] Major party leaders can be defined as government or official opposition leaders. As of this writing in the spring of 1992, Lyn McLeod led the Ontario Liberals in their official opposition status, and Nellie Cournoyea was the leader of the Northwest Territories Legislative Assembly.

[10] See, for example, Manon Tremblay, 'Les élues du 31e Parlement du Québec et les mouvements féministes: de quelques affinités idéologiques', *Politique* 16 (Fall 1989), 87-109; Debra L. Dodson, ed., *Gender and Policymaking: Studies of Women in Office* (New Brunswick, NJ: Center for the American Woman and Politics, 1991); Shelah Gilbert Leader, 'The Policy Impact of Elected Women Officials', in Louis Maisel and Joseph Cooper, eds., *The Impact of the Electoral Process* (Beverly Hills: Sage, 1977), 315-30; Kathleen A. Frankovic, 'Sex and Voting in the U.S. House of Representatives, 1961-1975', *American Politics Quarterly* 5:3 (1977), 315-30; and Elina Haavio-Mannila, 'The Impact of the Women's Movement and Legislative Activity of Women Members of Parliament on Social Development', in Margherita Rendel, ed., *Women, Power and Political Systems* (London: Croom Helm, 1981), 195-215. For a different interpretation of the connection between numbers and policies, see Lise Gotell and Janine Brodie, 'Women and Parties: More than an Issue of Numbers', in Hugh G. Thorburn, ed., *Party Politics in Canada* 6th ed.; Scarborough, Ont.: Prentice-Hall, 1991), 53-67.

[11] See Kornberg et al., *Citizen Politicians*, 14-15.

[12] Harold D. Clarke and Allan Kornberg, 'Moving Up the Political Escalator: Women Party Officials in the United States and Canada', *Journal of Politics* 41:2 (1979), 475.

[13] Kornberg et al., *Citizen Politicians*, 205.

[14] Statistics Canada, *Census of Canada: Population by Mother Tongue* (Ottawa: Supply and Services Canada, 1982).

[15] According to 1982 party records, no riding secretary positions existed in the Manitoba Conservative organization.

[16] Confidential interview with federal Progressive Conservative party organizer, 1990.

[17] See John C. Courtney, *The Selection of National Party Leaders in Canada* (Toronto: Macmillan, 1973); and Donald V. Smiley, 'The National Party Leadership Convention in Canada: A Preliminary Analysis', *Canadian Journal of Political Science* 1 (1968), 373-97.

[18] See Courtney, *Selection of National Party Leaders*, 108; Carl Baar and Ellen Baar, 'Party and Convention Organization and Leadership Selection in Canada and the United States', in Donald R. Matthews, ed., *Perspectives on Presidential Selection* (Washington, DC: Brookings, 1973), 59; and C.R. Santos, 'Some Collective Characteristics of the Delegates to the 1968 Liberal Party Leadership Convention', *Canadian Journal of Political Science* 3 (1970), 303.

[19] By way of contrast, political scientists in the US, UK and Australia gave more attention to women's representation in this phase of party life. See Leader, 'The Policy Impact of Elected Women Officials'; M. Kent Jennings and Norman Thomas, 'Men and Women in Party Elites: Social Roles and Political

Resources', *Midwest Journal of Political Science* 12 (1968), 469-92; M. Kent Jennings and Barbara G. Farah, 'Social Roles and Political Resources: An Over-Time Study of Men and Women in Party Elites', *American Journal of Political Science* 25 (1981), 462-82; Lorraine Culley, 'Women's Organisation in the Labour Party', *Power and Politics* 3 (1981), 115-22; and Marian Sawer, 'Women and Women's Issues in the 1980 Federal Elections', *Politics* 16 (1981), 243-9.

[20]Cleverdon, *Woman Suffrage Movement*, 60.

[21]One difficulty in reaching parity in Canada follows from *ex-officio* and, in the case of the NDP, union delegation to party conventions. Party rules that govern riding delegate selection generally do not apply to these other categories.

[22]Kornberg et al., *Citizen Politicians*.

[23]For further information on the structure of the Ontario parties, see Sylvia Bashevkin, Marianne R. Holder and Karen Jones, 'Women's Political Involvement and Policy Influence', in Graham White, ed., *The Government and Politics of Ontario* (4th ed.; Toronto: Nelson, 1990), 293-310.

[24]Sydney Sharpe and Don Braid, 'Feminism Anathema to most Reform Party Members', *Toronto Star*, 9 February 1992.

[25]For a journalist's view of this problem, see Charlotte Gray, 'The New Backroom Girls', *Chatelaine* (July 1980), 25-6.

[26]For earlier data on campaign management, see Sylvia B. Bashevkin, *Toeing the Lines: Women and Party Politics in English Canada* (1st ed.; Toronto: University of Toronto Press, 1985), Table 3.8.

[27]On the hierarchy of political involvement, see Lester Milbrath, *Political Participation* (Chicago: Rand McNally, 1965); and William Mishler, *Political Participation in Canada* (Toronto: Macmillan, 1979).

[28]Brodie, 'The Recruitment of Canadian Women'; Vickers, 'Where are the Women'; Brodie, *Women and Politics in Canada*; Cleverdon, *Woman Suffrage Movement*; M. Janine Brodie and Jill Vickers, 'The More Things Change . . . Women in the 1979 Federal Campaign', in Howard R. Penniman, ed., *Canada at the Polls: 1979 and 1980* (Washington, DC: American Enterprise Institute, 1981), 322-36; Liane Langevin, *Missing Persons: Women in Canadian Federal Politics* (Ottawa: Canadian Advisory Council on the Status of Women, 1977); and Chantal Maillé with Valentina Pollon, *Primed for Power: Women in Canadian Politics* (Ottawa: Canadian Advisory Council on the Status of Women, 1990).

[29]Vickers, 'Where are the Women', 46.

[30]Brodie and Vickers, 'The More Things Change', esp. 323, 326ff.

[31]Brodie, *Women and Politics in Canada*, 111.

[32]See Lynda Erickson and R.K. Carty, 'Candidate Selection in Canadian Political Parties', paper presented at American Political Science Association meetings, San Francisco, 1990; Alfred A. Hunter and Margaret A. Denton, 'Do Female Candidates "Lose Votes"? The Experience of Female Candidates in the 1979 and 1980 Canadian General Elections', *Canadian Review of Sociology and Anthropology* 21:4 (November 1984), 395-406; and Pippa Norris, R.K. Carty, Lynda Erickson, Joni Lovenduski and Marian Simms, 'Party Selectorates in Australia, Britain and Canada', *Journal of Commonwealth and Comparative Politics* 28:2 (July 1990), 219-45.

[33]These ridings were Scarborough West, vacated by Richard Johnston; Riverdale, vacated by David Reville; and Beaches-Woodbine, vacated by Marion Bryden.

[34]Margaret Stewart and Doris French, *Ask No Quarter* (Toronto: Longmans, 1959), 63.

[35]For a discussion of constraints on female participation, see Jeane J. Kirkpatrick, *Political Woman* (New York: Basic Books, 1974), chap. 1.

[36]See Langevin, *Missing Persons*. For more general treatments of legislative recruitment in Canada, see Allan Kornberg, *Canadian Legislative Behavior* (New York: Holt, Rinehart and Winston, 1967); and Allan Kornberg and William Mishler, *Influence in Parliament: Canada* (Durham, NC: Duke University Press, 1976).

[37]Langevin, *Missing Persons*, 37.

[38]Maillé with Pollon, *Primed for Power*, 8, 12.

[39]Interview with Hon. Ellen Fairclough, 16 April 1983.

[40]LaMarsh, *Memoirs*, 283. LaMarsh disliked the secretary of state and postmaster general positions offered to her in 1965 because both had been held earlier by Fairclough; LaMarsh wanted to avoid any such comparisons. See *Memoirs*, chap. 9.

[41]See Shirley Woods, *Her Excellency Jeanne Sauvé* (Halifax: Formac Publishing, 1986).

[42]See Susan Mann Trofimenkoff, 'Thérèse Casgrain and the CCF in Quebec', *Canadian Historical Review* 66:2 (June 1985), 125-53; reprinted in Linda Kealey and Joan Sangster, eds., *Beyond the Vote* (Toronto: University of Toronto Press, 1989), 139-68.

[43]See Keith Archer, 'Choices and Decisions in Leadership Selection: Explaining McLaughlin's Victory at the 1989 NDP Convention', paper presented at Canadian Political Science Association meetings, Kingston, 1991.

[44]See Sheila Copps, *Nobody's Baby: A Survival Guide to Politics* (Toronto: Deneau, 1986).

[45]See Hal Quinn, 'A Winning Way: Rita Johnston Wins her Party's Support, but can she Win an Election?' *Maclean's* (29 July 1991), 12-15; and Deborah Wilson, 'Johnston Resigns as Leader at BC Socred Convention', *Globe and Mail* (13 January 1992).

CHAPTER FOUR

Reforming the System: Efforts to Increase Representation on Elite Levels

Canada could benefit from the contribution of many more women than are now involved in the political process.

—Royal Commission on the Status of Women, *Report*, 1970[1]

The reality of women's limited numbers at the elite level in Canadian parties has been identified more and more widely as a serious problem of democratic representation. Beginning with the 1970 *Report* of the Royal Commission on the Status of Women and following through to the 1991 conclusions of the Royal Commission on Electoral Reform and Party Financing, a host of official documents have discussed the varied obstacles that limit female political mobility.[2] Together with a growing body of academic literature as well as women's own reflections on their political experiences, official sources reinforce earlier claims that systemic under-representation demands systemic response.[3]

This chapter considers a variety of efforts to increase women's numbers in elite-level party activity. Although these strategies are diverse and ever more numerous, they can be broken down into two main categories. First, we evaluate a 'rules and regulations' approach that challenges internal party and external electoral statutes. Among the measures falling under this heading are quotas for women in party office, dual-member constituencies and proportional representation. Second, the chapter examines informal organizational and consciousness-raising activities that employ a non-regulatory framework. These include sponsoring leadership campaigns, establishing party funds to support women candidates, increasing efforts to recruit women (outside the rubric of targets or quotas) and creating more training opportunities.

Overall, this second type of informal organizational and consciousness-raising work is unlikely—on its own—to increase significantly the numbers of women in elite-level positions. Women's under-representation would appear to be sufficiently severe in the Canadian case as to require the introduction of at least some regulatory reforms.

REPRESENTATION: CONCEPTS AND ASSUMPTIONS

On a theoretical level, the main focus of elite-level discussions has usually been the issue of representation. In general, the representativeness of key political institutions, including political parties, is regarded as a *sine qua non* of democratic government. As Hanna Pitkin argues in a major study of this subject, much of modern democratic thought and practice begins with the assumption of both a demographic similarity between mass and elite (which she terms descriptive or 'standing for' representation) and a substantive or policy-based linkage between the citizenry and political leadership (termed 'acting for' representation).[4]

Party activists and political scientists in Canada emphasize the representative character of existing institutions and processes. Discussions of party leadership conventions, for example, maintain that the selection of elite personnel in major party organizations is responsive to and representative of a broad variety of societal interests. According to one Liberal senator, these conventions were 'designed to obtain "the fullest possible representation of party views"'.[5] Similarly, in the words of Donald Smiley, Canada's amalgamation of US and British influences made it 'the only country in the British parliamentary tradition which chooses its party leaders through representative party conventions called for that purpose'.[6]

Despite its seeming importance as a subject of social and political analysis, however, the representativeness of Canadian parties received relatively little academic attention prior to the late 1970s and early 1980s, when much of the literature reviewed in Chapter 3 was published. This new literature had a direct and immediate impact on some party organizations, where women were experiencing first-hand the difficulties identified in research on female participation. Some studies considered responses *outside* Canada to the same set of circumstances, so that researchers and party activists began to explore how US and European systems were dealing with women's under-representation.

Structural reforms introduced during the 1970s in US party organizations were especially relevant to Canadian proponents of a 'rules and regulations' strategy. As early as the 1920s, the Democratic and Republican parties had adopted terms establishing numerically equal representation of men and women on national party committees. Both parties also urged their state and local committees to adopt similar by-laws, so that by 1947, 39 (81.3 percent) of Democratic state committees had adopted some form of equal representation, as had 30 (62.5 percent) of Republican state committees.[7] One problem with these by-laws, however, was that female representatives in American party organizations were often limited to designated co-chair or vice-chair positions that, according to Frank Sorauf, 'long confirmed their separate but unequal status'.[8]

It was not until 1972 that equal representation was established for national party conventions in the United States. At the 1968 Democratic convention, criticism of traditional party structures, including the delegate selection process, led to the formation of a Commission on Party Structures and Delegate Selection, popularly referred to as the McGovern-Fraser Commission. Perhaps the best-known guideline introduced by this commission was the 'affirmative action' provision requiring 'all states to "overcome the effects of past discrimination by affirmative steps to encourage representation on the national convention delegation of young people . . . and women in reasonable relationship to their presence in the population." An identical requirement applied to blacks and other minorities.'[9] This particular policy was adopted informally by the Republicans as well in 1972. These initiatives helped to increase female convention representation from 12.9 to 39.9 percent between 1968 and 1972 in the Democratic case, and from 16.7 to 30.1 percent during the same period in the Republican case.[10] As noted in Chapter 3, the number of women convention delegates subsequently increased in both major parties, reaching 50 percent by the 1980 Democratic presidential convention.

Aside from its obvious numerical impact, one of the major consequences of this rule change in the US context was its effect on party recruitment and policy. As indicated in research by Kirkpatrick as well as Jennings and Farah, both the Republicans and, especially, the Democrats were compelled to locate new female activists during the 1970s, many of whom turned out to be young, well-educated, employed and, not incidentally, feminist in their social and political orientations.[11] These new recruits helped to change the face of female party participation in the United States, arguing for the inclusion of significant 'women's issue' statements in party platforms and contesting increasingly powerful and visible positions within their organizations. As Sorauf reflected in the wake of US party reforms, 'the more activist women want a role in the regular party organizations, or else they prefer to become active in nonparty organizations (such as the National Women's Political Caucus).'[12]

Rule change south of the forty-ninth parallel held important implications for Canadian politics, especially for activists who believed that women could improve their status by working inside established political structures. Figures presented in the 1970 *Report* of the Royal Commission on the Status of Women, as well as internal party studies and academic research, all indicated that Canadian women were poorly represented in all major federal and provincial political parties, in all regions, and in virtually all sectors of elite-level activity; furthermore, very few women were nominated outside of marginal ridings and only a small handful attained public office.[13] Comparisons between Canadian figures and data from other Western industrialized nations showed that the numbers of women in Canadian legislatures remained relatively low despite fairly consistent increases over time.[14]

In light of the extent of women's under-representation in legislatures and extra-parliamentary party organizations, Canadian activists pursued two general strategies during the mid-1970s and following. One approach, employed primarily by women in the New Democratic party, involved the introduction of structural reforms modelled on earlier rule changes in the US Democratic party. In adopting this route, NDP women sought to obtain numerically equal representation across the board (on party committees, as convention delegates, and so on), as well as increased recognition as candidates in winnable ridings. Paralleling these demands for internal rule changes were the pressures exerted by women in the NDP and elsewhere for external or system-wide regulatory change.

A second strategy, pursued in most Canadian parties, employed less formal methods to support and recruit female activists. Among these relatively informal means were campaigns for party leadership by prominent women; party women's funds; conferences, caucuses and training sessions designed to attract and prepare new activists; campaign literature and speakers' notes on 'women's issue' policy questions; and personal out-reach or 'networking' activities by party gatekeepers.[15]

Common to both strategies was one very crucial assumption or expectation: that in the near future more women would join political parties, become active in them and, ultimately, contest positions of organizational leadership—thereby offering females a stronger collective voice and more policy input within Canadian politics. Increased numbers, it was assumed, would automatically produce greater substantive representation in major party organizations.

This key assumption has generally not been borne out by subsequent developments. Since the organized beginnings of both formal rule change and informal consciousness-raising, the disparity between women's numbers in the population and in the political elite has been more widely recognized as a problem of political representation. Yet powerful sanctions continue to restrict the attention paid to 'women's issues' by the very same female elites who understand and challenge both numerical and substantive under-representation. In short, the conversion from descriptive (or numerical) to substantive (or policy) representation by women in the major Canadian parties—which is assumed to follow from formal and informal approaches—seems blocked for some time to come.

EARLY RULE CHANGES IN PARTY ORGANIZATIONS

Early efforts to alter the rules governing Canadian parties included a resolution adopted by the federal NDP at its 1981 convention in Vancouver. This provision encouraged constituent party sections to recruit women candidates and to assist with child care costs; to seek out women for party office and to provide leadership training for them; and to study women's participation and the impact of voluntary affirmative action.[16] The NDP's strategy was later formalized at the 1983 Regina convention, where an official party nominating committee was, in the words of its chair, 'under constitutional obligation to implement affirmative action'.[17] Ultimately, twelve women (including an associate president and treasurer) were nominated and elected to the new twenty-member NDP federal council, and resolutions ensuring gender parity in the future on federal councils and executives were adopted. Although numerical representation was thus achieved among the elected elite at the federal level in 1983, constituent New Democratic parties were only urged or encouraged to implement similar procedures.[18]

Efforts undertaken during the winter of 1982 in the Liberal Party of Canada (LPC) established an Ad Hoc Committee on Affirmative Action and charged this body with gathering data on the participation of women, assessing party recruitment procedures as they affected women, and establishing short- and long-range goals 'to achieve the objective of parity between men and women'.[19] The introduction of specified targets or quotas for female involvement was rejected at the time by the LPC committee, which pursued data collection activities as well as consultation with various branches of the federal party organization.

One of the most sweeping rule-change initiatives by a Canadian party during the early 1980s was the affirmative action resolution adopted by the Ontario NDP. The resolution was developed by the party Women's Committee, established in 1973 for the purposes of: (1) increasing 'the participation of women in the Party at all levels'; (2) educating 'women in the NDP in all aspects of political activity'; (3) participating 'with women outside the Party in areas of mutual interest'; and (4) '[encouraging] these women to join the Party and work with the Party'.[20]

In the years between 1973 and 1980, the Women's Committee organized a series of policy conferences, presented resolutions on various 'women's issues' at provincial council meetings and party conventions, and monitored the participation of women in the party.[21] This approach culminated in the adoption of a comprehensive 'Policies for Equality' resolution at the 1980 Women's Committee conference, which was in turn approved at the provincial council and by delegates to a subsequent party convention in the same year. This lengthy policy document addressed such issues as economic rights for women, pensions, health, day care, housing and education; it was designed to replace existing and often outdated party policy on women's issues. The package was also expected to elevate the external feminist profile of the ONDP, as well as the status of women in the organization.[22]

Contrary to the expectations of many party activists, including some in the Women's Committee, 'Policies for Equality' encountered little serious opposition on the floor of the 1980 convention. In fact, the passage of these and a number of related resolutions led to the hiring of a women's organizer at the provincial party headquarters and of a women's co-ordinator at the NDP legislative caucus. Overall, it appeared as if the goal of the Women's Committee, to obtain greater organizational and policy voice for females in the party, was within reach.

A number of developments during the 1981 provincial election campaign, however, suggested that the commitment of the mainstream party organization to female participation and feminist policy directions remained limited. First, the visibility of the women's organizer, women's co-ordinator, and 'Policies for Equality' document during the campaign was very low—both of the former were assigned to routine inside responsibilities for the duration of the election—while the women's issues that had been expected to be a focal point were barely in evidence.[23]

Second, monitoring of internal party participation during this period suggested that although more women were involved in the NDP than in 1973, females remained substantially under-represented in most parts of the organization.[24] A third factor encouraging the Women's Committee to revise its approach was the advent of a party leadership campaign. Although no woman entered the leadership race, all three male candidates focused upon party renewal, which provided the Women's Committee with a useful opportunity to raise questions about what was increasingly identified as a problem of systemic discrimination.[25] In addition, the leadership convention was viewed as a large, prestigious and relatively captive forum for debate on these issues.

An affirmative action draft resolution, approved by the executive of the ONDP Women's Committee in October 1981, established four major objectives: (1) to broaden the female electoral base of the ONDP by emphasizing policies of particular relevance to women both between and during election campaigns; (2) to encourage equal ('at least 50%') representation of women in riding executives, and to require this in provincial council delegations, the provincial executive and party committees; (3) to develop a leadership training program for women; and (4) to recruit female candidates in strong ridings, and to assist with the childcare and household management expenses of all candidates.[26]

The initial response to this resolution was generally favourable. At ONDP riding association meetings held between November 1981 and February 1982, however, a number of convention delegates expressed opposition to the 'at least 50%' terms of the resolution, particularly when applied to local party executives. In light of these objections, the Women's Committee prepared a two-page 'fact sheet' for the convention; it offered contemporary statistics on female participation and emphasized that ridings were 'urged' rather than required to adopt equal representation.

At the February 1982 party convention, debate on affirmative action was scheduled between two important items, namely elections to the party executive and nomination of leadership candidates. The floor debate lasted approximately thirty minutes and covered a number of issues raised previously in other—primarily US—discussions of affirmative action. Speakers in favour of the resolution emphasized three main points:

1. In light of experiences in political parties and the labour force, voluntary 'targets' did not provide sufficient means to achieve numerically equal representation.[27]
2. The Ontario NDP organization as a whole would benefit from adoption of internal affirmative action, since this resolution would make party policy on women's issues more credible.[28]
3. The resolution as presented provided a 'minimum' for women, since it only urged ridings to act. Waiting for a more comprehensive study of underrepresentation, and possibly for a series of constitutional amendments in

this area (see below), would simply delay 'effective action' on the problem, to the detriment of both women and the provincial party.[29]

Delegates opposed to the resolution included three younger women from Metropolitan Toronto ridings. Their major criticisms were as follows:

1. The terms of 'at least 50%' representation, especially on the riding level, implied that gender would take precedence over merit, ability, and experience. According to one speaker, 'I would always want to be elected because I was good, not because I was a woman.'[30]
2. Affirmative action was unnecessary in the ONDP because individual women were already equal participants. In the words of one opponent: 'I have never in this party been denied the right to run for an executive position or to be a candidate. In fact, I have been encouraged to do so.'[31]
3. Insufficient attention had been given to the implementation of the resolution, and therefore it should be referred to a committee for further study.[32] (This referral motion was defeated.)

On a standing vote following the eleventh speaker, the resolution carried. Notably, post-convention tabulations showed that about 40 percent of the voting delegates had been women and 60 percent men. In addition, the results of a convention questionnaire indicated that approximately 62 percent of NDP respondents approved of the resolution as presented, with 25.3 percent of male and 32.4 percent of female delegates expressing strong approval.[33] These results suggest that affirmative action was supported by a majority of voting delegates on the convention floor, and opposed by a relatively small but vocal minority.

PARTY RULE CHANGES SINCE 1985

One of the most notable features of efforts at rule change since 1985 has been the contrast between the lack of interest shown in this strategy by the Liberal and Conservative parties and the increased pursuit of it by the NDP. After endorsing voluntary efforts to recruit more women during the early 1980s, the federal Liberal party moved briefly in the direction of formal rule changes later in that decade. LPC constitutional provisions adopted in 1986, for example, established that positions at the vice-presidential level must be held equally by women and men, but this requirement was dropped in constitutional reforms instituted in June 1990. According to the 1991 *Report* of the Royal Commission on Electoral Reform and Party Financing: 'The Liberal Party's two vice-presidential positions are occupied by men, while the six regional presidential positions are held by four men and two women. Women are thus far less well represented in the party's decision-making process than they were between 1986 and 1990.'[34] This shift by the Liberals away from specific quotas was consistent with decisions by the party women's commission (see Chapter 5). At the National Women's Liberal Commission conference in 1990, members opposed quotas for female representation in the party structure, instead approving a constitutional amendment that specified the ways in which the Commission would encourage and promote women. Other than stipulating that 50 percent of convention delegates from ridings be female, and that officials of the Women's Commission serve on the federal executive and some committees, Liberal constitutional provisions reflected an emphasis on voluntary, informal efforts 'to correct any imbalance in the representation of women and men'.[35]

A similar orientation *away* from formal changes can be discerned among the Conservatives. The constitution of the Progressive Conservative Association of Canada, for example, establishes that executives of the party women's federation (see Chapter 5) must also serve on the Association executive; moreover, members of the women's federation elite are—as in the Liberal case—usually appointed to federal party committees. Riding delegations to Conservative conventions must include two women out of six, and at least one alternate out of four must be female.[36] No other gender-mandated positions are identified in the Conservative constitution.

The relative absence of a 'rules and regulations' focus in Liberal and Conservative organizations contrasts clearly with *increased* reforms of this type in the NDP. The Ontario NDP, for example, extended its 1982 affirmative action initiative in a 1989 rule change affecting nomination and candidacy. The 1989 guidelines identify 'specific target groups', namely women, visible minorities, the disabled and aboriginal people; they establish that 'as a general policy, 50% of all ridings should have women candidates', as should 60 percent of 'winnable or priority ridings'.[37] The Ontario NDP provisions require that ridings include target group members on their Election Planning Committees (EPC). Furthermore, any constituency without a party incumbent must wait to 'hold a nomination meeting until they have at least one target group candidate for that nomination',[38] and must explain any failure to do so to the provincial EPC. Informal supports for candidates also mandated by the 1989 document include campaign training opportunities and reimbursement for child care expenses. According to the 1989 document, 'consideration will be given to imposition of limits on expenditures for nomination campaigns'.[39]

The federal NDP adopted similar affirmative action policies at its 1991 convention in Halifax. Under the federal provisions, 50 percent of all ridings would have women candidates, including a minimum of 60 percent females in winnable seats without NDP incumbents. As in Ontario, affirmative action target groups were identified as women, visible minorities, the disabled and aboriginal people. The federal policy established that regional clusters of federal ridings would determine how to accomplish the affirmative action plan for themselves. Each cluster plan was to be approved by the Council of Federal Ridings (CFR) and, as in Ontario, failure to meet the goals of the plan would have to be explained to the CFR.[40]

Discussions within the federal NDP affirmative action subcommittee after the Halifax convention indicated some internal disagreement. For example, were affirmative action provisions to be mandatory and, if so, would they apply to the next federal election? Would the strategy include targets or, alternatively, quotas for categories other than women? The general consensus reached by August 1991 was that 'the *process* to be followed with respect to affirmative action is mandatory'; the process would be undertaken immediately and monitored by provincial and territorial EPCs.[41] Finally, as in the Ontario NDP, informal supports for target group candidates would include training programs, reimbursement for child care expenses and spending limits on nomination contests.

CHANGING THE ELECTORAL SYSTEM

To proponents of voluntary, informal reform in Canadian political parties, many of the mandatory NDP provisions introduced during the 1980s and early 1990s seemed cumbersome, overly ambitious and regulatory to an extreme. Yet it is important to recognize that this impetus toward mandated *internal* change on the political left was accompanied by an equally challenging demand for major *external* reforms.

One such external change has involved a shift away from the single-member plurality (SMP), first-past-the-post electoral system, towards proportional representation (PR). Legislative elections in Canada, according to this line of thought, tend to distort the conversion from votes to seats and allow the dominant national parties to win unwieldy, politically unresponsive parliamentary majorities. Compared with proportional arrangements, the SMP system is claimed to be undemocratic and regionally divisive, as well as unrepresentative in numerical and substantive terms of women. As Doris Anderson, a former president of the National Action Committee on the Status of Women (NAC), argued in her 1991 book *The Unfinished Revolution*, proportional representation is part of the reason that women in Nordic countries are considerably better represented than those in Canada.[42]

This position favouring proportional representation was reflected in constitutional demands by NAC during the same period. Responding to federal proposals in the fall of 1991, NAC endorsed electoral reform in the direction of either 'one man and one woman in each riding' (see below) or else full PR for elections to a reformed Senate. NAC proposed 'that 50% of people elected to the Senate be women', a position adopted in at least one other constitutional proposal from the same period.[43]

Senate reform and the merits of PR were not within the purview of the federal Royal Commission on Electoral Reform and Party Financing.[44] The commission did, however, endorse a number of rule changes in 1991 that were intended to enhance women's access to elective legislative office. These recommendations included: (1) mandatory leaves of absence granted by employers to employees seeking nomination and candidacy;[45] (2) spending limits on nomination contests;[46] (3) tax receipts to nomination campaign contributors;[47] (4) tax deductibility for child care if the 'primary caregiver' sought nomination or election;[48] and (5) formal party search committees and other 'processes that demonstrably promote the identification and nomination of broadly representative candidates'.[49]

One of the most innovative royal commission recommendations outlined a system of party bonuses to increase women's numbers in the House of Commons:

> We recommend that should the overall percentage of women in the House of Commons be below 20 percent following either of the next two elections, then: (1) at the two elections following the next election, the reimbursement of each registered political party with at least 20 percent female MPs be increased by an amount equivalent to the percentage of its women MPs up to a maximum of 150 percent; (2) this measure be automatically eliminated once the overall percentage of women in the House of Commons has attained 40 percent; and (3) following the third election, if this measure is still in place, the Canada Elections Commission review it and recommend to Parliament whether it should be retained or adjusted.[50]

This proposal assumed that parties would be most likely to take heed and nominate women candidates in winnable seats if there existed a promise of financial reward.

A final—and arguably the most contentious—proposal for external rule change was offered by Christine Boyle of Dalhousie University Law School. In a 1983 article entitled 'Home Rule for Women', Boyle rejected both single-member and proportional systems on the grounds that they fail 'to overcome the inability and/or unwillingness of women to participate in the political structure'.[51] She proposed instead 'a system of separate male and female constituencies', based on the argument that men and women have distinct and identifiable group interests that require political recognition.[52] Boyle favoured this 'form of benign separation . . . at least on a temporary basis, in order to ensure representation of women by women and, I hope, in the interests of women'.[53]

Clearly, the major electoral overhaul recommended by Boyle pressed concerns about representation far beyond even the most ambitious changes in formal party rules. In suggesting that women legislators might—quite legitimately—speak only for their female constituents, Boyle intentionally merged Pitkin's concepts of 'standing for' and 'acting for' representation; such a change would fundamentally alter the 'rules of the game'.[54] The willingness of the National Action Committee to endorse dual-member constituencies in its 1991 response to federal constitutional proposals reflected the support for Boyle's ideas that had grown over time in some parts of the Canadian feminist community.

Having reviewed major regulatory changes proposed inside and outside the parties, we will now turn to less formal strategies.

INFORMAL EFFORTS TO INCREASE REPRESENTATION

Many types of activities have been pursued in the Canadian party system as part of a non-regulatory or informal approach to increasing elite-level representation. These efforts have sometimes involved partisans in a single organization; in other cases, they have drawn together multi-party and non-partisan coalitions under the rubric of 'women and politics'. In each case, the purpose of informal efforts was one or more of the following: first, consciousness-raising to alert both women and men to the challenge of attracting more women and addressing 'women's issues' more seriously; second, organizing to meet the administrative and political challenges posed by the results of successful consciousness-raising; and third, education to inform women about actual opportunities and obstacles at the elite level.

It is not surprising that many early efforts of this type were directed at consciousness-raising. One 1972 conference of Women for Political Action in Toronto began a long series of meetings organized by various women and politics groups around the country. As described in Chapter 1, these events frequently featured prominent female politicians speaking about their own experiences, as well as their hopes that more women would contest and win public office.

Over time, many of these conferences began to move beyond a simple consciousness-raising function. By imparting concrete knowledge of the electoral process and by helping to build organizational networks among politically motivated women, some conferences assumed direct educational and organizational roles. By the early 1990s, for example, the Committee for '94 in Toronto had developed a six-part television series as well as a nomination school program that integrated consciousness-raising, organizational and educational purposes.[55]

A second direction for early consciousness-raising efforts, and one that also assumed additional goals as time passed, involved party leadership campaigns. The 1975 decision by British Columbia MLA Rosemary Brown to seek the leadership of the federal New Democratic party was a watershed in this respect. As Brown reflected in her memoirs:

> We had come to the conclusion that although men and women share the same world, due to a combination of genetics, history and socialization women do inhabit the world and experience it differently from men. Personal experience, as well as study and observation, had led us to conclude that the world community of men and that of women are different; consequently the priorities of the two are different, and this difference is reflected in their political agendas. . . . consciousness-raising helped us to accept these differences without feeling that we were diminished by them.[56]

Similar efforts to raise feminist questions and bring women's leadership potential to the attention of party activists also helped to propel Flora MacDonald's 1976 campaign. MacDonald was a Conservative MP from Kingston, Ontario who, like Brown, was unsuccessful in her bid for national party leadership. What MacDonald and Brown *did* establish through their campaigns, however, was that Canadian women could raise funds, increase public awareness and challenge entrenched party elites in a collective manner.

Their consciousness-raising efforts were in many respects a response to the considerable barriers then facing women's aspirations to lead competitive political parties. Brown, MacDonald, Muriel Smith (who sought the Manitoba NDP leadership in 1979) and Sheila Copps (whose first bid was for the Ontario Liberal leadership in 1982) thus constituted a first generation of female leadership contenders. Their early campaigns differed from subsequent ones in that they had to contend with three specific questions raised by media commentators and partisans alike; each of these questions tended to weaken the candidate's chances of winning major party leadership. First, would a woman make a suitable political party leader? Second, what is the personal style or image of this particular candidate? And third, is she a 'token women's' or a 'real' candidate?

Although the attention paid to these points varied across parties and leadership campaigns, it generally obscured a more salient question: 'Would this individual make a good party leader?' Moreover, in suggesting that female candidates might represent only other women or other feminist women, enquiries of this type imposed a major constraint upon the practical conversion from numerical to substantive representation by female elites. That is, by labelling women candidates as 'women's candidates', political commentators and partisans tended to marginalize the significant policy issues raised by these participants.

During the 1975 federal NDP leadership campaign, Rosemary Brown was frequently described in the press as an elegant, eloquent, well-dressed black woman who resided with her American-born psychiatrist husband in the wealthy Point Grey neighbourhood of Vancouver. In addition, Brown was reported to hold an extensive portfolio of private stocks as well as real estate on the Gulf Islands.[57] Since comparable data on the other three (male) candidates for NDP leadership was not provided in journalists' accounts, it seems that personal background factors played a disproportionately large role in the media portrayal of Brown, as they did in accounts of Flora MacDonald, Sheila Copps and the female municipal candidates examined by Linda Archibald and her colleagues.[58]

The Brown campaign was also weakened by allegations of 'token' candidacy. It was particularly vulnerable in this area because of an identifiably pro-feminist orientation, reflected in campaign literature encouraging delegates to 'Celebrate International Women's Year by Nominating Rosemary Brown as Leader'.[59] This emphasis on such issues as affirmative action, child care and abortion produced mixed results. On the one hand, Brown was initially dismissed by journalists as well as party insiders who viewed her as a marginal candidate with limited legislative experience.[60] On the other hand, however, she showed unexpected strength at the convention—which led a number of reporters and supporters of the eventual winner, Ed Broadbent, to speculate that she was simply a 'token' candidate who would attract 'first ballot support to show there is no prejudice against blacks or women'.[61] In the words of former party leader T.C. Douglas (who endorsed Broadbent), this support for Brown constituted 'a sort of prejudice in reverse'.[62] Despite allegations of tokenism, Brown retained a strong second-place position through four rounds of voting. Similarly, in 1979, Muriel Smith managed a respectable second-place finish on the first (and only) ballot for the Manitoba NDP provincial leadership.[63]

Concerns about female suitability to party leadership, personal style and 'tokenism' were even clearer during Flora MacDonald's 1976 campaign for the federal PC leadership. The willingness of Conservative partisans to question explicitly the acceptability of a woman leader indicated that gender constituted an important criterion for a fair number of PC delegates.[64] In addition, MacDonald's attempts to raise much of her campaign money among women (including well-known feminists) who were not Conservatives suggested that she lacked solid support among important sectors of the party organization.[65]

Issues of personal style were also raised throughout the campaign. MacDonald was frequently referred to as 'Flora', the red-haired 'girl Friday' 'spinster' who was raised in a large Scottish family in Cape Breton, and who seemed to have had no existence outside of politics in her adult life.[66] Captions in one press account reflect the prominence accorded to these personal factors: 'I can barely boil an egg. My job is my life—yes! My constituency is my family.'[67] Compared with the accounts given of the other (male) contenders for PC leadership, the treatment of MacDonald was distinctly style- or image-oriented. However, since the MacDonald campaign itself was geared in a populist direction, the candidate was especially vulnerable to these kinds of characterizations.

Probably most damaging to MacDonald were the strong allegations that she was a 'token' candidate. MacDonald referred to herself as 'a politician who happens to be a woman, not a woman politician.'[68] Furthermore, she argued that 'women's issues' were in fact 'society's issues',[69] and suggested that her gender was an asset to the Conservative party. As she emphasized in her main address to the leadership convention: 'I am not a candidate because I am a woman. But I say to you quite frankly that because I am a woman my candidacy helps our party. It shows that in the Conservative Party there are no barriers to anyone who has demonstrated serious intentions and earned the right to be heard. It proves that the leadership of this great party is not for sale to any alliance of the powerful and the few.'[70]

Despite MacDonald's hopeful expectations, she finished in a disappointing sixth place on the first ballot. This weak showing, later termed 'the Flora syndrome', appeared to confirm the allegations regarding token female candidacies and tended for a time to overshadow the very credible leadership campaigns organized by other women, including Rosemary Brown.

Despite her youthful age, 'insider' connections and careful avoidance of a 'women's candidate' image, the response to Sheila Copps's Ontario provincial candidacy during 1981-82 suggested a continuation of first-generation experiences.[71] Like MacDonald, Copps was confronted directly with questions about female suitability to political leadership. For example, party delegates asked, 'Are we ready for a woman leader?' Or, 'Will Ontario vote for a woman', ' . . . a 29-year-old woman', ' . . . a 29-year-old single woman?' One prominent newspaper columnist posed the suitability issue as follows: 'The question facing the delegates of the OLP leadership convention when they gather here next February is simple. Will the voters of Ontario in 1985 choose a government led by a 32-year-old woman, albeit an attractive, intelligent one?'[72]

This same journalist went on to describe the personal style of the candidate, to whom he referred simply as 'Sheila', as 'brash, gutsy, impudent, even impatient'.[73] The article offered no such assessment of personality traits among the other four (male) leadership contenders, perhaps because these same characteristics would have been deemed acceptable, even advantageous, in a male candidate. Similarly, Copps was described by other commentators as a 'vivacious brunette', as a candidate 'with a fallen marriage six years behind her' and, in one especially biased treatment, as 'some jumped-up combination of Jayne Mansfield and Joan of Arc. Jayne of Arc?'[74]

Questions about a token candidacy were also raised during the Copps campaign. A number of discussions referred explicitly to the 'Flora syndrome'; for example, one *Globe and Mail* columnist noted that '"Sheila" even sounds a bit like "Flora".'[75] Copps vehemently, and apparently correctly, rejected such comparisons, making a strong second-place showing on both convention ballots— and this despite a concerted 'Stop Copps' effort by the party establishment on the last day of the convention.[76]

INFORMAL EFFORTS SINCE 1982

To a large extent, contemporary efforts to increase women's representation in political parties reflect a movement away from early consciousness-raising concerns. Women's leadership campaigns since the mid-1980s have been more clearly focused on the concrete pursuit of power and, in a growing number of cases, have actually resulted in victory. In the New Democratic party, Alexa McDonough and Audrey McLaughlin became leaders of the Nova Scotia and federal organizations in 1980 and 1989, respectively. Although neither party had held power and both were in relatively uncompetitive positions at the point of their selection, McDonough and McLaughlin both improved their competitive standings over time. A similar scenario unfolded during the 1980s in the Manitoba Liberal party, an organization that was nearly defunct when Sharon Carstairs took over in 1984, but that under her leadership became the official opposition from 1988 until 1990.

The arrival of second-generation conditions was probably clearest in competitive parties of the centre and right. For a brief period during 1991, Rita Johnston led the British Columbia Social Credit party and served as Canada's first female premier. In 1992, Lyn McLeod successfully contested the provincial Liberal leadership in Ontario, becoming that province's first female opposition leader. Most notably, Sheila Copps (who did not support McLeod's candidacy) ran once again for party leadership in 1990, this time in the federal Liberal organization. Although it was again unsuccessful, Copps's second bid confronted fewer public questions of a token candidacy and female suitability to party leadership than did her first effort.[77]

By the early 1990s, it seemed, Canadian women could run for party leadership *without* limiting their campaigns to a consciousness-raising focus. Yet at least one crucial barrier still remained for party women, and that concerned money. The problem of raising funds to contest public office was placed squarely on the partisan agenda with the establishment in 1983 of the Agnes Macphail Fund in the federal NDP, followed in 1984 by the creation of the Judy LaMarsh Fund in the federal Liberal organization and in 1986 by the founding of the Ellen Fairclough Fund in the federal PC party. These funds and their provincial counterparts helped to support female candidates in subsequent general elections; in 1988, for example, the federal NDP disbursed $1,000 to each of 85 women, the Liberals contributed $850 to each female candidate, and the Conservatives gave each new woman candidate $750 and each incumbent $100.[78]

The problem of money remained crucial, however, at the point of nomination and leadership candidacy. One informal response to the nomination question was attempted under the 1987 Women in Nomination (WIN) program in the Ontario Progressive Conservative party; any PC woman seeking nomination was allowed to apply for money from WIN.[79] WIN also organized workshops to train women to run for nomination, and acted as a consulting service on selecting ridings, setting up campaign teams and fund-raising.

With regard to party leadership, Sheila Copps spoke widely and vigorously about her experiences—particularly the financial obstacles she had confronted in 1990.[80] Copps, however, like many others, believed informal change was insufficient and recommended a formal regulatory reform that would bring leadership campaigns within the statutory purview of a reformed *Canada Elections Act*.

ARE INFORMAL REFORMS ENOUGH?

This review of informal strategies begs one obvious question: can consciousness-raising, organization and education *by themselves* elevate more women and women's issues within party elites? Are party funds, for example, likely to achieve their objective of improving access in the absence of other changes?

The answer to these questions is 'probably not'. One can easily argue that each dimension of the informal route is necessary and important on its own, yet even as a group these kinds of activities are unlikely to be sufficient to

challenge under-representation. Particularly with the passing of an older consciousness-raising orientation in women's leadership campaigns, informal efforts
tend to be short-term and episodic in their effects. Special women's funds, for
example, may form a lively pivot around which party women can focus their
networking and fund-raising energies. Yet such funds are usually available only
to candidates who have already overcome considerable obstacles *prior to* their
six- or eight-week campaign for public office; moreover, like the women's organizations discussed in Chapter 5, such funds can be seen as diverting party
women away from mainstream organizational activity.

Other informal mechanisms are also vulnerable to these same difficulties.
Women and politics groups that draw on a combined multi-partisan and non-
partisan membership can be exceedingly active in one period and virtually dorm-
ant in another; like all voluntary groups, they can exert palpable influence at
one level of government and almost none at others—again, with considerable
variation over time.

The point is that while informal efforts complement formal regulatory reforms,
they are *not* able to effect the same sustained level of change over time. This
conclusion must take account of ideological differences among parties, however.
Parties of the left in most political systems, including Canada's, are usually more
favourably disposed towards formal regulatory approaches than parties of the
centre and, especially, the right. New Democrats have consistently pursued more
sweeping internal party reforms related to the representation of women than
Liberals, who in turn have been more supportive of internal rule change than
Progressive Conservatives. As well, NDP organizations have taken many informal
initiatives, including the establishment of a federal party fund, sooner than Liberal
organizations, which in turn have usually preceded Conservative organizations.

The same pattern unfolds with respect to external rule changes. Demands
for proportional representation, party finance reform and other system-wide revisions have tended to take hold more firmly among left and centre partisans
than among those on the political right. As in the case of internal rule change,
conservatives usually prefer a non-interventionist and non-regulatory solution,
one that would see women gradually increase their numbers and influence
through existing political channels.

From the perspective of the early 1990s, this situation suggests that increased
representation of either a numerical or substantive nature will prove difficult
to achieve. The systemic changes endorsed by feminist interests are unlikely
to receive a sympathetic hearing from a federal Conservative government that
is challenged by the Reform party on its right flank. Even basic informal processes
such as skills training or targeted recruitment of party women can be curtailed
in circumstances that favour a traditionalist, 'pro-family' approach to political
organization.

Because the interests that have been willing to entertain changes in formal
systemic as well as internal partisan rules operate in opposition at the federal

level, the prospects for such reforms may be more promising at the provincial level. The existence, in the early 1990s, of NDP governments in Ontario, British Columbia and Saskatchewan, for example, could prompt a major round of innovation in at least some provinces. Nevertheless, this challenge to act on some of the systemic demands of party feminists may not be taken up. And if their concerns are not satisfied, politically active women may retreat once again from the partisan struggle and re-group in the independent arena.

One transitional space between these two settings can be found in party women's organizations, to which we now turn our attention.

NOTES

[1] Report of the Royal Commission on the Status of Women (Ottawa: Information Canada, 1970), 333.

[2] See ibid. as well as *Reforming Electoral Democracy*, vol. 2 of Royal Commission on Electoral Reform and Party Financing final report (Ottawa: Supply and Services Canada, 1991); and *Reforming Electoral Democracy: What Canadians Told Us*, vol. 4 of ibid.

[3] Among the most powerful of these reflections are Rosemary Brown, *Being Brown: A Very Public Life* (Toronto: Ballantine, 1989); and Sheila Copps, *Nobody's Baby: A Survival Guide to Politics* (Toronto: Deneau, 1986).

[4] Hanna Fenichel Pitkin, *The Concept of Representation* (Berkeley: University of California Press, 1967), 11. See also Anne Phillips, *Engendering Democracy* (University Park: Pennsylvania State University Press, 1991), chap. 3.

[5] Senator Chubby Power, quoted in John C. Courtney, *The Selection of National Party Leaders in Canada* (Toronto: Macmillan, 1973), 107.

[6] Donald V. Smiley, 'The National Party Leadership Convention in Canada: A Preliminary Analysis', *Canadian Journal of Political Science* 1 (1968), 373.

[7] Marguerite J. Fisher, 'Women in the Political Parties', *Annals of the American Academy of Political and Social Science* 251 (1947), 87-93.

[8] Frank J. Sorauf, *Party Politics in America* (Boston: Little, Brown, 1976), 123. See also Hugh A. Bone, *Party Committees and National Politics* (Seattle: University of Washington Press, 1958), 107-11; Louis Maisel, 'Party Reforms and Political Participation: The Democrats in Maine', in Louis Maisel and Paul M. Sacks, eds., *The Future of Political Parties* (Beverly Hills: Sage, 1975), 202-8; and Robert J. Huckshorn, *Party Leadership in the States* (Amherst: University of Massachusetts Press, 1976).

[9] Jeane Kirkpatrick, *The New Presidential Elite* (New York: Russell Sage Foundation, 1976), 43. On the background to US party reforms, see John S. Saloma and Frederick H. Sontag, *Parties* (New York: Knopf, 1972), 108-10.

[10] See Carl Baar and Ellen Baar, 'Party and Convention Organization and Leadership Selection in Canada and the United States', in Donald R. Matthews, ed., *Perspectives on Presidential Selection* (Washington, D.C.: Brookings, 1973), 59.

[11] Kirkpatrick, *The New Presidential Elite*; and M. Kent Jennings and Barbara G. Farah, 'Social Roles and Political Resources: An Over-Time Study of Men and Women in Party Elites', *American Journal of Political Science* 25 (1981), 462-82.

[12] Sorauf, *Party Politics*, 123.

[13] For a summary of this situation, see M. Janine Brodie and Jill McCalla Vickers, *Canadian Women in Politics: An Overview* (Ottawa: Canadian Research Institute for the Advancement of Women, 1982).

[14]Walter S.G. Kohn, *Women in National Legislatures: A Comparative Study of Six Countries* (New York: Praeger, 1980).

[15]For a review of these efforts, see Chantal Maillé with Valentina Pollon, *Primed for Power: Women in Canadian Politics* (Ottawa: Canadian Advisory Council on the Status of Women, 1990).

[16]See *Resolutions to the NDP Convention*, Vancouver, 1981, 165-6.

[17]Donald C. MacDonald, 'Affirmative Action: Moving From Talk to Reality in the NDP', *Toronto Star*, 31 July 1983.

[18]See *Report* of the Affirmative Action Committee of the NDP Federal Council, 1983.

[19]See National Women's Liberal Commission, 'Action Plan: Basic Elements and Strategies of an Affirmative Action Plan for Women in the Liberal Party of Canada', 1982.

[20]Constitution of the Ontario NDP Women's Committee, 1973, section 2, paras 1 and 2.

[21]This discussion draws heavily on interviews with the president of the ONDP Women's Committee at the time, Marianne Holder, as well as on participant observation in the Committee by the author during 1980-1.

[22]See *Resolutions to the Tenth Convention of the Ontario NDP*, Guelph, 20-22 June 1980, W1-W13.

[23]One staff member was appointed to the office of the party leader, while the other was assigned to manage an unsuccessful campaign in a Metropolitan Toronto riding vacated by an NDP incumbent. Both the women's co-ordinator and women's organizer positions were eliminated during post-election reorganization in the party.

[24]See Marianne R. Holder, 'Notes re. Internal Affirmative Action', prepared for the NDP Participation of Women Committee meeting, Ottawa, 5 July 1980.

[25]As defined in a 1983 report to the NDP federal council: 'Systemic discrimination refers to practices or systems which may appear to be neutral in their treatment of women and may be implemented impartially, but which operate to exclude women for reasons which are not related to the job to be done. In terms of the Party, there is no conscious intention of practicing discrimination; the discriminatory impact on women is either not recognized or is assumed to reflect actual inadequacies (or unavailability) of women to do the job.' See *Report* of the Affirmative Action Committee of the NDP Federal Council, 1983, 1.

[26]*Resolutions to the Eleventh Convention of the Ontario NDP*, Toronto, 5-7 February 1982, 93-4.

[27]On the failure of voluntary remedies in the US, see Nijole V. Benokraitis and Joe R. Feagin, *Affirmative Action and Equal Opportunity* (Boulder, Col.: Westview Press, 1970), 173-7.

[28]According to some supporters of affirmative action in the US, 'discrimination is more costly than remedial action' in an organizational context (ibid., 187).

[29]This argument maintains that rather than resulting in a loss of institutional autonomy, affirmative action enhances the operation of organizations, especially because it improves (or rationalizes) internal decision-making. See ibid.

[30]For a critique of affirmative action from the position of individual merit, see Lance W. Roberts, 'Understanding Affirmative Action', in W.E. Block and M.A. Walker, eds., *Discrimination, Affirmative Action and Equal Opportunity* (Vancouver: Fraser Institute, 1982), 159-62.

[31]The argument that affirmative action is unnecessary because discrimination remains unproved is presented in Walter Williams, 'On Discrimination, Prejudice, Racial Income Differentials and Affirmative Action', in ibid., 69-99.

[32]According to Block and Walker, little evidence is available to suggest that discrimination exists, and therefore 'what is needed for intelligent public policy is careful analysis, a measured and dispassionate outlook, well-documented research, convincing evidence, and a willingness to look at the world as it really is, and not only as we might like to see it' (ibid., xix).

[33]See Sylvia B. Bashevkin, 'Political Participation, Ambition and Feminism: Women in the Ontario Party Elites', *American Review of Canadian Studies* 15:4 (Winter 1985), 413.

[34] *Reforming Electoral Democracy*, vol. 4, 148.

[35] Constitution of the Liberal Party of Canada, 1990.

[36] Constitution of the Progressive Conservative Association of Canada, 1991.

[37] Ontario New Democratic Party, 'Affirmative Action Guidelines for Nomination and Candidacy', as approved by Provincial Council, 9-10 December 1989.

[38] Ibid.

[39] Ibid.

[40] New Democratic Party of Canada, Affirmative Action Policy, November 1991.

[41] New Democratic Party of Canada, 'Minutes of the Affirmative Action Sub-Committee Tele-conference Call', 15 August 1991; emphasis in original.

[42] Doris Anderson, *The Unfinished Revolution: The Status of Women in Twelve Countries* (Toronto: Double-day, 1991).

[43] National Action Committee on the Status of Women, 'Response to Federal Constitution Proposals', 25 October 1991, 9. See also Stephen Clarkson et al., 'Three Nations in a Delicate State', *Toronto Star* (4 February 1992), A17, reprinted as Christina McCall et al., 'Three Nations', *Canadian Forum* (March 1992), 4-6. This statement advocates 'equal representation of women' in restructured legislative institutions.

[44] See *Reforming Electoral Democracy*, vol. 1 of final report of the Royal Commission on Electoral Reform and Party Financing (Ottawa: Supply and Services Canada, 1991), 3.

[45] Recommendation 1.3.17 in *Reforming Electoral Democracy*, vol. 2 of final report of Royal Commission on Electoral Reform and Party Financing (Ottawa: Supply and Services Canada, 1991), 271.

[46] Recommendation 1.3.19 in ibid.

[47] Recommendation 1.3.20 in ibid.

[48] Recommendation 1.3.21 in ibid.

[49] Recommendation 1.3.23 in ibid., 272.

[50] Recommendation 1.5.11 in ibid., 280.

[51] Christine Boyle, 'Home Rule for Women: Power-Sharing Between Men and Women', *Dalhousie Law Journal* 7:3 (October 1983), 799.

[52] Ibid., 805.

[53] Ibid., 809.

[54] See Pitkin, *The Concept of Representation*.

[55] The Committee for '94 co-sponsored a 1986 conference at Ryerson Polytechnic Institute, which was later packaged into a series on TVOntario. See Carol Sevitt, ed., *Women and Politics Transcripts* (Toronto: Ontario Educational Communications Authority, 1988). In December 1990 and April 1991, the Committee organized additional conferences on the policy impact of elected women and the nominations process.

[56] Brown, *Being Brown*, 151. For a US study of the outlooks of elite-level political women, see Dorothy W. Cantor and Toni Bernay, *Women and Power: The Secrets of Leadership* (Boston: Houghton Mifflin, 1992).

[57] See, for example, Alan Fotheringham, 'BC's Mrs. Thatcher Embarrasses Barrett', *Toronto Star*, 14 February 1975; Malcolm Gray, 'Has Rosemary Brown's Socialist Image More Style than Substance?' *Globe and Mail*, 20 February 1975; and Lisa Hobbs, 'Why is Rosemary Running?' *Chatelaine*, July 1975.

[58] See Linda Archibald, Leona Christian, Karen Detarding and Dianne Hendrick, 'Sex Biases in Newspaper Reporting: Press Treatment of Municipal Candidates', *Atlantis* 5 (1980), 177-84.

[59] 'Rosemary for Leader of NDP', campaign literature, 1975.

60 On the initially dismissive attitude toward Brown's candidacy, see 'NDP Gathers Friday', *Winnipeg Tribune*, 2 July 1975; and Nick Hills, 'For Broadbent, the West is the Test', *Winnipeg Tribune*, 3 July 1975.

61 Stewart MacLeod, 'NDP Converges on City', *Winnipeg Tribune*, 4 July 1975.

62 T.C. Douglas, quoted in ibid. On Brown's reaction to this treatment by the party establishment, see *Being Brown*, chap. 8.

63 Interview with Muriel Smith (7 July 1982); Robert Matas, 'Pawley Supporters Eyeing Early Victory at Convention', *Winnipeg Tribune*, 2 November 1979; and Robert Matas, 'Pawley Wins Easy Victory to Lead NDP', *Winnipeg Tribune*, 5 November 1979.

64 Frank Jones, "Flora Keeps her Cool in 'Chauvinist Country,'" *Toronto Star*, 23 February 1976; and Harry Bruce, 'The Lady was for Burning: Why the Tories Gave Flora their Hearts but not their Votes', *The Canadian Magazine*, 10 April 1976.

65 Pat McNenly, 'Make Abortion Available to All, MacDonald Tells her Supporters', *Toronto Star*, 2 February 1976; and Jones, 'Flora Keeps her Cool'.

66 MacDonald's status as a 'girl' was emphasized in Tom Hazlitt, 'Girl's Fight for an "Independent" Canada', *Toronto Star*, 7 May 1971. For references to her as a 'spinster', see for example Frank Jones, 'Flora MacDonald is Finding her Kind of People', *Toronto Star*, 1 March 1975; and Heather Robertson, 'Delivering Politics Back to the People', *The Canadian Magazine*, 3 May 1975.

67 Robertson, 'Delivering Politics'.

68 Mary Janigan, 'Prime Minister Flora MacDonald? Why Not!' *Toronto Star*, 1 February 1975.

69 Frank Jones, 'Flora Keeps her Cool'.

70 Flora MacDonald leadership address, as quoted in Alvin Armstrong, *Flora MacDonald* (Toronto: J.M. Dent and Sons, 1976), 192.

71 Copps's father was a long-time mayor of Hamilton and federal Liberal leadership candidate. As well, she had been a constituency assistant and protégée of the retiring provincial leader, Dr Stuart Smith.

72 Hugh Winsor, 'A Dash of Spirit is Added', *Globe and Mail*, 8 December 1981.

73 Ibid.

74 On Copps's marital history, see Jonathan Fear, 'Five Hope to Beat the Tory Machine', *Kitchener-Waterloo Record*, 19 February 1982; and Jean Sonmor, 'Sheila: The Next Hurrah', *Toronto Sun*, 23 February 1982. The comparison with Mansfield and Joan of Arc appeared in the 24 November 1981 Slinger column in the *Toronto Star*.

75 Winsor, 'A Dash of Spirit'.

76 On the Sunday morning of the convention, a number of members of the provincial Liberal caucus announced that were Copps elected as party leader, they would expect resignations en masse from the caucus. Their statements, accompanied by the distribution of a list of 23 MPPs who were supporting David Peterson, were apparently meant to counter the endorsements that Copps had received from seven federal cabinet ministers. See Paul Palango, 'Peterson Runs Hard to Stay Ahead', *Globe and Mail*, 16 February 1982; and Pat Crowe, 'MP's Presence a Mixed Blessing', *Toronto Star*, 21 February 1982.

77 This change can be attributed to a number of factors, including growing numbers of female reporters covering political news, more women delegates at conventions, and a sense that older and more stereotypical questions about women candidates were less acceptable than in the past.

78 I am grateful to the following federal party officials for providing this information: Abby Pollonetsky of the NDP, Cynthia Cusinato of the Liberals and Mary Meldrum, Linda Scales and Suzanne Warren of the Progressive Conservatives. According to Pollonetsky, 'The Agnes Macphail Fund has generated over $388,000, and dispersed funds and material assistance to over 130 women candidates.' See Abby Pollonetsky, 'More Women Needed', letter to the *Globe and Mail*, 21 February 1992.

[79]The WIN project, chaired by Elizabeth Burnham, was a response to the findings of an internal party task force chaired by Jane Pepino. See 'Report of the Leader's Task Force on Women in the [Ontario] Progressive Conservative Party', August 1986.

[80]Copps spoke, for example, at the December 1990 conference of the Committee for '94 in Toronto as well as the October 1990 opening session of the Symposium on the Active Participation of Women in Politics, sponsored by the Royal Commission on Electoral Reform and Party Financing in Montreal.

CHAPTER FIVE

Women's Organizations in the Major Parties

Most parties hold together as an entity only because women's groups meet regularly, year in and year out; although they rarely concern themselves with the issues of the day, they are the muscle of all political parties.

— Judy LaMarsh, *Memoirs of a Bird in a Gilded Cage*, 1969[1]

We believe that the public life of Canada would benefit from the full participation of women and that women should be accorded full access to political affairs through the party structure. Therefore, *we recommend that women's associations within the political parties of Canada be amalgamated with the main bodies of these parties.*

— Royal Commission on the Status of Women, *Report*, 1970[2]

During the period of suffragist activism in English Canada, and for approximately the next fifty years, women's associations provided some of the only evidence of sustained female involvement in either the Liberal or the Conservative party. These associations, then referred to as clubs or auxiliaries, helped to channel women's energies into local, provincial and national party activities, in some cases before enfranchisement was formally obtained. For example, in Toronto, Vancouver and Charlottetown, women's Liberal associations were founded prior to the passage of provincial suffrage legislation, in 1913, 1915 and 1922, respectively.[3]

Many of the activities undertaken by these separate Liberal and Conservative women's associations, as well as a variety of standing committees of the main party organization in the CCF and NDP, were reflective of a 'ladies' aid' approach to volunteer party work. As providers of support services to mainstream party organizations, women's associations raised money through banquets, luncheons, bazaars, cookbook sales and other similar projects. Their members also performed valuable clerical, social and fund-raising tasks inside riding associations, particularly during election campaigns, and staffed registration, credentials and arrangements committees for various party meetings and conventions. As Judy LaMarsh observed in her memoirs (quoted above), these contributions were usually taken for granted by the parent party organizations, even though the latter would have been hard-pressed to operate without them.[4]

The fact that women's affiliates were constitutionally recognized in both the Liberal and Conservative parties, with separate membership dues, leadership structures and internal regulations, meant that some prominent female activists were appointed to the mainstream party executive and, in a few cases, Senate seats by virtue of their group involvement (see Chapter 1). Such appointments, however, rarely signified that women's associations or their leaders exerted substantive influence within the Canadian political system. Rather, their lack of tangible policy impact, combined with the minimal attention devoted to questions of representation by party women's associations, contributed to a major re-evaluation of their goals and purposes by the early 1970s. As reflected in one recommendation of the Royal Commission on the Status of Women (quoted above), separate associations were increasingly viewed as impeding full political participation by Canadian women. A majority of royal commissioners thus recommended 'that women's associations within the political parties of Canada be amalgamated with the main bodies of these parties'.[5]

The concept of amalgamation was favourably received by many people, including feminists and male party strategists who viewed traditional associations as politically ineffective and unattractive to younger recruits.[6] Despite consistent opposition by the older groups, both the national Liberal and Progressive Conservative women's associations were replaced, by the National Women's Liberal Commission (established in 1973) and the National Progressive Conservative Women's Caucus (established in 1981). Both of the latter were formally committed to improving the status of women within the parties rather than to providing support services for the mainstream organization; they were considered more appropriate to the changing socio-economic and political roles of Canadian women than their predecessors.

The dissolution of older women's groups and the establishment of more contemporary commissions and caucuses, however, revealed important conflicts regarding female participation in the major parties. In the Liberal and Conservative cases, one source of contention was the treatment of older associations and especially their participants, many of whom felt betrayed by both the party hierarchies and younger female activists. According to some, the latter had eliminated legitimate women's groups in order to 'impose' a feminist direction upon contemporary organizations.

A second problem affected not only the two established parties but also the NDP, in which a separate women's association had never existed at the national level. This difficulty concerns the relationship between contemporary associations of party women, on the one hand, and the broader party organization and feminist movement, on the other. The expectation that newer caucuses and commissions would function as conduits for feminist policy initiatives and for ascendant female activists has proved difficult to fulfil in all three major parties—even though the mandate for such groups rests precisely in this area of enhanced numerical and substantive representation.

The following sections explore the history and contemporary status of women's organizations in the three major parties. Although the study of both older and newer associations is essential for an understanding of wider changes in the party system, it has attracted little systematic attention from political researchers. This long-standing neglect requires that we begin with a brief survey of older women's associations in the Liberal and Conservative parties.

EARLY WOMEN'S LIBERAL ASSOCIATIONS

In the years prior to the awarding of the provincial franchise in Ontario, British Columbia and Prince Edward Island, associations of Liberal women were organized both to pressure for suffrage and social reform legislation and to contribute to the activities of existing Liberal parties. The earliest of these groups was the Toronto Women's Liberal Association (TWLA), established in 1913 and presided over at its inception by Mrs Newton Wesley Rowell, wife of the pro-suffrage Liberal opposition leader in the Ontario legislature. The first constitution of the TWLA, drafted with the assistance of Newton Rowell and Sir Wilfrid Laurier, permitted the group to acquire a provincial charter in June 1918. This charter specified three main objectives: first, improving the welfare of women and children in Ontario; second, establishing a Liberal government in the province; and third, striving for a united Canada. According to one internal history, members of the TWLA held fund-raising socials, worked in election campaigns and developed policy resolutions concerning social welfare issues (including pensions, equal pay and health care) during the early decades of this century.[7] In addition, at least one prominent activist in the organization, Mrs Wesley Bundy (who served as president from 1918 until 1920), ran as a candidate in the 1921 general elections.

During this same period the Ontario Women's Liberal Association (OWLA) was also founded. Established in 1914, with Mrs Rowell again as first president, the OWLA began as an attempt to impart central direction to the growing number of Liberal clubs in the province. With the encouragement of both Lady Aberdeen, wife of the former governor-general, and Prime Minister Mackenzie King, the OWLA set out to organize more women's clubs, to offer program materials to these groups and in general to promote Liberal principles.[8] In the years between 1914 and 1928, the OWLA established 47 clubs organized into 10 districts, each of which was responsible to a district vice-president. During the subsequent decade, the OWLA grew rapidly to embrace a total of 105 clubs, and at its twenty-fifth-year anniversary celebration, in 1939, it boasted an active membership of some 4,000 Liberal women.[9] This organizational strength weakened with the advent of the Second World War, however, so that by the mid-1940s, the OWLA included only 56 active affiliates.

Although the origins of early women's Liberal associations in British Columbia and Prince Edward Island are more difficult to document, both seem to have been established with essentially the same aims as the Toronto and Ontario groups. According to accounts by Catherine Cleverdon, Elsie Gregory MacGill and Diane Crossley, the Women's Liberal Association of Vancouver and the Women's Liberal Club of Charlottetown lobbied extensively for the provincial franchise, as well as for social reform legislation during the 1920s.[10] In the case of the Vancouver Women's Liberal Association, close ties developed with the provincial Liberal caucus, particularly following the appointment of one of the association's founders, Mary Ellen Smith, to the provincial cabinet in 1921. In addition to Smith, a number of other prominent suffragists and social feminists—including Helen Gregory MacGill and Evlyn Farris (founder of the University Women's Club of Vancouver)—assumed major roles in the establishment of the BC Women's Liberal Association in 1915.

THE NATIONAL FEDERATION OF LIBERAL WOMEN

Many of these same activists were also instrumental in founding the National Federation of Liberal Women of Canada (NFLW). The first assembly of the federation, held in Ottawa in April 1928, attracted about 500 women and was organized by Cairine Wilson, an Ontario Liberal who later served as NFLW president and as the first female member of the Canadian Senate.[11] Reports presented at the first meeting covered the activities of both the Toronto and the Ontario associations; for its new executive, the federation elected British Columbian Mary Ellen Smith to serve as first national president.

According to one study of the federation by Patricia Myers, the organization was generally inactive during its early years, since the work of the Liberal party overall was interrupted by both the Great Depression and the Second World War.[12] Following a formal end to hostilities, however, the federation established a network of one hundred constituent clubs, published a *Liberal Woman* newsletter and maintained an extensive list of French- and English-speaking members. In fact, Myers indicates that by 1967 the NFLW included some 450 affiliated clubs with a combined membership of approximately 31,000 women.

The relationship between the Women's Federation and the larger National Liberal Federation reflected an auxiliary-mainstream linkage throughout most of this period. Since the NFLW was a federation of local women's clubs, it developed as a less centralized and less policy-oriented organization than the parent party grouping. As Myers demonstrates, the Women's Federation newsletter focused its reports on individual club activities, while federation conventions were festive social occasions that included tours, teas, receptions and banquets with the federal leader as keynote speaker.[13]

Policy issues that were broached during NFLW meetings generally concerned such questions as family life, social welfare, and the appointment of women to boards, commissions and the Senate. The attention accorded these resolutions was limited by a number of important factors, including the marginal position of the Women's Federation in the broader Liberal party and the secondary role of policy concerns among organized women themselves. As Myers reports, it was not until the late 1960s that NFLW members as a group began to evaluate the partisan effectiveness of their organization, and to challenge its financial and political dependence upon the mainstream Liberal party. In the interim, the campaign and convention efforts of federation activists became increasingly important to the larger party organization and, in the words of Mackenzie King, continued 'a noble effort' on behalf of Canadian Liberalism.[14]

The post-war activities of other Liberal women's associations also reflected a growing, albeit unstated, reliance upon their recruitment efforts. Inside the Toronto Women's Liberal Association, for example, a group of 'new university women graduates' formed a Tuesday Luncheon Club in 1948. According to a statement marking its twenty-fifth anniversary in 1973: 'The club is a Women's Liberal Organization which provides a forum for visiting speakers to discuss topics of general interest. Members of the Senate, Cabinet, Commons, Legislative Assembly and the academic and business worlds are frequent speakers at the regular luncheon meeting on the first Tuesday of the month from October to May.'[15] In 1983 the club had a membership of some 90 women[16], but by 1992, its active members numbered only about 35.[17]

The establishment of the Tuesday Luncheon Club in Toronto, combined with the mobilization activities of the Ontario Women's Liberal Association during the post-war years (constituent clubs at its fiftieth anniversary meeting in 1964 numbered 110, with 275 delegates in attendance), suggest that the mainstream party organization became increasingly dependent upon the varied services that its female support structures could provide. As relatively well-educated and well-motivated party workers, Liberal women fulfilled crucial duties as poll captains, canvassers, volunteer publicists, coffee party hostesses, election day drivers and convention registrars. Their associations in the post-war years grew closely identified with basic social, fund-raising and clerical maintenance functions. In the words of one OWLA historian, recounting experiences during the 1963 federal election: 'The Liberal Women threw all their know-how and energy into the campaign, knocking on doors for the candidates, licking stamps and stuffing envelopes and pouring coffee at social functions to 'meet the candidate'. They spoke at Liberal rallies and on television and radio. They tacked up candidate placards along the roads and highways. Nothing was too difficult or too trivial to perform.'[18] In the following year, many OWLA members also attended an Ontario provincial leadership convention where, according to a group historian, they were 'convention hostesses, wearing their carnation corsages and pouring tea at the receptions'.[19]

This conventional tea-pouring role, however, became a source of concern and distaste to some Liberal women during the 1960s. Reflecting upon a year spent as OWLA president prior to her by-election victory in 1960, Judy LaMarsh concluded that 'women did the donkey work' in party organizations.[20] Although publicly appreciative of the important contributions made by women's associations and their members, including their work in her own campaigns, LaMarsh endorsed the growing, largely non-partisan effort to change the position of women in Canadian party politics.

Before examining these attempts at reform, we shall first review the development of older women's organizations in the Conservative and CCF/NDP organizations.

CONSERVATIVE WOMEN'S ASSOCIATIONS

Early records of Conservative women's groups are somewhat less detailed. One internal history of Tory women, published in 1966 by the Progressive Conservative Women's Association of Canada, suggests that isolated clubs existed in Vancouver as early as 1917 (the old Vancouver Women's Conservative Club), in Quebec City in 1918 (a district association encompassing four urban federal ridings), and in Montreal as early as 1920 (L'Association des Femmes Conservatives de Montréal).[21] According to this same account, 'in 1938, the first attempt at a national organization was made by the Honourable R.B. Bennett asking Mrs. Hugh MacKay of Rothesay to come to Ottawa. This meeting led to one at Port Hope where a national organization began to take shape and the decisions made there were formally confirmed at the Winnipeg Convention in 1942.'[22] The war impeded organizational development, however, and it was not until 1946 that the 'Women's Committee within the Progressive Conservative Association of Canada' became active, under the leadership of Hilda Hesson.[23]

As a full-time party organizer and president of the Committee, Hesson devoted her considerable energies to publishing a women's newsletter (which appeared in both English and French) and to establishing new or expanded associations in Nova Scotia, Newfoundland, New Brunswick, Prince Edward Island, Alberta, Manitoba, Quebec and Ontario. By 1950 the PC Women's *News Letter* reached a mailing list of approximately 10,000 readers, compared with only 1,500 at its inception in 1946, but it ceased publication following Hesson's retirement in 1956.

The exact size of the PC Women's Association during this early period is difficult to estimate, in part because constituent local and provincial groups expanded and disbanded with some frequency. For example, a biographical summary of leading Conservative women refers to the establishment in 1938 of a PC Women's Association of New Brunswick, which was founded by Katie MacKay upon her return from the Ottawa meeting with R.B. Bennett.[24] Later in this same report, a quotation from Lucy Sansom (who was elected president of the national association in 1954) suggests that the New Brunswick organization had grown moribund through the war years: 'When I came to New Brunswick after World

War II, I found no Women's Associations, although a few women had gone to meetings and tried to hold things together. I organized Women's Associations in the cities, towns, and villages and as the men of the province gave us no financial help, I had membership cards printed and sold. For membership we charged $1.00—of which 50 cents went to the Provincial Women's Association.'[25]

A similar pattern of wax and wane occurred in many other regions of Canada where Conservative women's associations were organized, only to succumb to the pressures of wartime work or an absence of local activists. Available sources indicate that PC activists in Fredericton attracted 'over one hundred women' to meetings held in 1948,[26] while the Victoria Women's Association 'had a membership of one hundred names' in this same period.[27]

In practical terms, the activities of Conservative women through the 1960s generally resembled those of their counterparts in the Liberal party. In campaign organizations, for example, Conservative women frequently performed stereotypically feminine tasks, as the president of the Alberta PC Women's Association observed following the 1962 federal elections. According to Eva MacLean, Tory women 'should be the best cooks in the world after the thousands of cookies, donuts and sandwiches they made for "meet-the-candidate" receptions'.[28]

The element of personal and collective ferment that developed in response to these tasks, however, surfaced somewhat later than in the Liberal case. One 1966 Progressive Conservative Women's Association report, for example, concluded that organized Tory women should 'oust the Liberal government' and defend Conservative philosophy.[29] The view that PC women should coalesce for the purpose of improving their own status in the party and broader political process did not take shape organizationally until 1981, approximately eight years after the establishment of newer women's groups in both the Liberal and New Democratic parties. In the interim, Conservative women provided valuable support services to the parent organization and, like their Liberal counterparts, made important contributions to the election of female legislative candidates, including federal MPs Margaret Aitken[30] and Sybil Bennett.[31]

WOMEN IN THE CO-OPERATIVE COMMONWEALTH FEDERATION

The development of women's organizations in the CCF/NDP is more complex than in either the Liberal or Conservative cases, in part because separate, constitutionally recognized women's associations were never established on a national scale. As the 1970 *Report* of the Royal Commission noted, the NDP 'has never had a separate women's organization. It has had federal and provincial women's committees which were, in effect, standing committees. Women, as well as men, are full members of the constituency, provincial and federal associations.'[32] The egalitarian ideology of the CCF and NDP, combined with the challenge involved in founding a new national organization, thus impeded the formation of the types of auxiliary support structures that evolved in the two older parties.

Although this institutional background suggests that from the outset CCF women were full and equal participants with men, historical research points toward a somewhat different conclusion. Studies by John Manley, Dean Beeby and Joan Sangster indicate that women were generally fewer in number, less politically influential and more likely to perform conventional feminine (including clerical, fund-raising and social) tasks in the party than men.[33] These patterns suggest that traditional gender role socialization cut across class and ideological lines; the existence of conflict within the CCF over female participation, therefore, is worth exploring in some detail.

Early materials on the CCF suggest that from the party's inception in 1932, the task of building a new national organization demanded sustained commitment from all members, whether male or female. Enormous human energy was required to establish a unified, grass-roots social movement, and to dislodge the entrenched two-party system.[34] Women were thus encouraged and expected to 'pitch in', which many did in such diverse capacities as legislator (federal MP and later Ontario MPP Agnes Macphail and BC MLA Dorothy Steeves are notable examples from the early years), party propagandist (Grace MacInnis, later an MP, co-wrote at least three publications during the 1930s), provincial functionary (both the Saskatchewan and Manitoba parties had women as provincial secretaries or directors during the 1930s), and general purpose volunteer. Clearly, this last category embraced many CCF women who were active as riding-level and especially campaign workers. In the words of one early activist, 'we were always trying to branch out, so whenever we found people, male or female, who would contribute, we put them to work. It was such a struggle to keep the party alive at all.'[35]

One significant dispute regarding female participation in the CCF during these early decades concerned separate versus integrated approaches to involvement—an issue that continued to draw attention in the NDP as well as the two older parties through the 1990s. In the province of Ontario in particular, CCF members frequently differed over questions such as the following. First, were women equal participants in the mainstream CCF organization and, if not, could the establishment of an affiliated women's committee remedy this situation? Second, should the party develop a distinctive electoral strategy to attract women voters and new female activists? And third, would the development and implementation of such a strategy be controlled by a formally constituted women's group in the party? These three questions, while deceptively simple, involved complex issues related to organizational cohesion, the power of central party bureaucrats and, particularly in the case of the early CCF, the role of 'united front' alliances with other leftist, especially Communist party, women.

Some disputes involving the role of women and women's organizations in the Ontario CCF came to the fore during the mid-1930s, when a group known as the Toronto CCF Women's Joint Committee attempted to establish what John Manley terms 'an autonomous agency of sexual and political struggle'.[36] Briefly, the Women's Joint Committee grew out of 'united front' activities by a number of left-wing CCF women in Toronto. For approximately six months during 1936, veterans of the Canadian League against War and Fascism (a Communist party front group) worked together in this committee 'to promote female activity on the widest possible basis'.[37] As critics of 'the standard party clubs [which] failed to provide their women members with adequate opportunities' in public speaking and political leadership, Joint Committee activists set out to establish an affiliated but independently directed women's organization.[38]

Their success in challenging the status of women in the CCF was limited by frequent charges of 'united front' collusion. In a period when the CCF was increasingly concerned with electoral respectability, party functionaries carefully avoided involvement in any activities which might be perceived as Communist-inspired or otherwise politically 'tainted'. The willingness of the Women's Joint Committee to violate official party doctrine on this point led to the eventual expulsion of many of its key activists, including Jean Laing and Elizabeth Morton. Those who remained within the CCF often became resigned to their traditional fate. As Caroline Riley (who later led the first Ontario CCF Women's Committee) observed in 1938, achieving electoral success meant that 'we must come back to the old business of women's organizations, for the present, that of financial aid. Little as some of us like that, we shall probably have to put on teas, bridges, raffles, etc., to fill the treasury.'[39]

Throughout the Depression and the Second World War, many CCF women indeed contributed valuable time and effort toward this end—as did their counterparts in the two older political parties. Therefore, although the ideological climate of the former was more egalitarian, and while a fair number of CCF women ascended to positions of political responsibility during this period (including Alice Loeb, a Joint Committee activist who became head of the Ontario CCF Literature Committee), the overall position of party women remained a source of concern to some members through the war years.

CCF WOMEN IN THE POST-WAR PERIOD

Conflicts concerning the role of affiliated women's groups, as well as an appropriate electoral approach to female voters, were particularly apparent in the Ontario CCF after 1945. Since these same issues continue to attract attention in all three major federal parties, the early Ontario debates warrant close consideration.

One issue of contention in the post-war CCF was the basic need for a women's organization in the party. Research suggests that opinions for and against were fairly clear cut.[40] On the affirmative side, such prominent CCFers as Marjorie Mann, Peggy Brewin and Alice Katool were convinced that, in order to achieve electoral success, the party needed to recruit more female activists and voters. In 1942, therefore, the Ontario party council established a women's committee, and three years later delegates to a CCF convention endorsed a resolution committing the party to 'draft a clear statement of CCF policy toward women'.[41]

Although a 1949 equal pay bill was among the only policy initiatives to follow from this resolution (it constituted one of the first efforts to introduce equal pay legislation in Canada), the organizational impact of the Women's Committee was substantial. As Dean Beeby reports:

> The Ontario CCF Women's Committee . . . was the first partisan female organization to be established as something other than an auxiliary to the main party structure. Whereas the Conservatives and Liberals had kept their women's groups organizationally separate, the CCF Women's Committee was established as a standing committee of the main party council and thus entitled to a continuing voice in CCF affairs.[42]

The central problem with this new committee was how it might go about influencing party activities. Would a separate network of local CCF women's groups provide the organizational base for the larger provincial committee? Many party members, both male and female, were uncomfortable with the idea of such a network, since it ran contrary to the basic CCF philosophy of integrated and unified party work.

A number of opponents of the committee either held major organizational responsibilities in the Ontario party or were close confidantes of party functionaries. Their perceptions, frequently grounded in a daily struggle for additional funds, members and electoral respectability, began with the assumption that there was little need for a separate women's section. According to this view, men or women who sought to become active in the CCF had abundant opportunities to do so, given that the party was in continual need of new volunteers.[43] Women who were active in the mainstream organization were particularly hesitant about the committee; in the words of one Ontario respondent: 'We didn't believe in separate associations because we didn't want to be set aside and apart. Marjorie Mann and Peggy Brewin felt that a Women's Committee could attract some of the non-political women, but we political women felt that the separate Committee would demote all of us within the larger organization.'[44]

The organizational strategy of the CCF Women's Committee was also of concern to party insiders, who questioned the ability of the group to recruit new members through women-oriented issue campaigns. These campaigns, which occasionally ran the risk of accusations of 'united front' collusion, attempted to draw housewives into the CCF through such activities as consumer price monitoring, cookbook projects and rummage sales. As stereotypically feminine activities, these projects were opposed by some CCF members who disagreed with the view that 'you should appeal to women where they were rather than where you thought they should be'.[45] Furthermore, the broader issue focus of the committee drew strong criticism on tactical grounds. According to one respondent who worked as a CCF organizer during the post-war years:

The Committee would do things that I thought were tactically wrong, like making women's issues separate, and letting them get hived off from the policy mainstream, whereas I wanted to see them integrated. I recall one resolution on day care which they brought to a provincial Council meeting during the 1950s. I was definitely sympathetic until they read a section calling for day care to be free. They were so ahead of their times—just think about day care in the 1950s, let alone making it free, and here we were, fighting against all those claims that the CCF was full of crazy spendthrifts. I successfully argued tactics against the free section, so it read something about day care being free only for poor women . . . Now looking back, I can see that they were trying to popularize issues and make an impact.[46]

Ultimately, these conflicts with party insiders, combined with internal strains between feminist activists and more traditional Women's Committee members, meant that by the late 1940s the group had become a relatively weak structure primarily 'engaged in activities reminiscent of a ladies' auxiliary'.[47] The very existence of such a committee, however, is important evidence that the question of female status in party organizations was significant as early as the Second World War period. Moreover, as a standing committee of the main party council, the Ontario Committee provided a useful model for subsequent feminist activists in the NDP and elsewhere—and foreshadowed important organizational problems that continue to confront party women's groups.

EFFORTS TOWARD REORGANIZATION IN THE NDP

A number of developments during the early 1960s and following helped to renew interest in questions of women's participation and, more specifically, in the issue of women's organizations inside the parties. One factor drawing attention to this subject was the establishment in 1961 of the New Democratic Party (known initially as the New Party), the formal successor to the CCF. In October 1961, Eva Latham was appointed to the newly created position of Director of Women's Activities in the federal NDP, a post that reported to the federal executive. During this same period, older CCF women's councils and groups were renamed as women's committees of the NDP, and a federal women's committee was established to advise the Director of Women's Activities. According to its initial statement of structure and purpose (dated August 1962), the national NDP Women's Committee was to include three members appointed by the federal council, as well as two members appointed from each constituent provincial council.

This federal committee believed that its mandate was similar to that of the Ontario CCF Women's Committee during the 1940s, namely to recognize 'that women in general, and housewives in particular, have specific interests, needs and problems'.[48] The NDP Women's Committee sought to mobilize, for partisan purposes, non-political women who were affiliated with 'trade union ladies' auxiliaries' and 'who are able to work for the party in special money raising or social events'.[49] By 1963 approximately 135 constituency-level women's committees had been established in the federal NDP, along with five provincial committees. In addition, through the mid-1960s a number of women's conferences were held in Ontario and British Columbia, and substantial monies were raised 'through the sale of cookbooks, earrings, and Christmas cards'.[50]

This traditional form of committee activity became increasingly outdated by the late 1960s, however. As Eva Latham, the director of NDP women's activities, observed in her report to a 1967 federal party council meeting, 'younger women were seeking answers to personal and community problems and were not just interested in fund-raising and social activities'.[51] Moreover, she explained, traditional committee activities drew limited interest because as a group, 'women were eager to improve their own financial, educational and career status'.[52] Latham's report was followed in 1968 by a federal executive decision to eliminate her position and, in 1969, by a constitutional amendment creating a new Participation of Women (POW) Committee at the federal level. This new group, a standing committee appointed by the federal council, was 'to assist and encourage women's participation in all forms of political activity'.[53]

This new mandate proved difficult to implement in the federal NDP, in part because of major organizational and ideological problems. On an organizational level, the appointment of a federal women's organizer, the relationship between this organizer and the POW Committee, and the method by which POW members would be selected remained contentious issues through the late 1970s. For example, delegates to the 1971 federal convention endorsed a resolution calling for the appointment of a women's organizer, but this position was not filled on a continuous basis until 1977, when Judy Wasylycia-Leis was hired by the federal executive. Prior to that year, a succession of hirings, dismissals and disputes between the federal executive and the POW Committee over the role of the women's organizer rendered the position largely inoperative.[54]

During this same period, conflict also developed around the selection of POW members. Proposals were offered as early as 1975 that committee members be elected by provincial women's groups, but it was not until 1977 that a federal constitutional amendment (article 8, section 1e) established POW representatives as specially designated delegates to the federal council, who were to be elected at their respective provincial conventions. Implementation of this change in turn was delayed until 1980, when all constituent provincial and territorial New Democratic parties chose designated POW delegates.

These organizational problems were frequently related to the ideologically conflictual atmosphere of the NDP during the late 1960s and following. The growth of a renewed women's movement, especially in the extra-parliamentary left of this period, held important consequences for NDP women, as did the development of a radical Waffle wing within the party. As reflected in a 1968 NDP brief to the Royal Commission on the Status of Women, two surveys of party women conducted in fifty-six communities across Canada showed growing identification with the grievances and ideals of the nascent feminist movement: 'Women expressed the view that they were conditioned, by tradition, to regard their role in public life as the quiet worker behind the scenes, the organizer for the more aggressive male . . . It is quite within the scope of this attitude that a woman would well find herself a recording secretary for a constituency association, but seldom its president.'[55] Ironically, this identification of a potential for discriminatory attitudes within the NDP was expressed in the same year that the federal party executive eliminated the Director of Women's Activities position. Major factional splits between right and left, establishment and anti-establishment, also developed in the NDP during this period. In particular, the organizational and ideological challenge presented by the radical Waffle group in 1970-72 included a demand that women's status within the party, as well as 'women's issue' policy concerns, receive increased attention.[56] A Waffle women's committee in the Ontario NDP was especially active during these years, and helped to organize a new ONDP women's committee following 1972.[57]

One apparent influence of the Waffle upon women's activities in the NDP continued long after the group's expulsion in June 1972. It involved a sense among some party insiders that the political loyalty of feminist activists was open to question; bluntly stated, associating with the Waffle had tainted party women much as 'united front' activities had contaminated them in the past. In the view of these establishment elites, newer women's caucuses, women's committees and demands for greater policy emphasis upon 'women's issues' were compromised by their connection with the Waffle, and thus constituted a potential threat to organizational unity. Moreover, the increasingly assertive position adopted by feminist women within the NDP—notably in the Rosemary Brown campaign for federal leadership in 1975—meant that the distinction between pro- and non-feminist party activists grew clearer over time.

In the longer term, though, the federal POW Committee, provincial women's committees and federal women's organizers did achieve meaningful gains for women in the NDP. The election of Audrey McLaughlin as party leader in 1989, the recruitment of greater numbers of females for party and public office, the development of policy initiatives on equal pay and other 'women's issues', the creation of the Agnes Macphail Fund and the adoption of internal party affirmative action rules (see Chapters 3 and 4) demonstrated the improved status of women both inside the NDP organization and in the political process more generally.

By the early 1990s the federal NDP had appointed two full-time staff members in Ottawa for their Women's Program, including a director who had run as a federal candidate (Abigail Pollonetsky).[58] Much of the work of this federal staff was devoted to overseeing the implementation of internal affirmative action, particularly through the recruitment of women candidates, and to continuing the fund-raising that would support those candidates via the Macphail Fund. These efforts involved co-ordination with provincial and territorial NDP affiliates, some of which had established their own affirmative action policies and fund-raising campaigns for women candidates.

AMALGAMATION IN THE LIBERAL PARTY

Just as the Liberal party in Ontario was the first to establish separate women's organizations during the suffrage period (the Toronto and Ontario Women's Liberal Associations were formed in 1913 and 1914, respectively), so it also initiated the movement towards amalgamating these older groups. In 1969, the Ontario Women's Liberal Association (OWLA) disbanded as part of an effort to increase female integration in the mainstream party organization. According to the minutes of a final OWLA executive meeting, the group was to integrate with the larger Liberal Party of Ontario (LPO) 'subject to the following provisions: (a) The Annual Meeting of the LPO on March 29, 1969, approve in their new constitution the guarantee of a minimum of two women on the Executive Committee of LPO'.[59]

Although the motion to amalgamate passed in 1969, its consequences for Liberal women remained problematical for some time following. First, a number of older activists who had long identified with OWLA became convinced that their organization was unjustly dissolved and, as evidence of their lingering dissatisfaction, wore OWLA pins at Liberal party functions through the 1980s. Furthermore, as will be discussed below, OWLA veterans maintained that the ability of Liberal women to become delegates to party meetings was impaired by efforts to integrate (and, in their view, destroy) older groups.

Second, amalgamation was organizationally complicated by the division of the LPO into separate federal (Liberal Party of Canada, Ontario; LPC(O)) and provincial (Ontario Liberal Party; OLP) wings following 1975. One effect of this division was that many Liberal feminists who supported integration became more involved with the federal than the provincial wing, so that although new national and Ontario Women's Liberal commissions were established (in 1973 and 1981, respectively), the provincial-level OLP was left without any women's affiliate. In short, the dissolution of OWLA in 1969, followed by a federal-provincial party split in the mid-1970s, meant that many older women's association activists grew disenchanted with the mainstream Liberal organization at the same time that younger female partisans were directing most of their energies towards the federal level.

The formation of the National Women's Liberal Commission in 1973 provided the focus for much of this activity. According to Joseph Wearing: 'Women at the national level first balked at the idea of integration, allegedly because the elderly members were afraid of losing their right to attend national meetings as women's delegates. In a final paternalistic coup de grâce, the national executive cut off their funding and in 1973 the women at last accepted the wisdom of disbanding the organization.'[60] An older Women's Liberal Federation was thus replaced in 1973 by the National Women's Liberal Commission (NWLC), whose membership encompassed all female members of all Liberal Party of Canada (LPC) organizations, including older women's clubs.

The Commission differed from its predecessor in a number of important ways. Perhaps most significantly, the executive of the NWLC was to be elected by and responsible to a caucus of all Liberal women, who would gather at each LPC convention to elect a national president and five regional represent-atives.[61] Unlike the older federation, which was constituted as a separate but affiliated support organization within the LPC, the newer NWLC was established as an integrated part of the larger party organization. Its statement of purpose reflected clearly the broader objectives behind amalgamation: 'The purpose of this organization shall be to represent and promote the interests of women within the Liberal Party of Canada and to encourage the active participation of women at all levels of the Party.'[62] As in the NDP, therefore, integrating more women inside the mainstream party organization was to be a key priority of the new Women's Liberal Commission.

Implementing this mandate inside the LPC, however, proved equally difficult. In terms of paid staff, the commission was frequently without a full-time liaison person in party headquarters; in February 1992, for example, budget troubles in the federal Liberal organization led to the loss of the women's director position. Furthermore, while the NWLC succeeded in publicizing internally the status of Liberal women, particularly through its informal recruitment activities, the Judy LaMarsh Fund (see Chapter 4) and an effective series of flyers and fact sheets,[63] the group evolved as an uneasy alliance between older auxiliary and newer fem-inist elements. In the words of one early member of the NWLC executive, 'I realized soon after my election that these women from across the country were *not* fem-inists—although eventually more feminists became involved.' The gap between auxiliary and feminist perspectives was also identified by one regional repre-sentative to the NWLC executive, who remarked that 'the Commission embraces women at very different stages of political development. At one extreme you find those . . . who are very integrated in the federal mainstream, while at the other you find groups of farm women, for example, who retain something of an auxiliary mentality.'

The challenge of reconciling older supportive with newer assertive notions regarding the role of party women's groups was also a problem for constituent bodies of the LPC, including the federal Liberal organization in Ontario (LPC[O]). As a result of the dissolution of OWLA in 1969, and the subsequent federal-provincial division of its parent party following 1975, women's clubs in the newly created federal wing in Ontario temporarily lost their right to elect delegates to party conventions. This loss remained a source of resentment among OWLA activists, who noted that older groups of Liberal women in New Brunswick and elsewhere had retained their constitutional right to delegate.

In an effort to reinstate women's delegates, and thus increase numerical rep-resentation at party conventions, members of a Standing Committee on Women in the LPC(O) recommended in 1981 that each recognized women's club or as-sociation in the province be allowed to send two voting delegates to every con-vention. This constitutional amendment permitting women's delegates was passed in November 1981, along with a number of modifications creating the Ontario

Women's Liberal Commission.[64] Older and newer perspectives on the role of Liberal women thus converged somewhat, as the need for province- or nation-wide organization and for increased numbers of female convention delegates became clearer to both sides. Yet the decline of traditional groups continued; by the early 1990s, fewer than twenty federal Liberal women's clubs existed in Ontario.[65]

At the federal level, the National Women's Liberal Commission remains entrusted with the job of certifying constituent women's clubs, each of which can send one delegate to federal conventions. As well, the president of the NWLC is appointed to the federal party executive and to the management committee of the Liberal Party of Canada. In addition to the loss of the federal women's director position (see above), budgetary problems in the Liberal organization have threatened to cut travel allowances for NWLC executive members attending federal party committee meetings. These financial difficulties further complicate the question of whether a women's commission can enhance female involvement in mainstream Liberal politics while actively encouraging participation in (and convention delegation through) separate clubs or associations at the local level.

We shall now consider the emergence of a similar dilemma in the Progressive Conservative party.

WOMEN'S ORGANIZATIONS IN THE CONSERVATIVE PARTY

Unlike the New Democratic and Liberal parties, which reorganized their federal women's organizations during the early 1970s, the Conservative party retained its older Women's Association through 1980. In fact, one summary of party involvement among Canadian women reports that as of 1967, the PC Women's Association had a membership of approximately 75,000.[66]

Attempts to reform this association emerged from discussions both inside the group and within the national executive of the parent PC party. According to a number of accounts, the last seven years of the association's existence (from 1973 to 1980) were marked by frequent internal questioning of the reasons for its existence. In the words of one respondent: 'The Association met during that period for about two hours at each national convention, asking itself whether or not to exist. Then, those in attendance went to lunch with the wife of the federal party leader. It simply grew into a blue-rinse set . . . They were a small group who were busy re-electing each other.'

Concern over the viability and direction of the PC Women's Association was also expressed in the national executive. By the summer of 1980, party elites began to question why they should continue funding an increasingly moribund organization. At the same time, a number of Association activists recognized the imminent demise of the older group and proposed to the executive a major reorganization along the lines of the National Women's Political Caucus in the United States. The purpose of a new women's group, in the view of PC caucus advocates, would be to recruit more female activists for involvement in the party mainstream; in fact, the proposed theme for the new PC Women's Caucus was 'Into the Mainstream'.[67]

The method by which party women were to be integrated, however, proved at least as contentious in the Conservative organization as it had in the New Democratic and Liberal parties. On the level of organization, the National PC Women's Caucus grew out of a name-change meeting of the older association in February 1981, but was frequently confused both with the latter and with new local caucuses established by the Women's Bureau (located in the national party headquarters). The National Caucus differed from its predecessor in that 'every women who is a member in good standing of any Association of the Progressive Conservative Party of Canada, Provincially or Territorially', was designated as a Caucus member.[68] Like the National Women's Liberal Commission, the PC National Caucus was composed of all female party members, with voting membership open to all female delegates to party conventions. The National Caucus executive, elected at each convention, included a president; a director of the Women's Bureau; ten provincial vice-presidents, each of whom presided over a provincial women's association; and ten provincial representatives.[69] In 1984, the National Caucus was replaced by the National Progressive Conservative Women's Federation (NPCWF), with a structure and purpose similar to those of the caucus.

One source of confusion that led to this name change involved the relationship between the national women's group, on the one hand, and local women's caucuses and riding associations, on the other. Following the contribution of more than $30,000 by former Ottawa MP Jean Pigott, the federal Conservatives established a three-member Women's Bureau in their national headquarters in January 1981.[70] The first director of the Women's Bureau, Barbara Ford, worked to establish a network of city or regional women's caucuses in urban areas with populations of more than 100,000.[71]

Although Ford's initiative began as an attempt to provide female partisans with an adjunct or alternative route to political mobility through riding associations, some of which were inactive between elections or not receptive to new female (and especially younger feminist) recruits, it tended to blur an important distinction between the national and local organizations. That is, the local or regional caucuses—generally referred to as Federal PC Women's Caucuses—were designed as relatively small-scale skills training groups, in contrast to the national group, which was established as an advisory and lobby organization at the national level.[72] The Federal Caucuses were perceived in some quarters as competing with established constituency associations, even though their original mandate was to operate as specialized recruitment vehicles for the eventual benefit of local ridings. Conservatives initially planned on about 30 local caucuses, of which only 14 had been established by the early 1990s.

On a more ideological plane, the PC caucuses received an uneasy reception among supporters of older party women's groups. In Nova Scotia and Ontario, in particular, traditional women's associations continued to operate even after the dissolution of the National Association, so that friction persisted between older and newer groups. As one National Caucus activist reflected in light of her experiences between 1980 and 1982, 'It's been a long two years trying to address these people who feel threatened.' Ten years later, more than 200 PC women's associations remained, although their membership—especially in urban areas—continued to decline.

Probably the most vocal opposition to change in the Conservative party came from the Ontario Progressive Conservative Association of Women (OPCAW), a provincially based group established in 1973. OPCAW primarily attracted older Conservative women who, although extremely active as party workers, remained loyal to an essentially supportive or auxiliary role in the mainstream PC Organization.[73] This purpose was reflected in one official statement of principles: 'OPCAW exists to strengthen the capability of women to be of service to the Party, to share information of importance with its membership and to draw the matters of concern of its membership to the attention of the Party and the Government.'[74] The Ontario group considered and rejected amalgamation at several meetings, including one in 1976 at which provincial MPP and cabinet minister Dr Bette Stephenson stated that women's associations were 'dangerously close to being irrelevant'.[75] This allegation was denied by a core of OPCAW activists, who maintained that PC success in Ontario was largely dependent on the existence of parallel female support structures at both the riding and provincial levels.[76]

Internal conflicts between older and newer approaches to the organization of Conservative women revealed themselves at a June 1982 meeting of OPCAW in Toronto. Since no executive positions in OPCAW were contested, the president of the National PC Women's Caucus, Elizabeth Willcock, was invited to address the group. Willcock began her speech by acknowledging the dedicated work of OPCAW activists, but followed these comments with a reference to the 'anachronistic' nature of women's associations in the party. Her description of the National Caucus, Women's Bureau and city caucuses concluded with the statement that younger women in particular desired 'fuller participation in the political process . . . and input into all issue areas. Canadian women must walk into the twenty-first century with full equality in all spheres of our society.'[77]

Willcock's address was followed by a question-and-answer session in which a number of OPCAW delegates expressed their confusion regarding the relationship among older associations, the National PC Women's Caucus, city caucuses and riding associations. More importantly, some participants challenged Willcock to explain why, in establishing a new national caucus in 1981, PC women on the federal level had forfeited their right to recognize independently local women's associations, which could in turn send delegates to party conventions.[78] This issue of delegation to conventions, combined with a general sense that the federally based caucuses were overly assertive and feminist, contributed to the defeat of an OPCAW constitutional amendment that would have formally recognized the National PC Women's Caucus. In the words of one strong opponent of the amendment, 'By recognizing this new National Women's Caucus, we automatically unrecognize existing federal women's associations in Ontario, which I don't think any of us in OPCAW would want to do.'

The integration of women within the Conservative mainstream, and the amalgamation of older women's groups at the federal level, was thus complicated by major organizational and ideological difficulties. Yet the forces of change in party organizations clearly had an effect in the Ontario Conservative organization: by 1992, OPCAW was nearly defunct, with only about 30 active members and constituent women's associations in only six rural ridings.[79]

CONCLUSIONS

This chapter has traced the historical development of women's associations in the Liberal, Conservative and CCF/NDP organizations from the early suffrage period through the present. Overall, it suggests that despite continuing tensions within party organizations, older auxiliary-type attitudes and women's groups are gradually being replaced either by more explicitly pro-feminist ones, or by integrated structures that do not include women's units of any type. Unlike traditional associations, which frequently functioned as support structures for mainstream parties, newer party women's groups tend to emphasize increased female representation in party activities.

We shall now turn to a cross-cultural examination of women and party politics, one portion of which considers the development of party women's groups in comparative perspective.

NOTES

[1] Judy LaMarsh, *Memoirs of a Bird in a Gilded Cage* (Toronto: McClelland and Stewart, 1969), 281.

[2] Report of the Royal Commission on the Status of Women in Canada (Ottawa: Information Canada, 1970), 348, emphasis in original.

[3] See Catherine L. Cleverdon, *The Woman Suffrage Movement in Canada* (Toronto: University of Toronto Press, 1974), 98, 114, 204.

[4] In this same vein, Cleverdon (ibid., 273) remarks that the willingness of Canadian women to be restricted to 'ladies' auxiliaries in the parties . . . has resulted in their doing much of the drudgery, with payment in the form of "window dressing" jobs and a gentle pat on the back'.

[5] *Report* of the RCSW, 348.

[6] See Joseph Wearing, *The L-Shaped Party: The Liberal Party of Canada, 1958-1980* (Toronto: McGraw-Hill Ryerson, 1980), 216 ff.

[7] Toronto Women's Liberal Association, Historian's Report, mimeo (undated).

[8]See Florence Tilden Harrison, 'Fifty Years with the Ontario Women's Liberal Association, 1914-1965', mimeo (undated).

[9]Ibid., 7.

[10]Cleverdon, *The Woman Suffrage Movement in Canada*; Elsie Gregory MacGill, *My Mother the Judge*, with an Introduction by Naomi Black (Toronto: Peter Martin, 1981); and Diane Crossley, 'The B.C. Liberal Party and Women's Reforms, 1916-1928', in Barbara Latham and Cathy Kess, eds., *In Her Own Right* (Victoria: Camosun College, 1980), 229-53.

[11]See Valerie Knowles, *First Person: A Biography of Cairine Wilson, Canada's First Woman Senator* (Toronto: Dundurn Press, 1988); and Franca Iacovetta, '"A Respectable Feminist": The Political Career of Senator Cairine Wilson, 1921-1962', in Linda Kealey and Joan Sangster, eds., *Beyond the Vote: Canadian Women and Politics* (Toronto: University of Toronto Press, 1989), 63-85.

[12]See Patricia A. Myers, '"A Noble Effort": The National Federation of Liberal Women of Canada, 1928-1973', in Kealey and Sangster, eds., *Beyond the Vote*, 39-62.

[13]See Patricia A. Myers, '"A Noble Effort": The National Federation of Liberal Women of Canada, 1945-1973', MA thesis, University of Waterloo, 1980, chaps 1, 2.

[14]Ibid., title page.

[15]Tuesday Luncheon Club, 25th Anniversary Certificate, 1973.

[16]Interview with Mary Lancitie, 1 March 1983.

[17]Interview with Marian Maloney, 30 April 1992.

[18]Harrison, 'Fifty Years', 14-15.

[19]Ibid., 18.

[20]LaMarsh, *Memoirs*, 5.

[21]Gladys Taylor, *Madam President* (Ottawa: Progressive Conservative Women's Association of Canada, 1966), 9, 27.

[22]Ibid., 10.

[23]See ibid. for a review of this period.

[24]Ibid., 16.

[25]Lucy Samson, as quoted in ibid., 23.

[26]Ibid., 23.

[27]Ibid., 20.

[28]Eva MacLean, as quoted in ibid., 14.

[29]Ibid., 14.

[30]See Margaret Aitken, *Hey Ma! I Did It* (Toronto: Clarke, Irwin, 1953).

[31]See Taylor, *Madam President*, 21-2.

[32]*Report* of the RCSW, 347.

[33]John Manley, 'Women and the Left in the 1930s: The Case of the Toronto CCF Women's Joint Committee', *Atlantis* 5:2 (1980), 100-19; Dean Beeby, 'Women in the Ontario CCF, 1940-1950', *Ontario History* 74:4 (1982), 258-83; and Joan Sangster, *Dreams of Equality: Women on the Canadian Left, 1920-1950* (Toronto: McClelland and Stewart, 1989).

[34]See Walter D. Young, *The Anatomy of a Party: The National CCF, 1932-61* (Toronto: University of Toronto Press, 1969).

[35]Interview with Marjorie Wells, 1 March 1983.

[36]Manley, 'Women and the Left', 101.

[37]Ibid., 111.

[38]Ibid.

[39]Caroline M. Riley, 'Women and the CCF', as quoted in ibid., 116-17.

[40]See Beeby, 'Women in the Ontario CCF'.

[41]CCF 12th Provincial Convention, 1945 (Ontario), as quoted in ibid., 266.

[42]Beeby, 'Women in the Ontario CCF', 269.

[43]Some of these opponents ackowledge that, in hindsight, the opportunities available to female recruits may have differed from those available to males.

[44]Interview with Margaret Lazarus, 5 April 1983.

[45]Ibid.

[46]Interview with Marjorie Wells.

[47]Beeby, 'Women in the Ontario CCF', 278. This same period was characterized by a weakening of recruitment activities in the Ontario CCF generally. On the increased use of women as sacrifice candidates following Second World War, see Leo Zakuta, A Protest Movement Becalmed (Toronto: University of Toronto Press, 1964).

[48]'Women's Committees, New Democratic Party', mimeo dated August 1962, 1.

[49]Ibid.

[50]'New Democratic Party, Development of Participation of Women', mimeo dated January 1982, 1.

[51]Ibid., 2.

[52]Ibid.

[53]Ibid.

[54]See ibid., 2-3.

[55]Brief submitted by the New Democratic Party to the Royal Commission on the Status of Women, 11 March 1968, 9-10.

[56]See Krista Maeots, 'The Role of Women in Canadian Society and the Implications of This for the NDP', paper presented to NDP Federal Council, 19 September 1970.

[57]Interview with Marianne Holder, 22 March 1983.

[58]See Abigail Pollonetsky, 'Coming out of the MS Closet', Globe and Mail, 20 April 1992.

[59]Minutes of the Executive Meeting of the Ontario Women's Liberal Association, 26 March 1969, 2.

[60]Wearing, The L-Shaped Party, 218. A recommendation that older women's organizations in the Liberal Party be integrated was made in the 1972 Final Report of the Liberal Party of Canada Task Force on the Status of Women. According to a summary of Task Force recommendations, 'The Commission encountered the opinion that the political women's associations are a deterrent to women who would like to contribute to politics in significant ways.' See Esther Greenglass, 'Summary of Task Force Recommendations', mimeo, 2.

[61]See Women's Liberal Commission By-Laws (July 1980), paras 5 and 6. The national executive of the WLC was to include provincial representatives, one French and one English vice-president, and the immediate past president of the WLC.

[62]Ibid., para. 2. This same mandate for the Women's Commission appears in the 1986 constitution of the federal Liberal organization.

[63]These included 'Women for a Change' flyer, undated; 'Canadian Women have Terrible Figures' fact sheet, May 1980; 'Exploding the Myths' fact sheet, May 1980.

[64]See 'Constitutional Amendments as Proposed by Kay Manderville, Chair LPC(O) Women's Committee', mimeo, 4-5.

[65]Interview with Marian Maloney.

[66]Jean Cochrane, *Women in Canadian Life: Politics* (Toronto: Fitzhenry and Whiteside, 1977), 60.

[67]Interview with Elizabeth Willcock, then president of the National PC Women's Caucus, 12 June 1982.

[68]Constitution of the National Progressive Conservative Women's Caucus, as amended 26 February 1981, article 3.

[69]Notably, 'the wife of the Leader of the Party automatically is to be an Honorary Member of the Executive as well as the wives of former Leaders of the Party'. See ibid., article 5, section 6.

[70]See 'The Ottawa Scene: A Not so Fond Farewell to Politics', *Globe and Mail*, 20 December 1980, 8.

[71]By 1982, 28 cities had been targeted for a federal PC women's caucus. See 'Politics Isn't Just a Man's Game', Women's Bureau leaflet, undated.

[72]Interview with Barbara Ford, 22 April 1982. According to the terms of article 4, section c, of the National PC Women's Caucus constitution, city caucuses could send four delegates and four alternates to vote at National Caucus annual meetings.

[73]On the age, party involvement and attitudes of OPCAW activists, see Sylvia B. Bashevkin, 'Social Background and Political Experience: Gender Differences among Ontario Provincial Party Elites, 1982', *Atlantis* 9:1 (Fall 1983), 1-12; and 'Political Participation, Ambition and Feminism: Women in the Ontario Party Elites', *American Review of Canadian Studies* 15:4 (Winter 1985), 405-19.

[74]'Progressive Conservative Associations of Women', mimeo, last para.

[75]Stephenson as quoted in Mary Trueman, 'Bette Stephenson says Conservative Women's Associations "Outdated"', *Globe and Mail*, 12 April 1976. Stephenson stands by her earlier statement that 'the P.C. women's Association is an anachronism . . . I simply cannot see any reason for segregation on the basis of sex in political or professional associations.' Interview with Dr Bette Stephenson, 5 October 1982.

[76]Interview with Aase Hueglin, then president of OPCAW, 1 December 1981.

[77]Elizabeth Willcock, address to OPCAW annual meeting, Downtown Holiday Inn, Toronto, 13 June 1982.

[78]As of the 1982 OPCAW meeting, federal riding associations rather than the National Caucus had the power to recognize women's groups.

[79]These data on the Ontario Progressive Conservatives were provided by Allan Williams and Elizabeth Burnham.

CHAPTER SIX

Comparative Perspectives on Women and Party Politics

One hundred years hence, what a change will be made
In politics, morals, religion, and trade,
In statesmen who wrangle or ride on the fence
These things will be altered a hundred years hence.
                    —Frances Dana Gage, 'A Hundred Years Hence', 1852[1]

The formal entrance of women to many political systems of North America and Western Europe was accompanied by widespread expectations of rapid moral improvement, particularly in the corrupt domain of party politics. As one women's rights advocate in the US, Frances Dana Gage, predicted in a song composed in 1852, enfranchised females would generate sweeping changes 'in politics, morals, religion, and trade'.[2]

The subsequent extent of women's political influence has, in popular terms, been associated with the individual careers of Golda Meir, Indira Gandhi, Margaret Thatcher, Gro Harlem Brundtland and others who obtained positions of major party leadership, followed by prime ministerial responsibility. The national and international profiles of these leaders suggested to some observers, including a number of Canadian writers, that women's political experiences were no longer defined by their suffragist beginnings, traditional patterns of gender role socialization or discriminatory treatment within political institutions.[3] Instead, the achievements of specific individuals were viewed as 'proof' that historical and social constraints no longer limited women in politics.

This chapter adopts a different perspective in its comparative examination of women and party politics. Rather than beginning with the careers of a handful of exceptional cases, such as Brundtland, Gandhi, Meir and Thatcher and questioning why Canada has thus far failed to elect a similarly exceptional female prime minister, it proposes that the general experiences of women in Western party systems closely resemble the patterns described above in Chapters 1 through 5. We argue, for example, that the political wedging of early feminism and suffragism in English Canada was paralleled in other North American and Western

European cultures, where broader demands for social reform as well as the events of the First and Second World Wars frequently combined to obscure basic women's rights concerns. Furthermore, it appears that patterns of public opinion and party participation in these same systems vary by gender. In short—to take one obvious example—women's involvement in British party politics generally bears a closer resemblance to the phenomenon of under-representation outlined in earlier chapters on Canada than it does to the popularly cited 'exceptional case' of Margaret Thatcher.[4]

In exploring these questions, we rely upon a growing comparative literature on women and politics.[5] Our discussion begins with a brief review of the historical context of enfranchisement in areas outside English Canada, using Richard Evans's distinction between Catholic and Protestant cultures as a starting point.[6] We then consider the relationship between this historical background and patterns of public opinion. The next section examines patterns of party involvement, including local constituency-level, campaign and legislative participation. As in Chapter 4, we consider efforts to increase female representation on elite levels and, as in Chapter 5, evaluate the effectiveness of women's organizations in political parties.

Although this chapter presents only a brief overview of comparative research on women and party politics, it does provide important cross-cultural perspectives on the political status of women. Moreover, in examining the Canadian case in light of these perspectives, it points towards a number of possible directions for future research.

THE HISTORICAL DIMENSION

In his comparative study of feminism in Western democracies, Richard Evans suggested a useful distinction between women's political experiences in Catholic and Protestant cultures.[7] He compared women's political development in predominantly Catholic societies (such as those of France and Quebec), where traditional values regarding women's roles were deeply entrenched and where feminists faced strong clerical as well as political opposition in their pursuit of political rights, with that in Protestant systems (such as those of the United States, Great Britain and English Canada), where women's roles were less strictly circumscribed and where feminist activists had somewhat less difficulty in pursuing legal reforms.

Because traditional norms regarding 'woman's sphere' were better established and more vigorously defended in Catholic than in Protestant cultures, Evans and others have suggested that attempts by nineteenth- and early twentieth-century feminists to alter conventional gender roles were more successful (and occurred at an earlier date) in the latter than in the former.[8] The fact that suffragists in major Anglo-American cultures were able to obtain the vote during the period of the First World War, while enfranchisement was restricted until the Second World War period in Quebec, France and Italy, clearly illustrates this argument.

As was noted in Chapter 2 with reference to Canada, historical research suggests that 'dual cultures' within systems have also shaped the political lives of women and men; this interpretation takes issue with the traditional view that a condition of 'lagged modernization' impeded women's political development. Many comparative studies, however, including an important empirical article by Margaret Inglehart, have borrowed the imagery of the conventional lag argument.[9] In analysing patterns of political interest in Western Europe, Inglehart maintained that 'the historical experience of a given nation (whether Catholic or Protestant) has left an imprint on the relative politicization of the respective sexes in that society as a whole'.[10]

Arguments that women remain less politically engaged than men neglect the greater involvement of females in community-based, informal politics;[11] as well, they can be interpreted as supporting the 'defective' or 'deviant politicization' thesis. As Thelma McCormack points out, proponents of the lagged modernization view assume that females will gradually be 'integrated' as they adopt male political beliefs and behaviours.[12] McCormack contrasts these integrationist assumptions with the dual cultures view, which essentially rejects male norms as a basis for measuring female 'deviance'. In conjunction with research on women's history and ongoing disparities between female and male experience, the two cultures perspective would predict distinctive patterns of political behaviour—and see full integration as neither normatively desirable nor empirically likely. As McCormack writes:

> We have a women's political culture which is more of a parallel and alternative culture rather than an oppositional or counter culture. But there is an enduring tension between the two gendered cultures based on the misperceptions and misunderstandings which arise out of sex-roles and differential power.[13]

McCormack's perspective helps to explain the substantial gender differences that have been observed in levels of political interest and awareness within cultures, as well as the differences across systems. Together with historical research by Evans, it points towards at least two common threads connecting women's early political experiences in Catholic and Protestant environments. First, an important alliance linked early feminist and suffragist activism, on the one hand, and broader social reform movements, on the other. Whether defined in terms of radical secularism and anti-clericalism (as in France), or urban improvement, temperance and child welfare (as in the US and English Canada), early feminism maintained a clear connection with wider reformist activities, particularly in those political systems where a divisive struggle over enfranchisement ensued. In the 'frontier societies' of the American West, Australia and New Zealand, such alliances and prolonged debates were rarely necessary, in part because of widespread assumptions that female voters would 'civilize' politics in rough frontier areas.[14]

Second, historical materials indicate that despite their alliances with broader reform movements, early feminists frequently saw their key legislative concerns excluded from the main political agenda of the day. In France, Quebec and other Catholic cultures, female enfranchisement was often opposed by clerical and political authorities for fear that certain social institutions, notably the family, would suffer, should women gain increased rights. Feminist arguments thus became wedged in wider systemic disputes involving right and left, clericalism and anti-clericalism, with the result that women themselves did not necessarily become an independent political force during these debates or even with the formal granting of political rights during the 1940s.[15]

In Protestant, Anglo-American societies, a similar type of wedging occurred as a result of the events of the First World War. In the United States, Great Britain and English Canada, enfranchisement was granted more in reward for women's wartime contributions than in recognition of a broad social consensus regarding female rights to legal equality. The large majority of non-suffragist women in Protestant cultures thus gained formal political equality following limited direct public debate over their rights and roles; in fact, their enfranchisement was generally overshadowed by wartime mobilization and by concurrent changes or realignments in the party systems of Great Britain, the United States and English Canada.[16]

Do comparative data support a dual cultures argument? What attitudinal evidence suggests a link between early feminism and social reform, or a political wedging of suffragism in both Catholic and Protestant contexts? The following sections begin to explore these questions.

THE DUAL CULTURES QUESTION

The relationship between women's political history during the enfranchisement period and subsequent attitudinal and participatory patterns can be evaluated most directly with reference to the French political system. In France, survey-based electoral research was initiated shortly after General de Gaulle decreed female enfranchisement in 1944; this coincidence makes it possible to examine trends in political interest, electoral abstention and survey non-response from a relatively early date. In view of the more lengthy gap between enfranchisement and the beginnings of electoral research in other Western cultures, including those of Great Britain, Italy, Canada and the United States, the value of this coincidence becomes especially clear. French data permit us to evaluate the behavioural impact of women's enfranchisement-period experiences and to trace subsequent changes in political engagement.

Table 6.1 shows that men reported considerably greater political interest in post-war France than women. As could be expected given the background to suffrage in Catholic cultures generally, the largest gender difference in political interest (32 percent) occurred in 1953, the first year for which data were available; levels of female political interest tended to increase nearly 20 percent through the late 1970s, while relatively little change occurred among men. Women therefore became increasingly interested in politics over time, even though their absolute level of interest remained substantially below that of men.[17]

To use the language of the modernization thesis, French women remained 'behind' men for decades after formal enfranchisement, whether measured with reference to political interest (Table 6.1) or electoral abstentions (Table 6.2). Figures on non-voting in 1951 versus 1973 legislative elections, for example, show little change over time in the turnout levels of either men or women: the gender differential in both years remained at a level of 7 percent (Table 6.2). Data on survey non-response indicate that gender differences in non-response for both 1968 and 1978 were in the 3 percent to 4 percent range, as compared with 14 percent in 1958. Decreases over time in both the level of female non-response and the gender differences in non-response indicate greater politicization of French women, especially between 1958 and 1968, but they also show a continuation of older differences.

The persistence of many patterns over time in the French case parallels the Canadian data presented in Chapter 2. Moreover, the same tendency for levels of political engagement to continue to vary by sex even decades after enfranchisement is evident in research by Marian Sawer and Marian Simms on Australia,[18] Carol Christy's study of the US and West Germany,[19] and Joni Lovenduski's summary of Italian, Austrian, British and West German sources.[20] As Lovenduski writes:

TABLE 6.1   POLITICAL INTEREST AMONG FRENCH WOMEN AND MEN, 1953-1978[a]

	1953	1958	1965	1969	1970	1976	1978
Women	40	46.8	53	53	31	59.9	59.4
Men	72	69.4	64	66	47	78.4	71.7
Difference, women – men	–32	–22.6	–11	–13	–16	–18.5	–12.3

[a]All data are derived from nation-wide samples with the exception of the 1965 figures, which are drawn from a study of Boulogne-Billancourt, a working-class area of Paris. Each entry represents the percentage of respondents professing any level of interest in politics, except for the 1976 and 1978 results which combine the percentage of cases reporting frequent or occasional political discussion.

SOURCES: 1958 French Election Study; Euro-barometres no. 6 (1976) and no. 10 (1978); Mattei Dogan and Jacques Narbonne, *Les françaises face à la politique* (Paris: A. Colin, 1955); Guy Michelat, 'Attitudes et comportements politiques dans une agglomération de la région parisienne', in Gérard Adam et al., eds., *L'élection présidentielle des 5 et 19 décembre 1965* (Paris: A. Colin, 1965); Gisèle Charzat, *Les françaises, sont-elles des citoyennes?* (Paris: Denoël, 1972); Philippe Braud, *Le comportement électoral en France* (Paris: Presses Universitaires de France, 1973); and Janine Mossuz-Lavau and Mariette Sineau, *Les femmes françaises en 1978* (Paris: CORDES, 1980).

TABLE 6.2 ELECTORAL ABSTENTIONS AMONG FRENCH WOMEN AND MEN, 1951-1978[a]

YEAR / TYPE OF ELECTION	1951 LEGIS.	1953 MUNIC.	1958 REFER.	1962 REFER.	1962 LEGIS.	1965 PARIS MUNIC.	1965 PRES.	1967 LEGIS.	1968 LEGIS.	1969 REFER.	1969 PRES.	1973 LEGIS.	1977 PARIS MUNIC.	1978 VIENNE LEGIS.
Female abstentions	24	25	53	27	30	32	18	24	27	23	32	25	31	18.9
Male abstentions	17	13	47	17	18	24	11	17	14	16	34	18	30	16.7
Difference, women – men	7	12	6	10	12	8	7	7	13	7	-2	7	1	2.2

[a]Cell entries represent the percentage of electoral abstentions, with figures on presidential elections derived from the second round of voting.

SOURCES: Georges Dupeux, Alain Girard and Jean Stoetzel, 'Une enquête par sondage auprès des électeurs', in Mattei Dogan et al., Le référendum de septembre et les élections de novembre 1958 (Paris: A. Colin, 1960); Guy Michelat, 'Attitudes et comportements politiques à l'automne 1962', in François Goguel, ed., Le référendum d'octobre et les élections de novembre 1962 (Paris: A. Colin, 1965); Alain Lancelot, L'abstentionnisme électoral en France (Paris: A. Colin, 1968); Charzat, Les femmes françaises; Albert Brimo, Les femmes françaises face au pouvoir politique (Paris: Editions Montchrestien, 1975); Mossuz-Lavau and Sineau, Les femmes françaises; and Monica Charlot, 'Women in Politics in France', in Howard R. Penniman, ed., The French National Assembly Elections of 1978 (Washington, DC: American Enterprise Institute, 1980).

The consistency of the available evidence is undeniable. Measurable levels of political interest are greater among men than amongst women. And women have been found to be less knowledgeable about politics than men, less psychologically involved and less ideological in their thinking.[21]

Given their consistency across time and space, and the magnitude of some gender differences within systems, these data do not support claims that a marginal but temporary lag exists in women's political 'integration'. A more useful interpretation would posit that women's historical experiences differ from those of men within individual societies—as well as from those of women and men in other systems. The dual cultures thesis emphasizes the continued impact of disparate structures and traditions, acknowledging the reality of gender differences without expecting women to conform in aggregate to male norms.

SOCIAL REFORM AND WOMEN'S ATTITUDES

A similar view helps to make sense of the association between organized feminism and wider social reform. In the United States, for example, suffrage and other feminist issues were allied with a larger progressive agenda encompassing pacifist, urban improvement and general social welfare concerns. Similarly, suffragists in Quebec established a partisan alliance following 1938 with the reform-oriented Liberal party. Although these early feminist alliances are generally overlooked in public opinion research, they could hold important implications for the development of women's attitudes in Western democracies.

The US case is especially relevant because of social feminist efforts there to establish non-partisan, reform-oriented organizations on a national scale.[22] Historical research by Stanley Lemons demonstrates that suffragist victory on the federal level was followed by the creation of a National League of Women Voters that engaged women in discussions and activities related to progressive social issues, including health care, education, the environment and urban improvement.[23] As a major volunteer organization, the League and its local affiliates likely increased support for social reform, especially in issue areas related to the older progressive movement.[24]

Studies that examine this linkage report significantly greater support for environmental, urban improvement and income redistribution programs among women than men; at the same time, females have been less willing to endorse increased military expenditures and capital punishment.[25] These results are consistent across a large attitudinal literature in the US that shows women to be more approving than men of federal spending on income maintenance and social services, and less approving of war, military expenditures and the death penalty.[26]

Although these studies cannot demonstrate a causal linkage between older social feminist influences and contemporary attitudes, they help to explain the origins of a 'gender gap' in political—including partisan—attitudes in the US.[27] For example, former president Ronald Reagan was identified by many women with a belligerent foreign policy and a weakening of the already limited US welfare state; Reagan tended to gain more electoral support among men than women.[28] Moreover, Reagan's lack of support for the equal rights agenda of the second-wave women's movement reinforced older patterns, with the result that feminist attitudes became part of a larger constellation of progressive, pro-social welfare orientations. Far from being politically conservative, therefore, US women's attitudes tended toward liberal, reformist positions by the 1980s.[29]

A second cultural milieu where the attitudinal implications of early feminist alliances can be traced is Francophone Quebec. Women obtained the provincial franchise following the 1940 election of a Quebec Liberal (PLQ) government. According to Catherine Cleverdon and Thérèse Casgrain, the PLQ regime had been strongly encouraged to implement its 1938 convention resolution regarding suffrage by officials of the Liberal government in Ottawa.[30] Since provincial suffrage legislation was therefore attributable in large part to a single political party— the PLQ—and since the federal Liberals appear to have pressured their provincial affiliate in the direction of enfranchisement, a fairly strong Liberal predisposition might have been expected to develop among women in Quebec. Female cohorts who came of age during the period of suffrage activism in the 1920s and following might be especially supportive of the PLQ, given that an important feature of their formal entry to politics was the Liberal granting of the vote, followed by government-sponsored legislation permitting women to participate in municipal politics and to practise law in the province.[31]

TABLE 6.3   PARTY IDENTIFICATION OF ANGLOPHONE AND FRANCOPHONE
QUEBECKERS, 1965 (%)[a]

| | ANGLOPHONES | | FRANCOPHONES | |
	WOMEN	MEN	WOMEN	MEN
Créditiste	—	3.3	8.5	11.7
Liberal	64.9	66.7	64.3	55.9
New Democratic	14.0	8.3	12.2	9.9
Progressive Conservative	21.1	21.7	13.8	19.4
Union nationale	—	—	1.2	3.1
Total N	(57)	(60)	(319)	(324)

[a]Respondents were asked, 'Generally speaking, do you think of yourself as Conservative, Liberal, Social Credit, Créditiste, NDP, Union nationale, or what?' Non-identifiers were probed a second time: 'Well, do you generally think of yourself as a little closer to one of the parties than the others?' (If yes) 'Which one?' All missing data have been excluded from this and the following tables.

SOURCE: 1965 Canadian Election Study.

To what extent did females in Quebec express greater support for the Liberals than males? As reported in Table 6.3, Francophone women in 1965 were approximately 8 percent more likely to identify with the Liberals than were Francophone men, and were about 6 percent less likely to support the relatively weak Conservative party.[32] By way of comparison, Anglophone women and men in Quebec held relatively similar levels of Liberal and Conservative partisanship in 1965, although Anglophone females were approximately 6 percent more likely to identify with the New Democrats than Anglophone males. Party identification data from 1979, not presented in tabular form, also indicate that at the federal level, 3.1 percent more females than males were Liberal identifiers (71.7 percent versus 68.6 percent), while on the provincial level, 10.7 percent more of the former were Liberals (51.5 percent versus 40.8 percent).[33]

The relationship between women's history and subsequent patterns of public opinion in Quebec is reflected more directly in cohort breakdowns. According to 1965 data, support for the Liberals was highest (80.4 percent) among women who came of age politically during the 1920s through late 1930s, when suffragist activism was at or near its peak. Females born between 1901 and 1915 tended to be more Liberal than any male cohort in the 1965 sample (the most Liberal— 65.8 percent—being men born before 1900). A similar pattern obtained in survey data from the late 1970s.[34]

Combined with US data on attitudes to social reform, English Canadian data on partisanship analysed in Chapter 2, and patterns of political engagement discussed in the previous section, these Quebec results point towards a number of conclusions. First, survey data suggest that the historical experiences of women, and especially their treatment by political organizations and institutions, help to shape their attitudes. Analyses in Chapter 2 showed relatively high levels of New Democratic and Liberal support among female enfranchisement cohorts in Western Canada—where suffragism was closely allied with Liberal as well as agrarian and labour organizations (which predated the CCF/NDP in that region). Similarly, research on France indicates that leftist partisanship in 1958 was relatively strong among women residing in regions where Communist and Socialist women's affiliates were active.[35] Although this evidence remains fragmentary and heuristic, it does offer a basis for further research on the relationship between women's political history, especially their treatment by established party institutions, on the one hand, and female public opinion, on the other.

Second, this analysis sheds critical light on older explanations of women's political attitudes. In proposing that women are affected by and involved in processes of institutional and social change in Western cultures, it rejects the conventional view that attributes female attitudes to a deviant isolation in the domestic household. Similarly, in examining partisan preferences, we take issue with descriptions of female opinion as 'conservative' or 'moralistic'; women's views seem to have been centrist or reformist in direction, rather than rightist or reactionary.

We shall now examine patterns of party involvement in comparative perspective.

PARTY PARTICIPATION

As was noted in Chapter 3, party activity in Canada has been characterized by an absence of females in upper-echelon elite positions, particularly in organizations that hold, or are likely to take over, the reins of government. Empirical evidence for 'the higher the fewer' and 'the more competitive the fewer' was found in data on local constituency executives, convention delegates, campaign managers, party office-holders, candidates for public office, legislators and cabinet appointees.

From a cross-cultural perspective, it is difficult to examine each of these individual activities. Delegation to party conventions, for example, can reflect a very different functional role in one system than in another.[36] In addition, comparative research is complicated by the absence of data gathered at a single point in time and by the relative lack of attention, in the women and politics literature, to party institutions.

These difficulties notwithstanding, we can begin by reviewing levels of party membership and local activity. Research on the political systems of Australia and Western Europe, summarized in Table 6.4, shows that female party membership tends to be highest in parties of the centre-right and right, and lowest in parties of the left.[37] One explanation for this pattern follows from the traditional mobilization of women by conservative, church-affiliated organizations, especially in Catholic cultures, and from the parallel development of leftist parties in more masculine, trade union milieus.[38] The one exception is West Germany, where no significant differences distinguished female party membership in the rightist CDU and leftist SPD; instead, the major difference was between these established parties and the newer Greens.

Overall, data presented in Table 6.4 show that the numerical representation of women at the baseline level of party membership was highest in the Australian Liberal (50 percent), British Conservative (51 percent), Spanish Conservative (35 percent), French Gaullist (RPR; 43 percent), Italian Christian Democratic (40 percent) and Swedish Conservative (41 percent) parties. At the same time, women's membership was generally lower in such parties of the left as the Australian Labour (33 percent), British Labour (40 percent), Spanish Socialist (9 percent), French Socialist (27 percent), Italian Communist (25 percent) and Swedish Communist (38 percent).

Do patterns of local party activity, however, reflect similar left-right differences? This question is difficult to address because most constituency-level research has been conducted in the United States, where ideological variation in the party system is limited. In fact, some US studies suggest that party identification is irrelevant in determining patterns of local activity, since women in both the

TABLE 6.4   COMPARATIVE LEVELS OF FEMALE PARTY MEMBERSHIP

COUNTRY	PARTY	% FEMALE MEMBERSHIP
Australia	Labour	33
	Liberal	50
Britain	Conservative	51
	Labour	40
	Social Democratic	40
France	Communist (PCF)	36
	Gaullist (RPR)	43
	Republican (UDF)	40
	Socialist (PS)	27
Italy	Christian Democratic (DC)	40
	Communist (PCI)	25
	Socialist (PSI)	19
Norway	Centre	33
	Conservative	43
	Labour	40
	Liberal	42
Spain	Centre Democrat	30
	Communist	11
	Conservative	35
	Socialist	9
Sweden	Centre	43
	Communist	38
	Conservative	41
	Liberal	45
	Social Democratic	30
West Germany	Christian Democratic (CDU)	22
	Christian Socialist (CSU)	14
	Free Democratic (FDP)	23
	Green	33
	Social Democratic (SPD)	25

SOURCES: Joyce Gelb, *Feminism and Politics: A Comparative Perspective* (Berkeley: University of California Press, 1989); Eva Kolinsky, 'Political Participation and Parliamentary Careers: Women's Quotas in West Germany', *West European Politics* 14:1 (January 1991), 56-72; Joni Lovenduski, *Women and European Politics* (Amherst: University of Massachusetts Press, 1986); Vicky Randall, *Women and Politics* (2nd ed.; London: Macmillan, 1987); and Marian Sawer and Marian Simms, *A Woman's Place: Women and Politics in Australia* (Sydney: Allen and Unwin, 1984).

Democratic and Republican organizations are expected to contribute significant political efforts for very limited political rewards.[39] As Diane Margolis shows in her study of Democratic and Republican town committees, female party activity at the local level is generally less visible, more routine and more maintenance- (as opposed to decision-) oriented than that of males. Even though time logs submitted by party respondents indicated that women were 'far more active than the men', a check of local office-holders indicated that males outnumbered females in titled party positions. This pattern enabled men to obtain visibility and final decision-making authority at the town committee level.[40]

Research on local campaign activity in the United States also shows that women have conventionally specialized in such volunteer activities as stuffing and addressing envelopes, licking stamps, telephoning, chauffeuring voters and candidates, canvassing door to door and hosting coffee parties.[41] Therefore, just as women's activity between elections appears to be routine and maintenance- oriented, so too do their campaign contributions. Ellen Boneparth's research on Santa Clara County, California, however, suggests that this pattern altered as more female partisans contested public office, and in turn elevated the status of women in their campaign organizations, and as younger women more generally rejected gender-stereotyped roles in the parties.[42]

Louis Maisel's data from Maine indicate that municipal party committees included disproportionately few female chairs (19.5 percent in 1972), while they relied heavily upon women to serve as local secretaries (79.4 percent in 1972). This finding parallels closely the 'pink-collar' phenomenon identified in local constituency organizations in Canada; as well, it echoes the results of a Labour party survey showing women in Southwestern England to be under-represented, relative to their membership, 'in all posts, except in the purely clerical jobs of minutes secretary and secretary. Only 13 percent of chairs and 16 percent of treasurers were women.'[43]

Maisel's study of Democratic activism in Maine also emphasizes the influence of competitive party position upon local involvement. During the early 1970s, when women as a group began to demand reforms in US politics, Democrats in Maine were less likely to accomplish this objective in competitive than uncompetitive party areas. According to Maisel:

> Many more women participated in more highly Republican areas, as identified by respondents to the questionnaire. This suggests that the Democratic organizations in these areas were dormant, and women saw an opportunity to participate in a meaningful way. In fact, the Democratic organization in one highly Republican city—and those in many of its towns—was completely taken over by a group of new Democrats who then chose a woman to head the city committee. The corollary of this finding, of course, is that it is harder for new women to participate where strong organizations already exist. That is, party leaders in office, where

that office has some potential influence, appear to be less anxious to encourage new participants to try to enter the system.[44]

As in Canada, therefore, women in the US who resided in uncompetitive party areas found access to local party office—and to public nomination—far easier than did those living in competitive party areas.

PARTY DELEGATION

One of the only comparative sources of information on delegates is the US literature on state and national convention participation. This research suggests that, as in Canada, women delegates traditionally performed primarily clerical and ceremonial functions at party conventions. In addition to assuming roles as credential and registration clerks, American women escorted speakers to the platform, seconded nominations and called the roll of the states at presidential conventions.[45]

The method by which women conventionally obtained delegate or, more frequently, alternate status was related to broader assumptions about these activities. As one urban Democrat in Maine stated:

> Because of the reforms the entire delegate selection process was more wide-open. In the past this was done solely by the city committee. We would get together and make a list of us and our friends and would choose whoever wanted to be delegates. Usually most of the women were wives. Like a husband would be the delegate and his wife the alternate. It made a nice weekend trip to wherever the convention was held.[46]

Women were thus assumed to be secondary, apolitical companion delegates (or alternates) to American party conventions, while men were perceived to be the primary political actors.

More recent studies of US convention delegation suggest that as the confidence, ambition and feminist consciousness of female partisans increased, so too did their dissatisfaction with traditional role assignments. Research by Kent Jennings indicates that even though greater numbers of women obtained convention delegate positions as time passed (see Table 6.5), these females remained different from their male peers.[47] As Jennings writes:

> The increasing involvement of women in the parties has not worked to lessen their sense of gender role consciousness. They have not been assuaged in that they are still more likely than men to see obstacles for women in politics. Thus there remains a lively tension between achievement and progress on the one hand and perceived inequalities and deprivation on the other.[48]

Paralleling other research on convention delegation in the US, these conclusions suggest that women's increasing numerical representation may help to sustain their interest in and commitment to political careers, despite the widespread recognition of elite-level barriers.[49]

PARTY OFFICE-HOLDING

Comparative study of party office-holding is complicated by differences both within and across party systems in the titles and responsibilities attached to elite positions. For example, party secretaries in a US state organization could be responsible for compiling minutes on occasional executive meetings, while in a European socialist grouping, secretaries may wield day-to-day control over a large and complex party bureaucracy.

Furthermore, the appointment or election of token female representatives to party office, frequently as a result of internal arrangements with older women's associations, suggests that it is important to distinguish between substantive and ceremonial office-holding. As Eleanor Roosevelt observed in 1954, the practice of appointing 50 percent women to US national party committees 'looks better on paper than it has worked out in practice. Too often the vice-chairmen and the committee women are selected by the men, who naturally pick women who will go along with them and not give them any trouble. Thus they are apt to be mere stooges.'[50] Subsequent research on party office-holding in Chicago, Minneapolis and Seattle offered strong empirical support for Roosevelt's assertion. According to studies by Porter and Matasar as well as Clarke and Kornberg, efforts to include a respectable number of females in urban party elites generally led to the recruitment of token women with limited political ambition, very minimal feminist consciousness and exceptional commitment to the male party selectorate that recruited them.[51]

One way of approaching the question of party office is to use the 'law of increasing disproportion' as a basis to compare levels of membership (Table 6.4) and office-holding (Table 6.6). In most countries considered, women were

TABLE 6.5   WOMEN DELEGATES AT US PARTY CONVENTIONS, NATIONAL
LEVEL, 1916-1988 (%)

YEAR	DEMOCRATIC PARTY	REPUBLICAN PARTY
1916	1	1
1948-68 average	13	15
1972	40	30
1976	34	31
1980	50	36
1984	50	44
1988	49	37

SOURCE: M. Kent Jennings, 'Women in Party Politics', in Louise A. Tilly and Patricia Gurin, eds., *Women, Politics and Change* (New York: Russell Sage, 1990), 223-4.

far less likely to hold office than membership. For example, comparison of female membership in the British Conservative and Italian Christian Democratic parties with office-holding in these same organizations shows fairly extreme percentage differences: from 51 percent membership to only 18 percent policy committee representation in the British case (a difference of 33 percent), and from 40 percent membership to zero Party Secretariat representation in the Italian case.

TABLE 6.6   COMPARATIVE LEVELS OF PARTY OFFICE-HOLDING BY WOMEN IN AUSTRALIA AND WESTERN EUROPE

COUNTRY	PARTY	OFFICE	YEAR	% WOMEN
Australia	Country National	Central Council	1980	41.9
		General Conference	1977	39.5
	Labour	National Conference	1979	4.6
		State Conference	1979	11.0
		National Executive	1979	14.3
		State Executive	1979	6.1
	Liberal	NSW State Council	1976	19.0
Britain	Conservative	Annual Conference	1986	38.0
		Executive Committee	1986	20.0
		Policy Committee	1986	18.0
	Labour	Annual Conference	1986	11.0
		Executive Committee	1986	27.6
France	Communist (PCF)	Federal Committee	1983	21.0
		Political Bureau	1983	18.0
		Federal Secretariat	1983	17.0
	Gaullist (RPR)	Political Council	1983	6.0
		Central Committee	1983	8.0
	Republican (UDF)	National Council	1983	32.0
		Political Bureau	1983	20.0
		Secretariat	1983	6.0
	Socialist (PS)	Executive Bureau	1983	15.0
		Management Committee	1983	19.0
		Secretariat	1983	14.0
Italy	Christian Democratic (DC)	Secretariat	1983	0.0
	Communist (PCI)	Central Committee	1983	14.5
		Executive	1983	9.1
	Socialist (PSI)	Executive Board	1983	7.5

COUNTRY	PARTY	OFFICE	YEAR	% WOMEN
Norway	Centre	Executive Board	1982	45.0
	Conservative	Executive Board	1982	19.0
	Labour	Executive Committee	1982	40.0
	Liberal	Executive	1982	56.0
Spain	Conservative	National Executive	1982	13.0
	Socialist	Executive Committee	1982	12.5
Sweden	Communist	Executive	1982	34.0
	Conservative	Executive Board	1982	30.0
	Liberal	Executive	1982	44.0
	Social Democratic	Executive	1982	30.0
West Germany	Social Democratic	Executive	1988	26.3
		Presidium	1988	27.3

SOURCES: Marian Simms, 'Australia', in Joni Lovenduski and Jill Hills, eds, *The Politics of the Second Electorate* (London: Routledge, 1981), 83-111; Joyce Gelb, *Feminism and Politics: A Comparative Perspective* (Berkeley: University of California Press, 1989); Joni Lovenduski, *Women and European Politics* (Amherst: University of Massachusetts Press, 1986); and Vicky Randall, *Women and Politics* (2nd ed.; London: Macmillan, 1987).

Among parties of the left these differences are generally less extreme, in part because female membership is usually lower in leftist than in rightist parties. Comparing membership and office-holding in the British Labour party, for example, we find a difference of approximately 12 percent (40 percent membership versus 28 percent representation in the National Executive), the same as among the French Socialists (27 percent membership versus 15 percent representation on the Executive Bureau).

Hypotheses regarding 'the higher the fewer' can also be applied within single party organizations. Intra-party data from the British Conservative party (see Table 6.6) are consistent with the view that women tend to become increasingly under-represented as one moves toward positions of higher, and presumably more competitive and powerful party office. At the level of delegation to the Conservative Annual Conference, where special provisions ensure at least one female from each local constituency, women were fairly well represented (38 percent), but this figure dropped sharply in the national Executive Committee of about 200 members (20 percent), and in the smaller, more influential Policy Advisory Committee (18 percent).[52]

Comparative figures on party office-holding point towards two overall conclusions. First, the thesis that women would be weakly represented at higher levels of party activity was confirmed by comparisons of membership and office-holding data: particularly in European conservative parties, females were far less numerous as party officers than as members. Second, intra-party comparisons indicated that very few women held competitive, upper-echelon party offices:

females were increasingly under-represented in numerical terms as one moved toward higher and more powerful levels in a single party organization.

Both of these conclusions shed valuable light on the question of candidacy for public office.

LEGISLATIVE RECRUITMENT AND PARTICIPATION

Of all the subfields of women and politics, the area of female legislative participation has probably attracted the greatest amount of empirical interest. Beginning with early monographs by Alzada Comstock, Maurice Duverger and Emmy Werner, the literature on public candidacy, election and legislative tenure has grown to include a sizeable number of book-length studies, and an even larger volume of articles, conference papers and research notes.[53] Since it is impossible to review each contribution to the comparative literature on legislative recruitment and participation, we shall focus instead upon two key questions that inform most research in the area. First, in simple numerical terms, how many women contest and obtain legislative office? Second, on an explanatory plane, what factors help to account for patterns of female legislative recruitment and election? Examination of these two points will provide an introduction to contemporary responses to under-representation at elite levels.

Historically, the numbers of women contesting and obtaining legislative office in most Western democracies have been limited. As Kathleen Newland observed in her study of this phenomenon, 'Most women who participate in party activities are cannon-fodder; they knock on doors, answer telephones, hand out leaflets, and get out the vote—usually in the service of a male candidate.'[54] The extent to which females have been under-represented as both candidates and legislators, and specifically the failure of many women nominees to win election in Western political systems, is thus related to their more general status within party organizations.

In order to evaluate comparative patterns of candidacy and legislative election, longitudinal data from eight countries are presented in Table 6.7. Taken as a group, these figures indicate that women have generally increased their numerical representation as both candidates and legislators over time, comprising as much as 38 percent of the Swedish national legislature (Riksdag) in 1991. In the Nordic countries generally, women comprised approximately one-quarter of national legislators during the late 1970s and about one-third by the early 1990s, while in other West European countries and the United States female legislators remained far less numerous, ranging between 5.9 percent (French National Assembly, 1991) and 12.9 percent (Italian Chamber of Deputies, 1991). Therefore, even though women's involvement as both candidates and legislators generally increased over time in European and North American political systems, their usual percentage within national legislatures has—with the exception of the Nordic countries—remained below 15 percent through the early 1990s.

What factors help to account for this fairly limited legislative representation, particularly outside the Nordic region? Two major sets of explanations have been proposed in the literature on candidacy and recruitment; one is grounded in structural or systemic evaluations of this problem, while the second emphasizes social psychological factors. On the level of political structures, writers frequently observe that women's legislative participation is considerably higher in countries

TABLE 6.7 COMPARATIVE PATTERNS OF FEMALE CANDIDACY AND LEGISLATIVE OFFICE-HOLDING, NATIONAL LEVEL

COUNTRY	YEAR	% CANDIDATES	YEAR	% LEGISLATORS
Britain	1918	1.2	1929	2.3
	1929	3.9	1975	4.4
	1979	8.2	1980	3.0
	1983	10.7	1987	4.3
			1991	6.8
Denmark	1979	21.8	1945	5.4
	1983	25.0	1970	11.8
			1979	23.0
			1985	24.0
			1991	32.4
Finland	1948	12.1	1907	9.5
	1970	17.3	1948	12.0
	1979	26.0	1970	21.5
	1983	29.0	1979	26.0
			1985	31.0
			1991	36.0
France	1968	3.3	1945[a]	5.5
	1973	6.7	1981[a]	5.9
	1978	15.9	1981[b]	2.3
			1985[a]	5.5
			1991[a]	5.9
Italy	n/a		1948	7.8
			1968	2.8
			1979	8.2
			1984	8.0
			1991	12.9
Norway	1945	13.2	1969	9.3
	1957	18.0	1975	16.1
	1969	19.7	1979	23.9
	1983	37.0	1984	26.0
			1991	34.5

COUNTRY	YEAR	% CANDIDATES	YEAR	% LEGISLATORS
Sweden	n/a		1971	14.0
			1977	22.9
			1980	27.8
			1985	31.0
			1991	38.1
United States	1979[c]	5.3	1975[d]	4.4
			1979[d]	3.7
			1983[d]	5.0
			1986[d]	5.3
			1991[d]	6.4

[a]Represents National Assembly members only.

[b]Represents Senate members only.

[c]Represents major party candidates only for House of Representatives.

[d]Represents House of Representatives members only.

SOURCES: Sylvia B. Bashevkin, *Toeing the Lines: Women and Party Politics in English Canada* (1st ed.; Toronto: University of Toronto Press, 1985), Table 6.10; Anna Coote and Beatrix Campbell, *Sweet Freedom: The Struggle for Women's Liberation* (Oxford: Basil Blackwell, 1987); Robert Darcy and Karen Beckwith, 'Political Disaster, Political Triumph: The Election of Women to National Parliaments', paper presented at American Political Science Association meetings, Washington, 1991; Joyce Gelb, *Feminism and Politics: A Comparative Perspective* (Berkeley: University of California Press, 1989); Ingunn Norderval, 'Party and Legislative Participation among Scandinavian Women', in Sylvia Bashevkin, ed., *Women and Politics in Western Europe* (London: Cass, 1985), 71-89; and Vicky Randall, *Women and Politics* (2nd ed.; London: Macmillan, 1987).

with proportional representation (PR) electoral systems than in those with plurality arrangements. Figures on representation in the Swedish Riksdag (see Table 6.7), a unicameral legislature elected through proportional representation since 1970, provide useful support for this view, as does the tendency for female Bundestag members in West Germany to be elected through Land lists rather than to single-member constituency seats.[55]

Empirical analyses confirm that, in Wilma Rule's words, 'the party list/PR system is the most favorable for women's recruitment to national legislatures'.[56] In parallel findings, Rule and others maintain that women are advantaged by multi-member as opposed to single-member districts, including within plurality systems like that of Australia, and that they benefit from high rates of legislative turnover.[57]

Structural analysts have also looked beyond the issue of electoral arrangements to question the political viability of female candidacies in plurality systems. In the United States, Great Britain and France before it changed to PR arrangements in 1986, women candidates tended to be disproportionately clustered on the electoral slates of weak parties and in the marginal constituencies of strong ones. In reference to the former, writers caution that part of the growth in female candidature in the UK and France was related to the increased number of minor parties in both systems, which in turn afforded women access to larger numbers of less competitive, essentially protest nominations. Whether one considers the British Social Democratic, Scottish Nationalist, French Ecologist or French Feminist (*Choisir*) cases, it seems that 'the increase in the *number* of women candidates in recent years reflects a more general increase in the number of candidates fielded by minor parties.'[58] Moreover, as Margaret Stacey and Marion Price point out, improvements in the electoral viability of minor parties usually produce increased competition for nominations: thus women may be eased out of candidates' lists once the minor party ceases to be 'simply a quixotic venture'.[59]

As nominees for the weaker seats of major parties, women confront similarly depressing prospects. Many are referred to as 'sacrifice candidates', since their role as loyal party standard-bearers takes precedence over any reasonable hope of electoral victory. US studies by Bernstein, Welch et al., Deber, Tolchin and Tolchin, Van Hightower and others argue that one of the major characteristics of female legislative candidates has been their nomination in incumbent-dominated districts, where prospects for electoral success were limited.[60] Some Western European research confirms this finding, showing that relatively few women in proportional representation systems are placed at the top of their party lists, while those in plurality systems rarely secure nomination in viable seats.[61] One major distinction, therefore, between female legislators and unsuccessful women candidates is simply the safeness of their list position or local constituency.

Paralleling these findings concerning minor party and marginal nominations, researchers report that uncompetitive political environments are characterized by comparatively high levels of female participation. For example, US states with small populations, large legislatures and, as a result, fairly limited competition for legislative seats have elected relatively high numbers of women.[62] Similarly, British, Australian and American constituencies that were previously held by men have on occasion been contested and won by the widows of these deceased incumbents; that is, temporary conditions of diminished political competition in such seats permitted a pattern of 'widows' succession' to develop.[63] Nevertheless, other studies show that the strength of feminist organization in a given area is positively associated with the number of elected female legislators. As Wilma Rule notes with reference to US state houses, 'the women's movement has made a considerable impact on women's election to public office.'[64]

In contrast to these structural or systemic explanations of female candidacy, other findings have shown important social psychological influences upon legislative involvement. In its simplest terms, the social psychological view maintains that major sources of political under-representation can be found in the roles, attitudes and perceptions of women themselves. More specifically, conventional patterns of gender role socialization teach females to be submissive, deferential, private beings, while defining elite-level political participation as masculine, public and thus inappropriate for women. As a group, therefore, women are not encouraged to develop the self-esteem, confidence and other personal resources (including advanced education and professional careers) that are needed for upward mobility in party organizations.[65]

The influence of role and attitudinal constraints has been demonstrated in a number of comparative studies. Beginning with a pioneering study of US state legislators by Jeane Kirkpatrick, this literature suggests the continued impact on female partisans of traditional role norms (particularly a problem of role incompatibility for younger women with children),[66] personal resource poverty (including lower income and education than male partisans),[67] and relatively low levels of political ambition.[68] The tendency for women activists to be motivated by 'expressive' factors such as public service, as opposed to 'instrumental' factors such as power and career mobility, has been a common concern of social psychological studies; some maintain that the human service orientation of females toward political work provides a major reason for their limited mobility within party organizations.[69]

One additional focus of social psychological research has been the argument that women's chances of election to public office are reduced because of biases or discriminatory attitudes held by voters at large. Studies of public receptivity to elites, however, generally conclude that Western European and North American voters do *not* discriminate against women candidates. That is, despite assumptions among some party elites that female candidates lose elections because of popular resistance to their gender, empirical research based upon election simulations, mass surveys and longitudinal analysis of actual election returns offers little evidence in support of this view.[70]

We shall now consider party women's organizations in comparative perspective.

PARTY WOMEN'S ORGANIZATIONS

As in the Canadian case, traditional women's associations developed in many party systems, only to evolve toward increasingly assertive feminist organizations in recent decades. The service-oriented rationale behind the formation of older women's groups is reflected in US as well as Western European studies; they illustrate how traditional auxiliaries tended to distance their constituents from channels of mainstream party influence. Ingunn Norderval describes this problem with reference to Scandinavia, where some party women's groups

> are ridiculed as ladies' sewing circles and coffee clubs which neither inform nor integrate women in the political system, and hardly threaten male elites in the larger party organisation. Women's associations have thus been described by their detractors as politically marginal, isolated and insignificant in terms of both party policy and the recruitment of female elites.[71]

Yet auxiliary-type women's organizations were entrenched in many Western party systems during the turn-of-the-century period. In Britain, for example, the

Conservative Women's Council was formed in 1885, while a Women's Organization of the Labour party (the Women's Labour League) was founded in 1906.[72] The Norwegian Labour party established its first women's group in 1895.[73] In Italy, paralleling the delay in the granting of formal political rights, party women's organizations developed somewhat later. Growing out of a women's branch of the anti-fascist movement, the largest Italian women's group—UDI, or *Unione Donne Italiane*—was formed in 1944 with strong links to the Communist party.[74]

As Norderval and others demonstrate, the philosophical intentions and actual impact of these early groups differed widely. If some set out to provide a springboard or training ground from which newly enfranchised women could enter party politics, this purpose was usually replaced by a far different mandate, namely the provision of volunteer social, fund-raising and clerical services to the mainstream party. According to one account, Norwegian legislators 'tended to see the women's clubs as more humanitarian and social organizations than political ones, and providing not political schooling, but the comfortable, cozy, and undemanding atmosphere of the coffee-klatch; a poor preparation for the rough-and-tumble of political life'.[75]

This same conclusion is echoed in much of the comparative literature on traditional party women's groups. Whether one considers the Democratic Women's Clubs chartered by US state committees, or the National Federation of Republican Women (established in 1938), Frank Sorauf argues, these organizations played a 'docile, subordinate role' throughout most of their history.[76] Virginia Sapiro's evaluation of US party women's sections suggests that while they performed important symbolic functions by offering the image of political influence and mobility, they frequently segregated females and thus 'are designed very much for appeasement or cooptive purposes'.[77]

Similar generalizations can be found in research on Italian party participation by David Kertzer and in a study of British Labour party women's sections by Lorraine Culley.[78] Kertzer suggests that even though the Communist (PCI)-affiliated UDI may have done a modicum of political education work, a far more frequent focus at the local level was the organization of dinners for the elderly, children's puppet shows and the like. Kertzer concludes that the UDI reinforced rather than challenged conventional gender role norms in the PCI: 'the primary sphere of women's activities in party affairs, indeed, comprises none other than the traditional women's chores: preparing food for the annual party *feste* and preparing snacks and meals for party pollwatchers on election day.'[79] Kertzer's findings are supported by another study of Italian party involvement that argues 'the UDI plays only a subordinate role in PCI strategy and has only limited mobilization capacity.'[80]

As in Canada, however, newer feminist movements challenged older party women's associations on the level of style, purpose and basic *raison d'être*. This challenge was especially clear in European parties of the left, where contemporary women's movements had a relatively early and direct impact upon both women and men. Lorraine Culley, for example, described this influence in terms of

> an increasing militancy of women in the [British] Labour Movement which has
> arisen in the context of the disillusionment of many women with the effects of
> the 'Equality Legislation' and the performance of recent Labour governments, the
> explicit attacks on women by the present Tory government and the general debate
> concerning democratization of the Party. This militancy has been expressed in
> the formation of two new groups in recent months . . . [which] are concerned
> with campaigning for changes in the Party in order to increase the representation
> of women.[81]

Studies of a parallel radicalization among women in the French and Italian
Communist parties, the French Socialist party, the German Social Democratic
party and the labour and socialist parties of Denmark and Norway point towards
the fusing of leftist and feminist commitments among an activist core of party
women. What distinguishes the latter from their predecessors is an explicit demand for increased numerical and policy representation in the larger political
organization.[82]

Contemporary feminism held important implications for women's organizations in contexts other than European socialist and communist parties, however.
As in Canada, criticisms of increasingly weak, outdated and politically segregated
auxiliaries were voiced in liberal as well as conservative settings, with the result
that centrist and rightist women's groups also changed in the 1970s and following.
Perhaps the clearest reflection of these shifts can be found in the US where,
as Sorauf comments, older party women's associations risked extinction in the
face of a demand for power and political integration by younger females. In
Sorauf's words, the latter 'more activist women want a role in the regular party
organizations, or else they prefer to become active in non-party organizations
(such as the National Women's Political Caucus). Certainly they do not have
in mind the docile, subordinate role that the auxiliaries traditionally had.'[83] This
search for 'a new and proper role' among women in the US led to a shift wherein
national women's divisions began to pursue leadership training and candidate
recruitment activities.[84]

The question of continuing women's organizations in any form has been a
subject of considerable controversy in many parties. As Sapiro points out, it is
important to examine

> formalization of the women's interest in terms of strategies of segregation and
> integration. Special offices within parties or governments have important symbolic
> meaning and they are generally, although not always staffed by activists and spe-
> cialists in women's problems. At the same time, however, segregation can 'ghettoize'
> the problems; it can segregate the issues both from other related problems and
> from experts and leaders in other fields.[85]

Few political organizations escaped these debates over amalgamation or integration as opposed to separate status. The West German Social Democratic party (SPD) did not have a history of separate associations; however, feminists pressured for the establishment of a constituent association (the *Arbeitsgemeinschaft Sozialdemokratischer Frauen*, or ASF) in 1971, which by 1977 had established a base of about 16,000 activists.[86] Despite this growth, though, the ASF was generally unsuccessful in its attempts to increase elite-level representation in the SPD; research on female legislators suggests that most were recruited via the mainstream SPD organization rather than through the ASF.[87]

At the same time, feminist participants in left-of-centre governing parties frequently questioned the institutionalization of their priorities and activities. During periods of Socialist government in France, SPD rule in West Germany and PASOK dominance in Greece, much of the policy focus of the organized women's movement—including party women's groups—was government-centred. Feminists thus devoted much of their attention to task forces, working groups, legislative lobbies and bureaucratic liaison. This unprecedented institutional legitimacy, in short, was accompanied by a very worrisome loss of movement autonomy.[88]

RESPONSES TO UNDER-REPRESENTATION

In the absence of clear answers to this dilemma over integration, women in many party systems focused their efforts on rule changes that would guarantee a specific level of numerical representation. Following the affirmative action guidelines introduced in the US Democratic party in 1972, guaranteeing numerically equal representation of men and women at presidential nominating conventions, feminists in a variety of other parties sought to obtain similar commitments.[89] As in the Canadian case, these rules were most likely to be adopted by party organizations of the left and centre.

Few parties, however, have pursued this strategy as effectively as the US Democrats. In the British Labour party, the Women's Action Committee of the democratization movement pressured for 50 percent representation in party executive and parliamentary short lists, yet women's status remained frozen at the level of a 1918 constitutional guarantee.[90] This statute reserved a special women's section, composed of five members, on the 29-member Labour National Executive Committee (NEC). All five reserved positions were elected by delegates to the annual Labour party conference—disproportionately comprised of male trade unionists—rather than by delegates to the yearly party women's conference. As Joyce Gelb has observed, 'most women selected for the NEC are not independent feminists.'[91]

A numerically based response to under-representation was also pursued by feminists in Norway and France. By 1979, the Liberal, Left Socialist and Labour organizations in Norway had adopted 40 percent across-the-board quotas for women.[92] Under the leadership of writer and later cabinet minister Yvette Roudy, French Socialist (PS) activists secured an important constitutional amendment in July 1977.[93] 'Article 6 was changed to institute a minimum female quota of ten per cent at all levels of the party from the Executive Committee to the grass roots, the quota to be revised at each party conference so as to take into account the proportion of women in the party. Article 46 also indicated that in all elections the ten per cent quota must be respected on every list.'[94] This quota was raised to 20 percent in 1979 but, according to one account, had not been fully realized by 1983.[95] Furthermore, although the French Socialist government attempted to ensure that women obtained at least 20 percent of municipal party list positions in 1981, the initiative was ruled unconstitutional in 1983.[96]

Efforts to obtain guarantees of numerical representation were pursued in West Germany by the SPD. Although early ASF activitists argued against quotas for women in 1971, they found that once these statutes were removed, 'only two women were elected to the national executive at the following party convention—rather than the five who had served until then'.[97] This experience led to attempts within the ASF to reintroduce a guarantee of numerical representation in both 1977 and 1979. However, proposals to establish guidelines for party office and legislative lists were twice

> defeated by a majority who argued that quotas would endanger the emancipatory movement, that women must become a political factor within the party to effectuate change, and that it would be insulting to women if they gained party positions on the basis of a quota system rather than their qualifications . . . a quota system violated the principle of intra-party democracy and was not in women's interest. It would put a psychological burden on women seeking public office, who if elected would be labelled as belonging to a 'percentage' category.[98]

Ultimately, the SPD adopted a 40 percent internal party quota, to be reached by 1994, and a 40 percent parliamentary quota, to be met by 1998. These changes paralleled the minimum 50 percent across-the-board quota established by the German Greens.[99]

DIRECTIONS FOR FUTURE RESEARCH

This discussion has tended to confirm at least three significant hypotheses, each of which points toward new directions for women and politics research. First, political history seems to hold meaningful implications for women's attitudes and participation. Second, higher echelons of party activity, particularly within politically competitive organizations (those holding or in a position to take the reins of government), continue to include relatively few women. Third, comparative data show that women have often performed stereotypical functions, notably in 'pink-collar' clerical positions at the local level as well as service-oriented work in older women's associations.

These findings suggest many interesting research questions. For example, how do organized feminist groups interact with political parties in the contemporary period? Do feminist voters receive explicit partisan cues during election periods? How effective are these cues? Are younger women less likely to reflect an expressive orientation to politics than older ones? Have younger women become as instrumental in their approach as younger men? What internal party incentives encourage men to do more of the work traditionally performed by women? Are numerical quotas useful at all levels of activity and, once implemented, are these rules effective in enhancing female political mobility? From the perspective of organizational development, what is the impact of affirmative action regulations upon party life?

A final and very crucial set of research questions concerns the policy consequences of growing female political participation. On a substantive or public policy level, do increased numbers of elite-level women make a difference? Can a linkage be established between numerical or descriptive representation, on the one hand, and policy or substantive representation, on the other?[100] Research on the Quebec party system by Manon Tremblay, as well as a number of US and Western European studies, suggests that party women are generally more supportive of feminist issue positions than their male colleagues.[101] Whether measured by attitudinal surveys, roll-call data or public statements, gender does seem to matter at the elite level.

Yet more comparative work is needed to identify the when's and why's of policy impact. For example, does female representation in opposition matter in a majority parliamentary setting? Is cabinet clout more significant than backbench numbers? Are subnational governments more open to feminist policy influence than national regimes? Of what significance is the election of more women in highly disciplined parliamentary systems?

These questions, explored in Chapter 7, are only a few of the many that challenge future comparative research. Each can begin to relate the attitudes and experiences of women to the many pressing policy, and especially representational, issues confronting contemporary political systems.

NOTES

[1] Frances Dana Gage, 'A Hundred Years Hence,' reprinted in Aileen S. Kraditor, ed., *Up From the Pedestal* (Chicago: Quadrangle, 1968), 285.

[2] Ibid.

[3] Treatments of the Flora MacDonald campaign for federal Conservative leadership in 1976 reflected many of these assumptions. See, for example, Jonathan Manthorpe, 'Can Flora Become Thatcher Matcher?' *Globe and Mail*, 12 February 1975; and Mary Janigan, 'Prime Minister Flora MacDonald? Why Not!' *Toronto Star*, 1 February 1975.

[4] On Thatcher's individual career, see Michael A. Genovese, 'Margaret Thatcher and the Politics of Conviction Leadership', paper presented at American Political Science Association meetings, Washington, DC, 1991.

[5]See Vicky Randall, *Women and Politics: An International Perspective* (2nd ed.; London: Macmillan, 1987).

[6]Richard J. Evans, *The Feminists* (London: Croom Helm, 1977).

[7]Ibid.

[8]In addition to Evans's study, see Joni Lovenduski, *Women and European Politics: Contemporary Feminism and Public Policy* (Amherst: University of Massachusetts Press, 1986), chap. 2.

[9]Margaret L. Inglehart, 'Political Interest in West European Women', *Comparative Political Studies* 14 (1981), 299-326.

[10]Ibid., 301.

[11]See Guida West and Rhoda Lois Blumberg, eds., *Women and Social Protest* (New York: Oxford University Press, 1990); and Ann Bookman and Sandra Morgen, eds., *Women and the Politics of Empowerment* (Philadelphia: Temple University Press, 1988).

[12]See Thelma McCormack, 'Toward a Nonsexist Perspective on Social and Political Change', in Marcia Millman and Rosabeth Moss Kanter, eds., *Another Voice* (New York: Anchor, 1975), 1-33.

[13]Thelma McCormack, *Politics and the Hidden Injuries of Gender: Feminism and the Making of the Welfare State* (Ottawa: Canadian Research Institute for the Advancement of Women, 1991), 37.

[14]Alan Grimes, *The Puritan Ethic and Woman Suffrage* (New York: Oxford University Press, 1967), passim.

[15]On the background to these debates, see Sylvie d'Augerot-Arend, 'Why So Late? Cultural and Institutional Factors in the Granting of Quebec and French Women's Political Rights', *Journal of Canadian Studies* 26:1 (Spring 1991), 138-65; and Chantal Maillé, *Les Québécoises et la conquête du pouvoir politique* (Montreal: Editions Saint-Martin, 1990), part 1.

[16]The neglect of equality issues in Canadian parliamentary debates regarding woman suffrage is evaluated in Diane Lamoureux and Jacinthe Michaud, 'Les parlementaires canadiens et le suffrage féminin: un aperçu des débats', *Canadian Journal of Political Science* 21:2 (June 1988), 319-29. On party realignments during this period, see Jorgen Rasmussen, 'Women in Labour: The Flapper Vote and Party System Transformation in Britain', *Electoral Studies* 3:1 (April 1984), 47-63; David Morgan, *Suffragists and Liberals: The Politics of Woman Suffrage in England* (Oxford: Blackwell, 1975); Virginia Sapiro, 'You Can Lead a Lady to the Vote, but What Will She do with It? The Problem of a Woman's Bloc Vote,' in Dorothy G. McGuigan, ed., *New Research on Women and Sex Roles* (Ann Arbor, Mich.: Center for Continuing Education of Women, 1976), 221-37; and Chapter 1, above.

[17]For a more detailed treatment of these data, see Sylvia Bashevkin, 'Changing Patterns of Politicization and Partisanship among Women in France', *British Journal of Political Science* 15:1 (January 1985), 75-96.

[18]Marian Sawer and Marian Simms, *A Woman's Place: Women and Politics in Australia* (Sydney: Allen and Unwin, 1984), 165.

[19]Carol A. Christy, 'American and German Trends in Sex Differences in Political Participation', *Comparative Political Studies* 18:1 (April 1985), 81-103.

[20]Lovenduski, *Women and European Politics*, 120-24.

[21]Ibid., 124.

[22]Historical research indicates that the early US women's movement was characterized by a cleavage between 'social' or maternal and 'hard-core' or political interests. According to O'Neill and Kraditor, political feminists maintained that equal rights for women were the primary objective of the movement, and that these rights should be secured on the basis of political justice. In contrast, prominent activists also employed a more dominant social feminist argument that elevated progressive social reform above demands for legal emancipation. See William L. O'Neill, *Everyone Was Brave: The Rise and Fall of Feminism in America* (New York: Quadrangle, 1971); and Aileen S. Kraditor, *The Ideas of the Woman Suffrage Movement, 1890-1920* (New York: Columbia University Press, 1965).

[23] See J. Stanley Lemons, *The Woman Citizen* (Urbana: University of Illinois Press, 1973), passim.

[24] On the policies of the League from its establishment through the late 1970s, see Ruth C. Clusen, 'The League of Women Voters and Political Power', in Bernice Cummings and Victoria Schuck, eds., *Women Organizing* (Metuchen, NJ: Scarecrow Press, 1979), 112-32.

[25] See Sylvia B. Bashevkin, 'Social Feminism and the Study of American Public Opinion', *International Journal of Women's Studies* 7:1 (January/February 1984), 47-56.

[26] See Pamela Johnston Conover, 'Feminists and the Gender Gap', *Journal of Politics* 50:4 (November 1988), 985-1010; Robert Y. Shapiro and Harpreet Mahajan, 'Gender Differences in Policy Preferences: A Summary of Trends from the 1960s to the 1980s', *Public Opinion Quarterly* 50 (1986), 42-61; and Sandra Baxter and Marjorie Lansing, *Women and Politics: The Visible Majority* (rev. ed.; Ann Arbor: University of Michigan Press, 1983), chaps 3, 9.

[27] See Bella Abzug with Mim Kelber, *Gender Gap* (Boston: Houghton Mifflin, 1984); Ethel Klein, *Gender Politics* (Cambridge: Harvard University Press, 1984), chap. 9; and Carol M. Mueller, ed., *The Politics of the Gender Gap* (Beverly Hills: Sage, 1988).

[28] See Louis Bolce, 'The Role of Gender in Recent Presidential Elections: Reagan and the Reverse Gender Gap', *Presidential Studies Quarterly* 15 (1985), 372-85; Ted George Goertzel, 'The Gender Gap: Sex, Family Income and Political Opinions in the Early 1980s', *Journal of Political and Military Sociology* 11:2 (Fall 1983), 209-22; and Val Burris, 'The Meaning of the Gender Gap: A Comment on Goertzel', *Journal of Political and Military Sociology* 12:2 (Fall 1984), 335-43.

[29] See Pippa Norris, 'The Gender Gap in Britain and America', *Parliamentary Affairs* 38:2 (Spring 1985), 192-201.

[30] Catherine L. Cleverdon, *The Woman Suffrage Movement in Canada* (Toronto: University of Toronto Press, 1950), chap. 7; and Thérèse Casgrain, *A Woman in a Man's World* (Toronto: McClelland and Stewart, 1972).

[31] On Liberal reform legislation during this period, see Cleverdon, *The Woman Suffrage Movement*, 261-64.

[32] The main empirical materials employed in this discussion are the 1965 Canadian National Election Study, directed by John Meisel, Philip Converse, Maurice Pinard, Peter Regenstreif and Mildred Schwartz, and the 1979 Social Change in Canada Survey, directed by Tom Atkinson, Bernard Blishen, Michael D. Ornstein and H. Michael Stevenson. The former study was based upon a stratified random sample of approximately 2,100 respondents weighted to a total of about 2,700 cases, while the latter employed a multi-stage probability selection sample weighted to about 3,000 respondents. Both studies were made available by the Institute for Social Research at York University. Neither the Institute nor the original investigators bears responsibility for the analyses or interpretations presented here.

[33] For a more detailed examination of these data, see Sylvia B. Bashevkin, 'Social Change and Political Partisanship: The Development of Women's Attitudes in Quebec', *Comparative Political Studies* 16:2 (July 1983), 147-72.

[34] See ibid.

[35] See Bashevkin, 'Changing Patterns of Politicization and Partisanship'.

[36] See Carl Baar and Ellen Baar, 'Party and Convention Organization and Leadership Selection in Canada and the United States', in Donald R. Matthews, ed., *Perspectives on Presidential Selection* (Washington, DC: Brookings, 1973), 49-84.

[37] For a more detailed confirmation of this pattern, see Ingunn Norderval, 'Party and Legislative Participation among Scandinavian Women', in Sylvia Bashevkin, ed., *Women and Politics in Western Europe* (London: Frank Cass, 1985), Table 2.

[38] See Lovenduski, *Women and European Politics*.

[39] See Allan Kornberg, Joel Smith and Harold D. Clarke, *Citizen Politicians—Canada* (Durham, NC: Carolina Academic Press, 1979); and Harold D. Clarke and Allan Kornberg, 'Moving Up the Political Escalator: Women Party Officials in the United States and Canada', *Journal of Politics* 41:2 (May 1979), 442-76.

[40] Diane Margolis, 'The Invisible Hands: Sex Roles and the Division of Labor in Two Local Political Parties', in Debra W. Stewart, ed., *Women in Local Politics* (Metuchen, NJ: Scarecrow Press, 1980), 26. See also Mary Cornelia Porter and Ann B. Matasar, 'The Role and Status of Women in the Daley Organization', in Jane S. Jaquette, ed., *Women in Politics* (New York: Wiley, 1974), 85-108; Ellen Boneparth, 'Women in Campaigns: From Lickin' and Stickin' to Strategy', *American Politics Quarterly* 5:3 (July 1977), 289-300; Louis Maisel, 'Party Reform and Political Participation: The Democrats in Maine,' in Louis Maisel and Paul M. Sacks, eds., *The Future of Political Parties* (Beverly Hills: Sage, 1975); and Janet A. Flammang, ed., *Political Women: Current Roles in State and Local Government* (Beverly Hills: Sage, 1984).

[41] See Boneparth, 'Women in Campaigns'; and Martin Gruberg, *Women in American Politics* (Oshkosh, Wisc.: Academia, 1968).

[42] See Boneparth, 'Women in Campaigns'; as well as Janet A. Flammang, 'Female Officials in the Feminist Capital: The Case of Santa Clara County', *Western Political Quarterly* 38:1 (March 1985), 94-118.

[43] Anna Coote and Polly Pattullo, *Power and Prejudice: Women and Politics* (London: Weidenfeld and Nicolson, 1990), 176.

[44] Maisel, 'Party Reform and Political Participation', 205.

[45] See Gruberg, *Women in American Politics*, 60ff. On the low percentage of female party delegates to British and Australian party conventions, see Joni Lovenduski and Jill Hills, eds., *The Politics of the Second Electorate* (London: Routledge and Kegan Paul, 1981), chaps 2, 5.

[46] Maisel, 'Party Reform and Political Participation', 207.

[47] See M. Kent Jennings, 'Women in Party Politics', in Louise A. Tilly and Patricia Gurin, eds., *Women, Politics and Change* (New York: Russell Sage Foundation, 1990), 221-48; M. Kent Jennings and Barbara G. Farah, 'Social Roles and Political Resources: An Over-Time Study of Men and Women in Party Elites', *American Journal of Political Science* 25:3 (August 1981), 462-82; and M. Kent Jennings and Norman Thomas, 'Men and Women in Party Elites: Social Roles and Political Resources', *Midwest Journal of Political Science* 12:4 (November 1968), 469-92.

[48] Jennings, 'Women in Party Politics', 246.

[49] See also Jeane Kirkpatrick, *The New Presidential Elite* (New York: Russell Sage Foundation, 1976).

[50] Roosevelt as quoted in Martin Gruberg, *Women in American Politics*, 62. See also Susan and Martin Tolchin, *Clout: Womanpower and Politics* (New York: Coward, McCann, 1974), 64.

[51] See Porter and Matasar, 'The Role and Status of Women in the Daley Organization'; and Clarke and Kornberg, 'Moving Up the Political Escalator'.

[52] See Lovenduski, *Women and European Politics*, 138.

[53] See Alzada Comstock, 'Women Members of European Parliaments', *American Political Science Review* 20 (1926), 379-84; Maurice Duverger, *The Political Role of Women* (Paris: UNESCO, 1955); Emmy E. Werner, 'Women in Congress, 1917-1964', *Western Political Quarterly* 19:1 (1966), 16-30; and Emmy E. Werner, 'Women in the State Legislatures', *Western Political Quarterly* 21:1 (1968), 40-50. On the contemporary literature, see Randall, *Women and Politics*, chap. 3; and Susan J. Carroll, *Women as Candidates in American Politics* (Bloomington: Indiana University Press, 1985).

[54] Kathleen Newland, *Women in Politics: A Global Review* (Washington, DC: Worldwatch Institute, 1975), 22, 23.

[55] Wilma Rule, 'Electoral Systems, Contextual Factors and Women's Opportunity for Election to Parliament in Twenty-three Democracies', *Western Political Quarterly* 40:3 (September 1987), 485. On

the case for proportional representation, see Douglas J. Amy, 'Improving Representation for Women and Minorities: Is Proportional Representation the Key?' paper presented at American Political Science Association meetings, Washington, 1991; Pippa Norris, 'Women's Legislative Participation in Western Europe', in Bashevkin, ed., *Women and Politics in Western Europe*, 98-9; and Marian Sawer, 'Women and Women's Issues in the 1980 [Australian] Federal Election', *Politics* 16:2 (1981), 246.

56 Rule, 'Electoral Systems, Contextual Factors and Women's Opportunity', 481. See also Norris, 'Women's Legislative Participation.'

57 Rule, 'Electoral Systems, Contextual Factors and Women's Opportunity', 487; Wilma Rule, 'Why More Women are State Legislators: A Research Note', *Western Political Quarterly* 43:2 (June 1990), 437-48; Carroll, *Women as Candidates in American Politics*; Robert Darcy, Susan Welch and Janet Clark, *Women, Elections and Representation* (New York: Longman, 1987); Richard Engstrom, 'District Magnitudes and the Election of Women to the Irish Dail', *Electoral Studies* 6 (1987), 123-32; Susan Welch and Donley T. Studlar, 'Multi-member Districts and the Representation of Women: Evidence from Britain and the United States', *Journal of Politics* 52:2 (1990), 391-412; Kristi Andersen and Stuart J. Thorson, 'Congressional Turnover and the Election of Women', *Western Political Quarterly* 37:1 (March 1984), 143-56; and Robert Darcy and Karen Beckwith, 'Political Disaster, Political Triumph: The Election of Women to National Parliaments', paper presented at American Political Science Association meetings, Washington, 1991.

58 See Margaret Stacey and Marion Price, *Women, Power and Politics* (London: Tavistock, 1981), 147.

59 Ibid.

60 See Robert A. Bernstein, 'Why are There so Few Women in the House?' *Western Political Quarterly* 39:1 (March 1986), 155-64; Susan Welch, Margery M. Ambrosius, Janet Clark and Robert Darcy, 'The Effect of Candidate Gender on Electoral Outcomes in State Legislative Races', *Western Political Quarterly* 38:3 (September 1985), 464-75; Raisa B. Deber, 'The Fault, Dear Brutus: Women as Congressional Candidates in Pennsylvania', *Journal of Politics* 44:2 (1982), 463-79; Tolchin and Tolchin, *Clout*, chap. 2; and Nikki R. Van Hightower, 'The Recruitment of Women for Public Office', *American Politics Quarterly* 5:3 (1977), 301-14.

61 See Karen Beckwith, 'Women and Parliamentary Politics in Italy, 1946-1979', in Howard R. Penniman, ed., *Italy at the Polls, 1979* (Washington, DC: American Enterprise Institute, 1981), 230-53; Beverly Parker Stobaugh, *Women and Parliament, 1918-1970* (Hicksville, NY: Exposition Press, 1978); Monica Charlot, 'Women in Politics in France', in Howard R. Penniman, ed., *The French National Assembly Elections of 1978* (Washington, DC: American Enterprise Institute, 1980), 171-91; and Ingunn Norderval Means, 'Political Recruitment of Women in Norway', *Western Political Quarterly* 25:3 (1972), 491-521. For an autobiographical view of this problem, see Edith Summerskill, *A Woman's World* (London: Heinemann, 1967).

62 See Werner, 'Women in the State Legislatures'; and Irene Diamond, *Sex Roles in the State House* (New Haven: Yale University Press, 1977).

63 Melville E. Currell, *Political Woman* (London: Croom Helm, 1974); Stobaugh, *Women and Parliament*; Sawer, 'Women and Women's Issues'; Marian Simms, 'Australia', in Lovenduski and Hills, eds., *Politics of the Second Electorate*, 83-111; Charles S. Bullock III and Patricia Lee Findley Heys, 'Recruitment of Women for Congress: A Research Note,' *Western Political Quarterly* 25:3 (1972), 416-23; Irwin N. Gertzog, 'The Matrimonial Connection: The Nomination of Congressmen's Widows for the House of Representatives', *Journal of Politics* 42:3 (1980), 820-33; and Diane D. Kincaid, 'Over His Dead Body: A Positive Perspective on Widows in the US Congress', *Western Political Quarterly* 31:1 (1978), 96-104.

64 Rule, 'Why More Women are State Legislators', 45. See also Carroll, *Women as Candidates in American Politics*, 160-3; as well as Jill M. Bystydzienski, 'Women in Politics in Norway', *Women and Politics* 8:3/4 (1988), 73-95.

65 For a more complete statement of this view, see Jeane J. Kirkpatrick, *Political Woman* (New York: Basic Books, 1974), 13-19.

[66]See ibid. as well as Susan J. Carroll, 'The Personal is Political: The Intersection of Private Lives and Public Roles among Women and Men in Elective and Appointive Office', *Women and Politics* 9:2 (1989), 51-67; Virginia Sapiro, *The Political Integration of Women* (Urbana: University of Illinois Press, 1983); Susan J. Pharr, *Political Women in Japan* (Berkeley: University of California Press, 1981); Marcia Manning Lee, 'Why Few Women Hold Public Office', *Political Science Quarterly* 91 (1976), 297-314; Emily Stoper, 'Wife and Politician: Role Strain among Women in Public Office', in Marianne Githens and Jewel L. Prestage, eds., *A Portrait of Marginality* (New York: David McKay, 1977), 320-37; and M. Janine Brodie, 'The Constraints of Private Life: Marriage, Motherhood and Political Candidacy in Canada', paper presented at Canadian Political Science Association meetings, Halifax, 1981.

[67]See Jennings and Thomas, 'Men and Women in Party Elites'; Jennings and Farah, 'Social Roles and Political Resources'; and Paula J. Dubeck, 'Women and Access to Political Office: A Comparison of Female and Male State Legislators', *Sociological Quarterly* 17:1 (1976), 42-52.

[68]See Janet Clark, Charles D. Hadley and R. Darcy, 'Political Ambition among Men and Women State Party Leaders: Testing the Countersocialization Perspective', *American Politics Quarterly* 17:2 (April 1989), 194-207; Diane L. Fowlkes, 'Ambitious Political Woman: Countersocialization and Political Party Context', *Women and Politics* 4:4 (Winter 1984), 5-32; Diane L. Fowlkes, Jerry Perkins and Sue Tolleson Rinehart, 'Gender Roles and Party Roles', *American Political Science Review* 73:3 (1979), 772-80; Virginia Sapiro and Barbara D. Farah, 'New Pride and Old Prejudice: Political Ambition and Role Orientations among Female Partisan Elites', *Women and Politics* 1:1 (1980), 13-36; and Kirkpatrick, *The New Presidential Elite*, 411ff.

[69]On expressive versus instrumental orientations, see Werner, 'Women in the State Legislatures'; Fowlkes et al., 'Gender Roles and Party Roles'; Edmond Costantini and Kenneth H. Craik, 'Women as Politicians: The Social Background, Personality and Political Careers of Female Party Leaders', *Journal of Social Issues* 28:2 (1972), 217-36; and Clarke and Kornberg, 'Moving Up the Political Escalator', 458ff.

[70]See Monica Boyd, 'English-Canadian and French-Canadian Attitudes toward Women: Results of the Canadian Gallup Polls', *Journal of Comparative Family Studies* 6:2 (1975), 153-69; E.M. Schreiber, 'The Social Bases of Opinions on Women's Role in Canada', *Canadian Journal of Sociology* 1:1 (1975), 61-74; Myra Marx Ferree, 'A Woman for President? Changing Responses, 1958-1972', *Public Opinion Quarterly* 38:3 (1974), 390-9; E. M. Schreiber, 'Education and Change in American Opinion on a Woman for President', *Public Opinion Quarterly* 42:2 (1978), 171-82; Ronald D. Hedlund, Patricia K. Freeman, Keith E. Hamm and Robert M. Stein, 'The Electability of Women Candidates', *Journal of Politics* 41:2 (1979), 513-24; Laurie E. Ekstrand and William E. Eckert, 'The Impact of Candidate's Sex on Voter Choice', *Western Political Quarterly* 34:1 (1981), 78-87; Susan Welch and Lee Sigelman, 'Change in Public Attitudes toward Women in Politics', *Social Science Quarterly* 63:2 (1982), 312-22; Malcolm Mackerras, 'Do Women Candidates Lose Votes?—Further Evidence', *Australian Quarterly* 52:4 (1980), 450-5; Ian McAllister, 'The Electoral Consequences of Gender in Australia', *British Journal of Political Science* 13:3 (1983), 365-77; Ottar Hellevik, 'Do Norwegian Voters Discriminate Against Women Candidates for Parliament?' *European Journal of Political Research* 7:3 (1979), 285-300; and Jorgen Rasmussen, 'The Electoral Costs of Being a Woman in the 1979 British General Election', *Comparative Politics* 15:4 (1983), 461-75.

[71]Norderval, 'Legislative Participation among Scandinavian Women,' 78.

[72]See Stobaugh, *Women and Parliament*; and Lorraine Culley, 'Women's Organisation in the Labour Party', *Politics and Power* 3 (1981), 115-22.

[73]Norderval, 'Legislative Participation among Scandinavian Women', 78.

[74]See Karen Beckwith, 'Feminism and Leftist Politics in Italy: The Case of UDI-PCI Relations', in Bashevkin, ed., *Women and Politics in Western Europe*, 19-37.

[75]Means, 'Political Recruitment', 518.

[76]Frank J. Sorauf, *Party Politics in America* (Boston: Little, Brown, 1976), 123.

[77] Virginia Sapiro, 'When are Interests Interesting? The Problem of Political Representation of Women', *American Political Science Review* 75:3 (1981), 712.

[78] See David I. Kertzer, *Comrades and Christians* (Cambridge: Cambridge University Press, 1980); David I. Kertzer, 'The Liberation of Evelina Zaghi: The Life of an Italian Communist', *Signs* 8:1 (1982), 45-67; and Culley, 'Women's Organisation.'

[79] Kertzer, 'The Liberation', 68.

[80] Maria Weber, 'Italy', in Lovenduski and Hills, *Politics of the Second Electorate*, 194.

[81] Culley, 'Women's Organisation', 119.

[82] See Jane Jenson, 'The French Communist Party and Feminism', in Ralph Miliband and John Saville, eds., *The Socialist Register 1980* (London: Merlin Press, 1980), 121-47; Judith Adler Hellman, 'The Italian Communists, the Women's Question and the Challenge of Feminism', *Studies in Political Economy* 13 (Winter 1983), 57-82; Wayne Northcutt and Jeffra Flaitz, 'Women, Politics and the French Socialist Government', in Bashevkin, ed., *Women and Politics in Western Europe*, 50-70; Gerard Braunthal, *The West German Social Democrats, 1969-1982* (Boulder, Col.: Westview Press, 1983), chap. 7; and Norderval, 'Party and Legislative Participation among Scandinavian Women'.

[83] Sorauf, *Party Politics*, 123.

[84] Ibid. See also Barbara Burrell, 'A New Dimension in Political Participation: The Women's Political Caucus', in Githens and Prestage, eds., *A Portrait of Marginality*, 241-57.

[85] Sapiro, 'When are Interests Interesting?' 712. See also Riitta Jallinoja, 'Independence or Integration: The Women's Movement and Political Parties in Finland', in Drude Dahlerup, ed., *The New Women's Movement* (Beverly Hills: Sage, 1986), 158-78.

[86] Braunthal, *The West German Social Democrats*, 130.

[87] Eva Kolinsky, 'Political Participation and Parliamentary Careers: Women's Quotas in West Germany', *West European Politics* 14:1 (January 1991), 67.

[88] See Northcutt and Flaitz, 'Women, Politics and the French Socialist Government'; and Linda Briskin, 'Autonomy, Integration and Legitimacy: A Comparative Analysis of Socialist Feminist Practice in Canada, the United States and Western Europe', 1990 ms.

[89] See Jennings, 'Women in Party Politics'; and Jeane Kirkpatrick, 'Representation in the American National Conventions: The Case of 1972', *British Journal of Political Science* 5:3 (1975), 265-322.

[90] See Culley, 'Women's Organisation'; and Lovenduski, *Women and European Politics*.

[91] Joyce Gelb, *Feminism and Politics: A Comparative Perspective* (Berkeley: University of California Press, 1989), 54.

[92] See Bystydzienski, 'Women in Politics in Norway', 89; and Norderval, 'Party and Legislative Participation among Scandinavian Women', 80.

[93] See Yvette Roudy, *La femme en marge*, with a preface by François Mitterrand (Paris: Flammarion, 1975).

[94] Charlot, 'Women in Politics in France', 190.

[95] Lovenduski, *Women and European Politics*, 150.

[96] Ibid.

[97] Braunthal, *The West German Social Democrats*, 129.

[98] Ibid.

[99] Kolinsky, 'Political Participation and Parliamentary Careers,' 56.

[100] See Hanna Fenichel Pitkin, *The Concept of Representation* (Berkeley: University of California Press, 1967).

[101] Manon Tremblay, 'Quand les femmes se distinguent: féminisme et réprésentation politique au Québec', *Canadian Journal of Political Science* 25:1 (March 1992), 55-68; Shelah Gilbert Leader, 'The

Policy Impact of Elected Women Officials', in Louis Maisel and Joseph Cooper, eds., *The Impact of the Electoral Process* (Beverly Hills: Sage, 1977), 265-84; Kathleen A. Frankovic, 'Sex and Voting in the US House of Representatives, 1961-1975', *American Politics Quarterly* 5:3 (1977), 315-30; Sirkka Sinkkonen and Elina Haavio-Mannila, 'The Impact of the Women's Movement and Legislative Activity of Women Members of Parliament on Social Development', in Margherita Rendel, ed., *Women, Power and Political Systems* (London: Croom Helm, 1981), 195-215; and Debra L. Dodson, ed., *Gender and Policymaking* (New Brunswick, NJ: Center for the American Woman and Politics, 1991).

CHAPTER SEVEN

Epilogue:
Prospects for Political Representation

This study has examined women's political history, attitudes and participation, including the responses to under-representation that have been pursued by activists in a variety of party systems. Yet it has not addressed one complex and very frustrating question: where are women in general to go? If party politics remains a difficult challenge in Canada and elsewhere, then what prospects exist for improved representation in the future? How might women as a group obtain an increased and, one hopes, equitable share of policy influence?

The factors that limit female political involvement are well documented and provide a useful starting point for this discussion. With respect to social psychological barriers, analysts generally agree that both women and men are constrained by conventional patterns of gender role socialization; traditional norms define the former in terms of passive, private and apolitical roles, and the latter in terms of aggressive, public and political ones. Socialization thus restricts female access to elite positions in two ways: first, by defining women in a collective sense as properly outside of politics; and second, by perpetuating a masculine 'ideal type' of political activist.

Like their counterparts elsewhere in North America and Western Europe, Canadian feminists have responded to gender role norms by arguing against the use of stereotypes in advertising, school texts, career counselling and political recruitment. Although these arguments have met with opposition from various quarters, notably from groups of 'new right' women, the basic act of identifying socialization as an obstacle to gender equality remains crucial to future political mobilization.[1] That is, as greater numbers of women acquire the confidence and organizational ability necessary to confront school boards, advertising councils, party selectorates and other bodies, they build an invaluable groundwork for subsequent political activity—including within parties. Small-scale independent lobbies thus offer an attractive alternative to conventional (and, in light of this study, not very promising) constituency routes toward elite-level political involvement.

Similarly optimistic conclusions can be drawn from ongoing changes in a less apparent but, from the perspective of role socialization, no less important environment: the family. Long defined as a private realm, immune to both social change and political analysis, the family has become a focus of research and debate during recent years. Academic studies point toward three trends that could hold positive implications for women and politics.[2] First, females who enter into stable, long-term relationships can expect a somewhat more egalitarian sharing of household and child-rearing responsibilities with their spouses and are more likely to defer child-bearing and plan smaller families than were previous generations. This general pattern suggests that younger married women take their careers (including political careers) more seriously and organize their family lives more carefully than did either their mothers or grandmothers. As well, there is some evidence that family considerations are increasingly taken into account by politically ambitious men. As Susan Carroll writes, 'few men make decisions to run for office without some consideration of family responsibilities and reactions.'[3]

Second, researchers note that women of the baby-boom era in particular are more likely to remain single or, if married, to become separated and divorced than earlier generations of North American females. This trend away from the nuclear family model of the post-war period, combined with a third set of data showing relatively high educational attainment and earnings among younger women, indicate that decreasing numbers of females are encumbered by conventional family and household responsibilities—because they either contract (with spouses), buy (with earnings) or opt (with single lifestyle) out of traditional arrangements. Taken together, these developments bode well for the career mobility of middle-class women who possess the education and employment opportunities necessary to circumvent established family roles.

Among working-class women, however, and even among some middle-class professionals, the obstacles to participation remain formidable. Those whose educational and occupational opportunities are circumscribed often lack the money, contacts and confidence necessary for elite-level activism—whether they are women or men. And although trade union involvement has helped to compensate working-class men for their lack of the resources available to middle-class men, many unions have historically provided a less than welcoming environment for working women. Clearly, the women's movement has challenged trade union practices in Canada and elsewhere, but obstacles continue to exist in unions as well as in private sector corporations and political parties—especially for females from immigrant and minority backgrounds.[4]

Even for women in the legal profession, traditionally a conduit for men's entry into politics, research shows a less than overwhelming interest in elective office. One California survey, for example, found that female attorneys 'generally agreed that politics is a dirty business . . . Women attorneys appear to be in cross pressures. A few will move to the positions of power, while most will build their reputations in the positions that pay well in the field of the law.'[5]

Aside from these limits facing women, major structural or systemic obstacles exist. Perhaps the most obvious contemporary barrier is money. In Canada, candidates for constituency-level nomination, party office and party leadership benefited little from the campaign finance reforms that helped to democratize fund-raising in general elections after 1974.[6] Female candidates were directly affected by the absence of meaningful spending limits for party nomination and leadership campaigns, since employed women on average were paid less than seventy cents for each dollar paid to a man, while household labour (overwhelmingly done by women) was virtually non-remunerative. Hence, an average employed woman contesting local party nomination could be expected to have at least 30 percent less income to put toward her campaign than an average employed man, even though whoever won nomination could expect to raise funds under reformed campaign expenses legislation. These inequities were emphasized by women's groups in their submissions to the federal Royal Commission on Electoral Reform and Party Financing; the Commission's final report recommended important reforms, but none had been implemented as of this writing (see Chapter 4).

Women's economic condition is thus connected to their access to party elites. Without equal opportunity and remuneration in employment, affordable child care, and systematic reform of the party finance process, the pool of women available for elite-level participation will remain small. The costs of pursuing nominations in winnable constituencies, as well as party executive and leadership positions, rose throughout the 1980s; these costs effectively discouraged all but the most wealthy competitors. And women suffered disproportionately as a result of income differentials and the absence of serious party finance reform.

An additional but no less significant barrier was the practice, conscious or unconscious, of tracking women away from influential political positions. This discriminatory treatment served to perpetuate a 'pink-collar' party service corps responsible for social, clerical and fund-raising activities; it had little if any role in campaign strategy or internal policy-making. One response to this feminization of 'donkey work', as Judy LaMarsh referred to it, entailed pressuring for an equitable distribution of routine trench labour—including 'pink-collar' assignments—as well as the more challenging tasks of party policy, strategy and leadership.[7] Assertiveness on the part of female partisans, combined with greater egalitarianism among their male colleagues, continues to be essential in order for political organizations to recruit new cohorts of women—few of whom are likely to find fulfilment in tea parties, bake sales or clerical assignments.

This discussion of obstacles to party involvement is inseparable from a number of other questions concerning women in politics. First, in simple tactical terms, should contemporary feminists get involved in party organizations? Could not non-partisan interest groups or municipal-level political work serve a more direct and useful purpose? Given the long tradition of political independence among women's movements in Canada and elsewhere, this point poses far more than an academic dilemma; it addresses the very heart of the 'where should women go' question.[8]

From a Canadian perspective, arguments for exclusively non-partisan or independent action are flawed because they reflect an American-style interest group approach to what remains a party-based parliamentary system. Unlike the US political process, in which feminist and other lobby groups can expect regular access to more clearly delineated legislative and executive branches, and in which party discipline is relatively limited, the Canadian one is characterized by highly disciplined legislatures, dominant executives and fewer established points of access for interest groups. In other words, the non-partisan interest group approach on its own is unlikely to achieve the policy changes sought by any stream of the Canadian women's movement; existing parliamentary arrangements establish parties as pivotal actors in the legislative process. Changes having to do with abortion, violence against women, pay equity or child care all involve some elements of both legislative reform and budgetary commitment, neither of which can be accomplished outside party-dominated legislatures. Moreover, independent municipal alternatives to party activity can ghettoize women in the lowest paid, and arguably least powerful, echelon of Canadian politics.

Second, it is important to consider whether electing more women to party and legislative elites constitutes a politically worthwhile exercise. Do these elites indeed wield power? And would more women make a difference? One response to these questions is to maintain that some senior public servants in Canada exercise greater policy influence than most legislators, and probably some cabinet ministers.[9] Electing more women to the pinnacle of legislative office, the House of Commons, may thus prove futile in policy terms unless attention is given at the same time to recruitment to senior-level bureaucratic positions, particularly in central agencies of the federal government.[10]

As for the relationship between numbers of women and substantive policy changes, research shows that this conversion is by no means automatic. Accounts of political women who oppose reproductive choice, maintain that gender constitutes no barrier to career mobility and, in the oft-quoted case of Margaret Thatcher, question what the women's movement has 'ever done for me' point towards a crucial distinction between the biological fact of sex and the political phenomenon of feminist consciousness.[11]

Yet these examples hardly prove that, as a group, women in politics make no policy difference. In fact, studies in this area suggest precisely the reverse: that is, politically active women in Western Europe and North America are generally more supportive of feminist issue positions than either women in the general population or men who are active in politics.[12] The most comprehensive study to date of this question, undertaken by the Center for the American Woman and Politics at Rutgers University, concluded that

> women in public office are having a distinctive impact on public policy and on the political process . . . The cumulative message of these studies seems unavoidable: the under-representation of women in public office has profound consequences for society because it affects both the nature of the policies that are considered and enacted and the voices that are heard in the policymaking process.[13]

This finding demonstrates the importance of eliminating barriers and recruiting more women to all political systems, not only for the purposes of policy reform but also as a step towards reshaping the systems themselves.

NOTES

[1] See Andrea Dworkin, *Right Wing Women* (New York: Putnam, 1983); and Rebecca E. Klatch, *Women of the New Right* (Philadelphia: Temple University Press, 1987) on the US case. On Canada, see Karen Dubinsky, *Lament for a Patriarchy Lost: Anti-Feminism, Anti-Abortion and R.E.A.L. Women in Canada* (Ottawa: Canadian Research Institute for the Advancement of Women, 1985); and Lorna Erwin, 'R.E.A.L. Women, Anti-Feminism and the Welfare State', in Sue Findlay and Melanie Randall, eds., *Feminist Perspectives on the Canadian State*, special issue of *Resources for Feminist Research* 17 (September 1988), 147-9.

[2] See Margrit Eichler, *Families in Canada* (Toronto: Gage, 1983).

[3] Susan J. Carroll, 'The Personal is Political: The Intersection of Private Lives and Public Roles among Women and Men in Elective and Appointive Office', *Women and Politics* 9:2 (1989), 62.

[4] See Julie White, *Women and Unions* (Ottawa: Canadian Advisory Council on the Status of Women, 1980).

[5] Jerry B. Briscoe, 'Perceptions that Discourage Women Attorneys from Seeking Public Office', *Sex Roles* 21:7/8 (1989), 564-5.

[6] See Khayyam Zev Paltiel, 'Canadian Election Expense Legislation, 1963-1985: A Critical Appraisal or Was the Effort Worth It?' in Robert J. Jackson, Doreen Jackson and Nicolas Baxter-Moore, eds., *Contemporary Canadian Politics* (Scarborough: Prentice-Hall, 1987), 228-47.

[7] Judy LaMarsh, *Memoirs of a Bird in a Gilded Cage* (Toronto: McClelland and Stewart, 1968), 282.

[8] For a comparative view of this dilemma, see Riitta Jallinoja, 'Independence or Integration: The Women's Movement and Political Parties in Finland', in Drude Dahlerup, ed., *The New Women's Movement* (Beverly Hills: Sage, 1986), 158-78.

[9] See Richard French, *How Ottawa Decides* (Toronto: Lorimer, 1980); and Colin Campbell and George Szablowski, *The Superbureaucrats: Structure and Behaviour in Central Agencies* (Toronto: Macmillan, 1979).

[10] See Lucinda Sue Flavelle, 'Women Senior Civil Servants in Canada, the U.K. and the U.S.', (MA thesis, York University, 1982); and Nicole Morgan, *The Equality Game: Women in the Federal Public Service, 1908-1987* (Ottawa: Canadian Advisory Council on the Status of Women, 1988).

[11] Thatcher as quoted in Donna S. Sanzone, 'Women in Politics', in Cynthia Fuchs Epstein and Rose Laub Coser, eds., *Access to Power* (London: Allen and Unwin, 1981), 44.

[12] See Chapter 6, above, as well as Susan B. Hansen, Linda M. Franz and Margaret Netemeyer-Mays, 'Women's Political Participation and Policy Preferences', *Social Science Quarterly* 56:4 (1976), 576-90.

[13] Susan J. Carroll and Debra L. Dodson, 'Introduction', to Debra L. Dodson, ed., *Gender and Policymaking: Studies of Women in Office* (New Brunswick, NJ: Center for the American Woman and Politics, 1991), 7, 11.

Acknowledgement of Informants

In any study of this type, the author relies very directly upon materials supplied by informants. Some of the following individuals kindly agreed to provide access to publications, party records, personal archives and their political memories, while others helped to facilitate interviews and a convention delegate study. To each, I am deeply grateful.

Doris Anderson	Marianne Holder	Catherine Mustard
Ruth Archibald	Chaviva Hosek	Hon. Aideen Nicholson
Becky Barrett	Aase Hueglin	Bruce Ogilvie
Deanna Beach	Mary Humphrey	Wanda O'Hagan
Carol Beckman	Jackie Isbester	David C. Peterson
Hon. Monique Bégin	Nancy Jamieson	Dale Poel
Monica Bell	Janis Johnson	Abigail Pollonetsky
Margaret Birch	Karen Jones	Diane Poole
Margot Bowen	Reva Karstadt	Jan Port
Margaret Bryce	Joan Kouri	Marilyn Roycroft
Marion Bryden	Helen Lafountaine	Laura Sabia
Elizabeth Burnham	Mary Lancitie	Iona Samis
Hon. Iona Campagnolo	Margaret Lazarus	Kathy Sanderson
Jacquie Chic	Morden Lazarus	Lynda Scales
Sandra Clifford	Kay Macpherson	Margaret Scrivener
Marjorie Cohen	Marian Maloney	Hon. Muriel Smith
Barbara Colantonio	Kay Manderville	Lynda Sorenson
Sheila Copps	Hon. Lorna Marsden	Kay Stanley
Joseph Cruden	Jill Marzetti	Margaret Steeves
Cynthia Cusinato	Bari Maxwell	Hon. Bette Stephenson
Ed Dale	Thelma McCormack	Shelby Toderel
Ranne Dowbiggen	Lynn McDonald	Anne Venton
Jim Evans	Alexa McDonough	Suzanne Warren
Hon. Ellen Fairclough	Mary McGowan	Judy Wasylycia-Leis
Hon. Susan Fish	Mary Meldrum	Marjorie Wells
Joseph Fletcher	Irma Melville	Alan Whitehorn
Barbara Ford	Maria Minna	Elizabeth Willcock
Audrey Gill	Annalea Mitchell	Allan Williams
Esther Greenglass	Joe Morrow	Harriet Wolman
Jean Haliburton	Jack Murray	Wendy Wolnec

Index